A Matter of Record

A MATTER OF RECORD

Documentary Sources in Social Research

John Scott

Polity Press

First published 1990 by Polity Press
in association with Basil Blackwell

Editorial office:
Polity Press
65 Bridge Street,
Cambridge CB2 1UR, UK

Marketing and production:
Basil Blackwell Ltd
108 Cowley Road, Oxford OX4 1JF, UK

Basil Blackwell Inc.
3 Cambridge Center
Cambridge, MA 02142, USA

ISBN 0 7456 0030 1
ISBN 0 7456 0070 0 (pbk)

British Library Cataloguing in Publication Data
A CIP catalogue record for this book is available from the British Library.

Library of Congress Cataloging in Publication Data
A CIP catalogue record for this book is available from the Library of Congress.

Typeset in 10 on 12pt Times
by Hope Services (Abingdon) Ltd

Contents

List of Figures   vii
Preface   ix

1 **Social Research and Documentary Sources**   1
   Evidence and data in social research   2
   What are documents?   10

2 **Assessing Documentary Sources**   19
   Authenticity: soundness and authorship   19
   Credibility: sincerity and accuracy   22
   Representativeness: survival and availability   24
   Meaning: literal and interpretative understanding   28

3 **The Use of Documents in Social Research**   36
   The search for King Arthur   38
   Who wrote the Zinoviev letter?   43
   The social meanings of suicide   48
   Social research and the relativity of accounts   54

4 **The Official Realm: Public and Private**   59
   The State, surveillance and secrecy   60
   Official documents in the State   63
   Official records in the private sphere   78

5 **Administrative Routines and Situated Decisions**   83
   Conceptual instruments and administrative routines   84
   Situated decisions   90

6 **Explorations in Official Documents**   96
   Occupation, class and inequality   96

Class schemas and the problem of meaning 111
Measuring the class structure 117
The records of health, welfare and education 123
Business and industrial records 129

7 **The Public Sphere and Mass Communication** 136
Public opinion, the media and the audience 137
Images, content and meaning 143
Directories, almanacs and yearbooks 156
The annals of the rich and powerful 163

8 **Personal Documents** 173
Diaries, letters and autobiographies 174
Photographs and visual sources 185

Notes 198
Index 227

Figures

1.1 Sources of evidence: proximate access   3
1.2 A classification of documents   14
5.1 The Registrar-General's classifications   90
6.1 The Hall–Jones classification   112
6.2 The Goldthorpe classification: version 1   114
6.3 The Goldthorpe classification: version 2   115
7.1 Women's magazine covers, 1949–74   153
7.2 A typology of directories   171

Preface

Documentary sources of information, of all kinds, figure centrally in the research of sociologists. Official statistics on crime, income distribution, health and illness, censuses of population, newspaper reports, diaries, reference books, government publications, and similar sources are the basis of much social research by academics and their students. Yet these materials have rarely been given the attention that they deserve in accounts of sociological research methods. Questionnaires and participant observation figure centrally in texts and courses on research methods, but documentary sources are considered in only a fragmentary way.

The aim of this book is to attempt to remedy this situation by illustrating the diversity of documentary sources available for social research, and to discuss some of the ways in which they can be used. In doing this, I emphasise the similarity of the methodological problems faced by sociologists, historians, and other social scientists who use these sources in their work. This argument implies certain claims about the drawing of disciplinary boundaries – I am an unashamed 'sociological imperialist'. But I have deferred these general considerations to another occasion. My focus is on the handling of documents in relation to specific problems in social and historical research.

I also make the claim that the methodological issues involved in handling documentary sources are similar to those that arise in handling any sources of evidence in social research. I introduce four criteria for assessing the quality of social research evidence – authenticity, credibility, representativeness, and meaning – and I outline their application to the whole range of social research before proceeding to a detailed consideration of documentary sources. These criteria are used throughout the book as organising principles for my discussion. Although it is unnecessary that a researcher use them in the same systematic way, my argument is that an appreciation of their importance can only be learned through considering them systematically.

The examples of research that I have used in the book are drawn from a number of different substantive areas, and I have used both American and British source material and studies. My belief is that the uses and limitations of documentary sources can only be fully appreciated when they are understood in their social context as historical products. To this end, I have concentrated my attention on British source materials and have shown their emergence in the context of the British state and economy. Wherever appropriate, however, I draw parallels with the wider European and American experience and the types of source material that emerged in other countries.

My initial concern to write this book was stimulated by an important article by Jennifer Platt, which is referred to at numerous places in my text. Her path-breaking article not only suggested the need for such a book, but it also advanced some of the ideas that underlie my own development of the four appraisal criteria for social research materials. I am greatly indebted to her for pointing the way. The argument of the book has also been shaped by my involvement in the teaching of research sources and methods over a number of years, and by my own involvement in documentary research. I am grateful to Tony Giddens and Polity Press for the patience that they have shown in waiting for the final manuscript, my production of it being delayed by the administrative pressures of modern academic life and an overloaded mainframe computer.

John Scott

1 Social Research and Documentary Sources

The handling of documentary sources – government papers, diaries, newspapers and so on – is widely seen as the hallmark of the professional historian, whereas the sociologist has generally been identified with the use of questionnaires and interview techniques. In fact, documentary investigation was the main research tool of the classical sociologists: Marx made extensive use of the reports of the factory inspectors, Weber utilised religious tracts and pamphlets, and Durkheim employed official statistics on suicide. The bulk of the historical and comparative work that is undertaken in contemporary sociology involves the use of documentary materials, as does much work on contemporary societies. But textbooks on research methods have generally failed to recognise this and have given most of their space to discussions of questionnaires, interviews, and participant observation. The aim of this book is to rectify this imbalance by considering some of the issues involved in dealing with documentary evidence.

My argument is that the general principles involved in handling documents are no different from those involved in any other area of social research, but that the specific features of documentary sources do require the consideration of their distinguishing features and the particular techniques needed to handle them.[1] This argument rests upon the stronger claim that the logic of social investigation is no different from that employed in those areas of research concerned with physical objects, chemical substances and living bodies. All research involves the systematic and disciplined search for knowledge of the world that exists outside of the researcher's laboratory, institute or department. This is not to say that no methodological peculiarities arise in the study of social phenomena. There are, indeed, features of concept formation and theorisation in the social sciences which derive from the inherently 'meaningful' and 'value laden' character of social reality. These features do not, however, require any departure from a 'scientific' frame of reference. The meaningful character of social reality, moreover, does not constitute a 'problem' for social science methodology. It does mean that it is difficult to achieve the kind of unambiguous descriptions produced in the natural sciences, but the social scientist has certain compensating advantages. The inert phenomena of physical and chemical science are unable to communicate meaning to the scientist in the same way that human beings are able to, through written documents and through conversation. The argument of this book, therefore, is that sociology is a science and that documents should be handled scientifically.

The social researcher has available to him or her an enviable array of source materials from which scientific data can be constructed. The researcher can interview people, observe their behaviour, interact with them, study the administrative records of their dealings with official agencies, read their letters and diaries, examine the newspapers they read, and so on. Each particular source requires slightly different handling: the mechanics of participant observation, for example, are radically different from those involved in the use of official statistics. Written documents of all types, however, share certain features which distinguish them from other kinds of source material. For this reason, it is necessary to understand written documents in the wide context of the whole gamut of sources which are utilised in social research.

Evidence and data in social research

The aim of social research is to describe and explain the actions of agents and the structures that they produce and reproduce in the course of their lives. But neither 'actions' nor 'structures' are actually observable: they are inferred from the behavioural and other observational evidence through which they are manifested. It is important therefore to examine the types of evidence available to the social scientist as source material for data construction. This can best be approached by considering two contrasting relationships between the observer and the observed.

Proximate or 'direct' access by the observer exists where the observer and his or her source material are contemporaneous and co-present. In such a situation the observer is a direct witness of the audible, visible, and tactile signs of human action: the observer and the observed are 'coincident'; they have the same spatio-temporal location, and the observer may therefore use eyes, ears and other senses to observe and question the current behaviour of those being observed. *Mediate* or 'indirect' access by an observer exists where past behaviour must be inferred from its material traces, the visible signs of what happened or existed at some previous time. In this case the observer and the observed are not co-present and the observer may only obtain evidence indirectly from the buildings, books and so forth produced by people in the past. The distinction between proximate and mediate access should not, perhaps, be drawn too sharply, as much everyday 'observation', for example, involves both processes. We see people move and hear them speak, and we are also able to see the houses and cars they have bought and the clothes they wear. Nevertheless, the distinction is important as a way of sensitising us to some of the variations in sources of evidence.

Proximate access involves the use of one or more *channels* of access and the adoption of a particular *interactional stance*. The channel or means of observation may be aural or visual, involving listening or looking. The interaction between observer and observed may be 'reactive' or 'non-reactive', depending on the extent to which the observer intervenes or responds in order to communicate with those under observation. In non-reactive research, the observer strives to remain unnoticed as an observer in order to minimise his or her influence on the 'natural' course of events.

Figure 1.1 *Sources of evidence: proximate access*

		Channel	
		Aural	*Visual*
Interactional stance	Non-reactive	1	2
	Reactive	3	4

Note. I ignore tactile channels as in social research they are generally adjuncts of aural and visual channels.

Figure 1.1 shows a cross-classification of these two dimensions of proximate access to generate four sources of evidence. Type 1 is exemplified by natural, everyday conversation, in which our sense of hearing is the primary channel through which we learn about others.[2] Non-reactive interaction through a primarily visual channel, type 2, provides evidence of non-verbal behaviour, such as deportment and manner, and, like type 1, is a form of covert observation. This is not to say that non-reactive researchers habitually hide their physical presence behind screens or one-way mirrors: it is the researcher's presence *as a researcher* which is masked. Similarly, a covert participant observer is, to all intents and purposes, 'merely' a participant in the normal course of events.

Reactive observation through an aural channel, type 3, occurs when the observer questions those under observation in order to elicit responses relevant to the research, and the clearest example of evidence produced in this way would be interview responses. It should perhaps be emphasised that the contemporaneity of observer and observed does not mean that information may only be elicited about the present: the techniques of 'oral history'[3] have exploited interview techniques to obtain evidence about the past. Reactive observation through the visual channel, type 4, involves an attempt to elicit written responses, for example, from those under observation; the observer reads the written evidence in order to acquire knowledge. The clearest example of such research would be the use of self-completion questionnaires, where the subject of the research is invited to answer a series of written questions for later processing by the investigator.

Proximate access therefore characterises a number of the forms of evidence obtained by sociologists through such methods as participant observation, interviewing, and questioning. The communication between observer and observed in situations of proximate access is always direct, even if the observer records this communication for ease of handling. In mediate access, however, the evidence has already become 'fixed' in some material form which the observer has to 'read'. The researcher has no direct access to the situation in which the evidence was produced. When the results of past actions become fixed in a material form which is capable of survival for a period of time, it is possible for a researcher to study the material medium to obtain indirect evidence about those actions. The central question in considering mediate access, therefore, is the nature of the medium in which the message is fixed. The media may range from solid and substantial forms, such as houses, clay tablets and dead bodies, through the less substantial, such as paper, to completely insubstantial electronic media, which carry their information only for so long as they are supplied with a suitable supply of energy.[4]

Particularly important forms of such evidence have been those used in archaeological studies, where bones and other remains, artefacts, and waste products have been subjected to investigation. The archaeological method typically consists of excavation to disclose the strata of earth and remains which have accumulated on site, successive layers being removed and their details recorded. Items of interest might include the nature of the earth material, holes made by posts, remnants of walls, human remains, and pots, clothing, jewellery, weapons and coinage. Excavation may extend over a large area in order to produce not merely a cross-section but a three-dimensional view which combines vertical stratification with the lateral arrangement of each layer – showing, for example, house plans and street patterns. Through such means as radio-carbon dating, tree-ring dating and fluorine testing of the source material, the archaeologist attempts to construct a relative and, so far as is possible, an absolute chronology of the site. The physical evidence yielded by human and animal remains shades over into that provided by the physical conditions of landform and geology. Historians have shown that the Anglo-Saxon field patterns discovered and used as evidence of settlement and property distribution may be conditioned by an enabling geology.[5]

The use of physical evidence is not limited of course to the distant past. Webb and his colleagues have argued that physical traces may be used for studies of contemporary social action. The number of different fingerprints on the page of a book or magazine, for example, can be used to measure the number of readers, and the contents of dustbins can be used as indicators of consumption patterns.[6]

I have so far considered material traces as indicators of social actions and relations without reference to any intended messages they may contain. Much archaeological research, for example, sees remains and artefacts as unintentional testimony to past actions. When the material media also contain intentional messages, then they may be considered as 'documents'. A document is an artefact which has as its central feature an inscribed text. The material base for the script is irrelevant: it may be a clay tablet, a sheet of paper, or a visual display unit. The term script should not be taken to include only pictorial or patterned decoration – no matter how important these may be as sources of evidence. Script is the written expression of a spoken language and therefore contains a 'text'. The text is the central and most obvious feature of a document, and a book may be considered a paradigm of a document. Inscribed objects such as coins, clocks and cars are not documents in this strict sense because their inscriptions are peripheral to their main significance. There are of course marginal cases, such as stamps, cheques, tickets and gravestones; however, the distinctiveness of documentary evidence should be clear.[7]

Through the various means of proximate and mediate access, the researcher is able to obtain evidence about agents and structures. Observations of natural objects, artefacts (both documentary and non-documentary) and actual behaviour yield evidence about other people. These three types of source material are intrinsically inter-dependent: artefacts are natural objects which have been transformed in some way by human behaviour. It is for this reason that many source materials cannot be allocated unambiguously to one type or another, and also, therefore, why research will often involve a combination of proximate and mediate access. For example, a hill or a valley, a natural object, will generally be observed only in the state that results from transformation through human settlement and farming, as sharing a characteristic of artefacts. Even in cases where such obvious signs of human action as fields, footpaths and settlements are not apparent, a landscape may still be partly the result of human activity – as with the North American dustbowl and the Norfolk Broads. Nevertheless, natural geology, geomorphology, and climate will impose constraits on the transformative power of human action, and so any landscape will reflect both natural and human processes.

Much of the evidence available to the social researcher is, of course, analogous to that available to people in their everyday life: people read documents and talk to one another all the time; the issuing of questionnaires is a regular practice in many spheres of life; and police are not the only people to carry out interviews and engage in covert observation. What distinguishes the stance of the social researcher from that of people in their everyday activities is that sociological and historical data are constructed with a scientific, theoretically informed intent; great care is taken – or should be taken – about the quality of the evidence and therefore about the validity and reliability of the data constructed from the evidence. The foundation of scientific research is the quality of the evidence available for analysis. The assessment of its quality is central to the whole argument of this book, and I wish to argue that a simple set of criteria can be used for this purpose, regardless of the type of evidence. There are four criteria:

1 *Authenticity*. Is the evidence genuine and of unquestionable origin?
2 *Credibility*. Is the evidence free from error and distortion?
3 *Representativeness*. Is the evidence typical of its kind, and, if not, is the extent of its untypicality known?
4 *Meaning*. Is the evidence clear and comprehensible?[8]

Authenticity is a fundamental criterion in social research, as question-able sources of evidence can mislead the researcher unless he or she knows that they are inauthentic. The field-worker carrying out interviews, for example, must be sure of the identity of the interviewee before undertaking the interview, and the participant observer must know that he or she is in the right locale for the observations to be undertaken. Similarly, users of the physical evidence of human remains must be sure of the authenticity of those remains – Is the skull that has been discovered really one of a hominid, or is it, perhaps, an animal skull or a plausible forgery?[9] The secondary analyst handling questionnaires from an earlier study will want to know whether the material available is actually from the study in question (its 'known provenance'), where it has been stored since the original study, and whether there has been any editing or copying from the original. Unless the researcher is able to come to a conclusion about the authenticity of the evidence, there is no possibility of an informed judgement about the quality of the data eventually constructed.

Credibility refers to the extent to which the evidence is undistorted and sincere, free from error and evasion. Interviewers must be sure that their interviewees are taking the interview seriously and are therefore saying things which can be regarded as *prima facie* credible. If the interviewee is lying, or regards the interview as a humorous diversion, the responses must be handled differently from those acquired in a serious and sincere interview. Participant observers must know whether the things they are observing are credible events for that situation or are, perhaps, staged for their benefit and are therefore to be regarded in a different light. The secondary analyst will want to know whether responses to questions on, say, sexual behaviour which were asked thirty years ago are more or less likely to exhibit coyness and oblique answers than responses to similar questions asked today.

Representativeness refers to the general problem of assessing the typicality, or otherwise, of evidence. But it should not be assumed that the researcher always desires 'typical' evidence: what is important is that the scientist should know how typical it is in order to be able to assign limits to the application of any conclusions drawn.[10] The researcher handling physical evidence, for example, will want to know whether the surviving artefacts on the site (such as jewels and tools) are typical of the range of artefacts once in use by those living on the site. Have clothes or tools made of more perishable materials failed to survive the years buried under the ground? A central issue is the nature of any sampling techniques used by the present researcher or by those responsible for granting or securing access to the sources. If interviews are to be carried out on a random sample of workers, then the researcher must be confident that the sampling frame and procedures are adequate for the production of such a sample; and the secondary analyst of questionnaires will have to know what sampling methods were employed in the original study and whether the archivists or clerks responsible for storing the schedules have used additional selection or sampling methods to reduce the bulk of the material to be stored. In the latter case it is important to know whether any schedules have been destroyed and, if so, whether this was because of storage problems or in order to hide some flaw in the initial research design.

The final quality control criterion, *meaning*, refers to the extent to which the evidence is clear and comprehensible to the researcher: what is it, and what does it tell us? The observer of arcane tribal practices in the Sudan, for example, will need to ask such questions as 'Is this witchcraft?', a matter of how the actions under investigation are to be described.[11] The contemporary observer of violence at football matches will similarly need to know whether the 'hooligans' involved are engaged in 'ritualised' aggression or 'real' violence. An observer may be sure that he or she is in the right place, is not being faced with staged events, and is not observing unusual events, but may still be unclear as to *what* those events are and how they are to be described. In handling physical evidence, the researcher will ask such questions as whether the position of a body indicates ritual killing or domestic violence, and whether the pattern of holes discovered on a site should be seen as the remains of a dwelling or a temple, Finally, the secondary analyst can only assess the evidence available from the schedules if the original instructions given to interviewers and coders are known; without this knowledge it may be impossible to interpret the meanings of particular responses.

Data construction involves the use of methods and procedures for the derivation of data from evidence of known quality. In the natural sciences it may often involve systematic theories of observation and measurement, but this is far less common in the social sciences. In the absence of theories of measurement, resort must be made to rule-of-thumb techniques based on implicit, everyday theories. Accepted theories of measurement are far from evenly developed in the social sciences. While the assessment of authenticity and the construction of authentic data through interviewing and the use of documents often involves implicit and loosely established techniques, the archaeological use of physical evidence involves rigorous theories of authentication rooted in accepted scientific knowledge about, for example, the behaviour of carbon and fluorine atoms. Areas of social research where well-founded theories of measurement and data construction have emerged are those concerned with the assessment of representativeness and, to a lesser extent, credibility and meaning.[12]

The theory of sampling, for example, is well established. It was introduced into the social sciences by A. L. Bowley,[13] a statistician who carried out a follow-up to poverty studies undertaken by Booth and Rowntree.[14] While the earlier writers had each attempted to survey the whole population of their area, Bowley appreciated that advances in the theory of probability showed that a randomly drawn sample from the population could yield valid information about the population as a whole, even when the sample size was fairly small. Sampling theory, therefore, is an attempt to spell out the grounds on which generalisations from the sample to the wider population can legitimately be made. Bowley's intention in introducing sampling theory, apart from reducing the time and cost necessary for social research, was to make it possible to calculate the size of sample necessary in order to achieve a satisfactory degree of accuracy.[15] The researcher can be confident of producing accurate results so long as he or she is confident that the sample is unbiased. 'Bias' depends upon the representativeness of the sampling frame, the randomness of the method of sampling, and the number of sampled cases which are unavailable, inaccessible, or fail to respond. Because numerical values cannot be assigned to these factors, the assessment of bias is always a qualitative judgement, but it is nevertheless based on an understanding of the theory of sampling.

There is no single, widely accepted theory for the measurement of meaning. There are, instead, a number of competing and complementary theories alongside a number of more generally accepted principles. 'Measurement' should be here understood to refer to the processes of coding and classifying source material into the theoretically defined categories required for the researcher's purposes. Measurement is not always a quantitative procedure. The absence of generally accepted procedures for the measurement of meaning has led many researchers to treat coding as if it were a theoretically neutral process in which the sole consideration is the convenience and parsimony of the categories employed. Researchers have often taken over administrative categories, such as those for criminal offences, and have failed to consider the correspondence, or lack of correspondence, between these administrative categories and the sociological concepts in which they are interested. To assume that this relationship is unproblematic, and that coding categories are mere technical devices, is to ignore the theoretically grounded nature of scientific research and to run the risk of what Mills has termed 'abstracted empiricism'.[16] It is, of course, the case that a useful coding system must meet certain technical criteria – the categories must, for example, be exhaustive and mutually exclusive – but the codings are essentially ways of operationalising theoretical concepts. Research cannot be theoretically and empirically progressive unless the concepts of the theoretical framework are adequately operationalised. It is for this reason that questions of coding rest upon theories of meaning which tell the researcher how to 'read' and interpret evidence.[17]

What are documents?

Questions on the nature and use of documents have figured prominently in the methodological writings of historians, but it would be wrong to see documents as exclusively historical sources. Historians have often been concerned with only a very narrow range of documents, especially State documents of constitutional or diplomatic origin. Nevertheless, the methodological views of the classic historians remain the essential starting-point for a more general consideration of the use of documentary sources in social research.

In their classic compendium of research practice, Langlois and Seignobos remark that 'Documents are the traces which have been left by the thoughts and actions of men (*sic*) of former times',[18] and it is only through these traces, they argue, that we can know the past. 'For there is no substitute for documents: no documents, no history'.[19] This contention is rooted in the nineteenth-century revolution in historical writing initiated by Ranke, and it became the corner-stone of professional academic history. Written documents discovered in libraries and archives were regarded by Ranke as superior to observational and archaeological evidence, and to reminiscences and oral traditions. Learning to handle documentary evidence became the central feature of the research training of the historian because it was seen as the characteristic method of history, the method which distinguished it from other disciplines and gave the voice of authority to the expertise of professional historians. The historian was an expert in the handling of documents, and this expertise was a bulwark against the intrusion of uninformed judgements from outside the discipline.[20]

The rationale for preferring documentary evidence to all other sources of evidence about the past is, in part, a sheer matter of survival. For the distant past it is generally the case that interviewing and observation are impossible,[21] and that documents have survived in great numbers. The expansion of the State and the growth of the economy in the modern period have generated massive quantities of written material which appear to give a direct insight into past events. These documentary survivals are regarded as especially valuable because they 'are not deliberately designed for the benefit of the historian'[22] and so can be seen as the objective residue of the past; they provide the historian with the unwitting testimony of people in the past. It has, nevertheless, been recognised that such documents do not speak for themselves. The task of the historian is to speak objectively on their behalf. Langlois and Seignobos claim that the craft of the historian lies in moving from the *source* to the *fact*: 'The document is his starting point, the fact his goal.'[23] These writers voiced the prevailing view in German historical writing of the late nineteenth and early twentieth centuries, when the historian's task was seen as that of hermeneutic reconstruction. Echoing Dilthey's philosophical underpinning of history, they argue that the historian must 'revive in imagination the whole of that series of acts performed by the author of the document'.[24] Only by doing this can the document be placed in context and an understanding of its meaning and significance be achieved. While many of their contemporaries might not have accepted the philosophical notion of 'reliving' the experience of others, the general point was accepted that the historian had to place the document in the context of its conditions of production before an appraisal of its message could be made.

As has already been remarked, the range of documents considered by historians of the classical school tended to be remarkably narrow. The exemplary documentary source might be the manuscript report of a minister to a king, with the reports, letters and diaries of those active in the service of the State coming a close second. Printed documents of all kinds were poorly regarded, though Acts of Parliament and other official records might be used in studying the more recent period when the printing of documents had become more routine. But only those documents concerned with constitutional and diplomatic events were highly regarded. An important feature of the development of the discipline of history in more recent years has been a broadening of attention to other documentary sources, allied with the growth of economic and social history, and a willingness to supplement documents with other sources of evidence.

The legacy of the classical tradition has had a great influence, however, on attempts to define what exactly a 'document' is. A particularly influential view among those social researchers who have considered such matters is that of Sidney and Beatrice Webb, who argued that the manuscript and printed sources which the social researcher may legitimately consult can be divided into two classes: 'documents' and 'contemporary literature'. A document, they argue, is 'an instrument in language which has, as its origin, and for its deliberate and express purpose, to become the basis of, or to assist, the activities of an individual, an organisation, or a community'.[25] Documents are, therefore, 'exclusively for the purpose of action' and are not written to inform historians, sociologists or any other detached observer. The Webbs are here generalising the classical historian's view from the realm of the State to all organised groups and all purposive action. 'Documents' are the accounts, returns, statutes and proclamations that individuals and groups produce in the course of their everyday practice and that are geared exclusively to their immediate practical needs.

'Contemporary literature', on the other hand, is a residual term for all other written sources, such as treatises, sermons, newspapers, poems and biographies, which are contemporary with the events or people under investigation. The Webbs argue for the primacy of 'documents' over 'literature' in the study of social institutions on the grounds that it is never possible to be sure that the literature accurately and unbiasedly records what actually happened or what is contained in the original documents. 'Literature' does give, however, the 'background' which is often missing from the documents, and so enables the researcher to uncover, for example, the conflicts and struggles which lay behind the apparent consensus of a government statement.

There are clearly a number of problematic features in the Webbs' argument. While they correctly recognise the possible sources of inaccuracy and bias in contemporary literature, they fail to see that similar problems beset the 'documents' and that they cannot, therefore, be given the privileged status conventionally accorded to them. An adequate approach to the use of documentary sources must adopt a more general definition of 'document' than that of the Webbs and the classical historians.

The position that I wish to take here is that a document in its most general sense is a written text, as defined in the previous section. Writing is the making of symbols representing words, and involves the use of a pen, pencil, printing machine or other tool for inscribing the message on paper, parchment or some other material medium. The introduction of paper in place of clay, stone and parchment as the receptacle of writing, and the invention of printing as a supplement to handwriting created the archetypal document: the text printed or handwritten on paper. But to recognise this as the archetype or exemplar does not mean that it is not possible to regard hieroglyphic and cuneiform tablets, for example, as documents in essentially the same sense. All that differs in these cases is the physical embodiment of the document. Similarly, the invention of magnetic and electronic means of storing and displaying text should encourage us to regard the 'files' and 'documents' contained in computers and word processors as true documents. From this point of view, therefore, documents may be regarded as physically embodied texts, where the containment of the text is the primary purpose of the physical medium.

This purpose, however, is the purpose of the author of the text, and it is always necessary to establish through empirical research what purpose may, or may not, lie behind the production of artefacts. As the imputation of purpose may always be thrown into question, it is inevitable that the borderlines of the category 'document' will be somewhat fuzzy. The inclusion of an inscription on a coin, for example, does not necessarily make the coin a document, as the primary purpose of the inscription may simply be to denote the monetary value of the coin in transactions and to identify its country of origin. Even so, coins sometimes contain especially fulsome inscriptions which may have been intended, for example, to proclaim the authority and majesty of an emperor. Similarly, gravestones have the primary purpose of marking a place of burial though are sometimes inscribed with texts which serve as documents.[26]

This hazy borderline surrounding the archetypal document is especially obvious in the case of so-called printed ephemera. Advertisements, handbills, invoices and so on are clearly recognisable as documents, but the status of bus tickets, stamps and postcards is less clear-cut. The latter are circulatory or commercial devices, like coins, but are embodied in paper and so bear a closer physical resemblance to the archetypal document. A particular problem arises with maps, paintings, films and similar sources. Maps, for example, embody a text in pictorial and written form and are indistinguishable, in this respect, from other documents. Oil paintings on the other hand might be regarded as aesthetic remains rather than documents, though this is not to deny their importance to the social researcher. Photographs fall on the borderline between these two; whether they are the aesthetic products of the studio photographer or the physical residue of ritualised holiday snapshots, they are often used by families and organisations as documentary records of events to be stored in an album or archive. My aim in this book is to recognise this diversity in documentary sources as a valuable feature of social research. The discussion in it will concentrate on the mainstream of written documents, but the general principles of documentary research apply equally to those on the borderlines.

It is possible to classify documents by their content – as business, political, religious, etc. – but this tends to result in a myriad of overlapping categories, as many documents contain information on more than one area. Therefore, it is preferable to explore the range with a more analytical approach. Figure 1.2 uses the two dimensions

Figure 1.2   *A classification of documents*

		Authorship		
		Personal	Official	
			Private	State
Access	Closed	1	5	9
	Restricted	2	6	10
	Open–archival	3	7	11
	Open–published	4	8	12

of *authorship* and *access* to generate a typology of modern documents.[27] The dimension of authorship refers to the origin of the documents, and its applicability is clearly dependent upon the existence of a separation between the 'personal' and the 'public' or 'official' spheres and, within the latter, between the State and private bureaucracies. The distinction between the personal and the official world was central to Weber's discussion of the rise of modern bureaucratic administration, with its separation of the 'household' from the 'office'.[28] This differentiation is a hallmark of the modern period and the classification in figure 1.2 has less relevance to the medieval and earlier periods, when the distinction between 'personal' papers, 'Church' papers, and 'State' papers was not made at all sharply – if, indeed, it was made at all; and it is only in recent history that official prime ministerial documents in Britain, for example, have ceased to be regarded as the personal property of the Prime Minister.[29]

The dimension of 'access' refers to the availability of the documents to people other than their authors. Documents subject to 'closed' access are those which are available only to a limited circle of eligible insiders, normally to those who produce them and to their bureaucratic superiors. By contrast, 'restricted' documents are accessible on an *ad hoc* basis under specified conditions to those outsiders who are able to secure the permission of insiders; they are therefore, normally closed to outside access, though their authors or custodians may be willing to grant access on application. 'Archival' access exists where the documents have been lodged in a place of storage which is open to all comers; researchers and the general public therefore may use an archive subject only to minimal administrative restrictions – such as the need to apply for a reader's ticket, supply references, and attend during opening hours – and can consult all documents lodged in that archive.[30] Finally, 'published' documents are the most 'open' of all, in the sense that they are printed for public circulation, generally on a commercial basis, and so are accessible to all who can afford them or can obtain them in a library. (As will be seen, however, the fact that particular documents may be openly published does not mean that they are any less difficult to interpret: openness of access is not at all the same thing as openness of meaning!)

Personal documents which are subject to closed access, type 1 in figure 1.2, are perhaps very familiar from the letters, diaries, household account books, address books, and domestic ephemera which are kept by many people. Diaries, for example, are normally completely 'closed' documents – accessible only to the individual author – unless they take the form of an appointment book, when a wider family circle or a secretary may have routine access. But a diary may sometimes be written with the self-conscious intent of informing a wider public through eventual publication, as a diary or in the form of a memoir or autobiography. In such circumstances the diary becomes a document of type 4. As will be shown in a later chapter, however, the closed and the open diary are often of a very different character and require different handling, as the intention to publish may have coloured the author's style and attitude. Even the discovery and publication of a closed diary by a third party involves critical problems of interpretation. Besides the published diary are other published personal documents such as novels, plays, poems and non-fiction works (biographies and scientific works, for example), as well as such things as 'letters to the editor' in a newspaper, and printed sermons and speeches. What unites all these varieties of document is authorship outside the public sphere and the fact of publication.

Some personal documents (type 3), mainly those of wealthy and well-known families, have been deposited in archives, libraries and record offices, and this makes it more possible for the researcher to study them than if they had remained in private hands. The records of many landed estates and lords of the manor, for example, were produced before the distinction between the personal and the official was institutionalised, and remained as part of the day-to-day document-ation of the household. In many cases such documents remain still in private ownership and are, therefore, closed to public access unless the owners are able to establish a private archive in their own house and grant restricted access to the archived documents (type 2). There is thus a progression from the completely closed personal document to the completely open. Some may move from one category to another over the course of their lifetimes: the household accounts of a wealthy landowner, for example, may be 'closed' when in current use, but may eventually pass into the hands of a public archive; and if a researcher 'discovers' a document in an archive and regards it as important source material it may be commercially published and thus become more readily available to other researchers.

Official documents in the private sphere – produced by businesses, schools, hospitals, the church, and so on – may also range from the closed to the open. Typical of private closed documents (type 5) are confidential records and reports produced in organisations and which remain in current use: medical records of the treatment given to patients by their doctors and in hospitals, for example, are normally accessible only to those with responsibility for the patients.[31] Some private organisations have records falling under each of the four categories of access. For instance, businesses registered under the American Securities Exchange Act and quoted on the Stock Exchange have to publish annual reports and accounts (documents of type 8), but the current records of sales, wages, etc., which are contained in their ledgers, minute books and memos, and which are used to compile the published accounts, are normally accessible only to the company's managerial and accounting staff (type 5 documents). A requirement of the British Companies Act has been the public disclosure of certain documents for storage in the Companies Registration Office, a massive government archive for business documents of type 7: copies of annual reports and supporting documents such as registers of shareholders and lists of mortgages. Business documents normally subject to closed access may become available to researchers, such as business historians, when they are no longer of current operating relevance; when, as is usually the case, they remain in the company's own offices, they are restricted documents of type 6, but if they have been deposited in public archives (as in the case of some old or defunct companies) they are in the 'open' category, type 7.

Published documents of private origin (type 8) are particularly widespread in libraries and constitute a major source of research material. Typical of such documents are the timetables and directories produced by many commercial and professional organisations on an annual or more frequent basis, but the category also includes pamphlets, newspapers, and other products of the mass media.[32]

Documents produced by governmental authorities, both national and local, comprise the single largest class of documents available to the social researcher, many more being closed to research access. Police records and security reports, local authority housing records, current taxation records and so on are accessible only by those actually involved in their production and official assessment. In Britain such documents (type 9) are generally protected by the Official Secrets Act, which forbids the unauthorised disclosure of anything learnt by a servant of the State in the course of his or her work. Disclosure is generally not authorised for documents which are deemed to have defence or security implications or to contain information which the Government and its senior civil servants wish to keep private. The operation of official secrecy is such that official documents are either closed or open; relatively few are in the intermediate 'restricted' category (type 10):[33] one example is the British royal papers maintained in a private archive to which access is granted only with permission of the monarch.

Archival access (type 11) is very common for those governmental papers which are classified as 'open', though the vast majority never reach this stage. Examples of archived state documents are the vast range of papers stored in the Public Record Office in Britain or the Library of Congress in the United States. Such documents are available to anyone applying for a reader's ticket and include military and diplomatic dispatches, cabinet minutes, presidential papers, official correspondence and case files, census returns, army and navy records, revenue and taxation records, and so on. In addition to the national record offices, there are various specialist archives which store official documents of type 11 and with varying levels of access. The General Register Office in Britain, for example, maintains an archive of birth, marriage and death registers, the index to which is open to the public who may also purchase certified copies of register entries identified from the index. The registers themselves, however, are closed to all except GRO staff.

The final category of State document (type 12) encompasses a huge range of British official publications: reports of Royal Commissions, the Hansard record of parliamentary debates, Acts of Parliament, Census Reports, and an array of statistical publications such as *Social Trends,* and the *Annual Abstract of Statistics.*

Each of the various types of document involves distinct problems and advantages, and I shall use the typology to organise my discussion of documentary sources in chapters 4 to 8. Chapters 4 and 5 explore the emergence of the official sphere of action and the main classes of public and private documents. Chapter 6 examines the way in which official documents have been used in social research. Chapter 7 is concerned specifically with private documents which have been produced for publication, and chapter 8 discusses the range of personal documents. I have argued, however, that the issues involved in handling each type of document are manifestations of a common set of issues centered on the criteria through which the quality of evidence is assessed. Before discussing each type of document separately therefore, I shall explore these criteria a little further in chapter 2. In chapter 3 I shall show how the criteria can be used to undertake and to assess particular pieces of research.

2 Assessing Documentary Sources

I have argued in the previous chapter that 'documents' comprise a range of research sources, varied in origin and access, stretching from the archetypal government papers to the more marginal cases of photographs, invoices and stamps, and merging imperceptibly with printed ephemera and material remains. A social researcher will normally need to use a number of different sources, of which documents will be simply one kind; and I have also argued that the general principles governing social research are similar for all forms of evidence. I have claimed, however, that each class of source material involves the use of specific techniques through which these general principles are applied. The key to understanding these techniques is provided by the quality control criteria of authenticity, credibility, representativeness and meaning, and application of these to documentary sources will highlight the methodological features of documentary research.[1] Each of these criteria will be considered in turn.

Authenticity: soundness and authorship

Consideration of the authenticity of a document concerns its genuineness: whether it is actually what it purports to be. It may be thought that this is a relatively marginal consideration which arises only in extreme cases, but it constitutes a persistent and routine question in documentary research. An initial problem for the researcher is to decide whether the document to hand is an original or a copy and, if a copy, whether it is a copy of the original or a copy of a copy. Even an original must be assessed for unnoticed but possibly significant errors of spelling and grammar; and copies involve the further problem that a human copyist may have introduced additional errors in the process of copying so that the copy is not an authentic version of the original. Such errors can arise in manuscript, typed or printed copies, and even a purely mechanical process such as photocopying or microfilming may create problems of authenticity if the quality of reproduction is low. Minor smudges and blurs are especially common, as are such major problems as missing pages.

Langlois and Seignobos discuss the authentication of a copy in terms of its 'soundness'. An unsound document is one which is not close enough to the original because it has been corrupted in various ways. The problem is that 'In using a text which has been corrupted in transmission, we run the risk of attributing to the author what really comes from the copyists'.[2] Accidental corruption which results in unintelligibility can often be detected on the basis of a general knowledge of the likely sources of error that arise during copying: transpositions of words and letters, repetition, illogical punctuation, and mistranscription of similar words. Langlois and Seignobos recommend the use of such general knowledge to achieve what they term a 'conjectural emendation', duly footnoted, which reconstructs a sound version of the original.

But conjectural emendation may be insufficient to ensure a sound copy. This will be the case whenever the errors do not result in obvious unintelligibility, if whole sections are missing, or if there have been deliberate or fraudulent interpolations and excisions during the copying. If a document is incomplete, the researcher may attempt to reconstruct it from its fragmentary parts, but this is a difficult task which runs the risk of producing an inauthentic copy. If two or more independently produced copies are in existence, it may be possible to compare the various copies in order to reconstruct a sound version of the original. It is not, however, sufficient simply to compile a version through majority agreement among the copies, as most surviving copies may contain the same error. Langlois and Seignobos argue that the researcher's task is to try to work out the relation in which the various copies stand to one another – to construct their geneaologies – and so to reject all copies of copies which themselves survive.[3] Comparison of the remaining copies, grouped by their genealogical links to the original, may allow the researcher to identify the various 'traditions' which have evolved from the original and so to assume that agreement between traditions is indicative of agreement with the original.

Having established that a document is sound – either an original or a technically sound copy – the researcher must authenticate the identity of those responsible for its production. This is the question of authorship. Even where a particular name, and perhaps a date and place, are inscribed on the documents, these facts will have to be authenticated, as errors of a number of distinct kinds may occur. There may have been incorrect naming of the author by an editor or copyist; or the named author may be merely a nominal author, masking the reality of authorship by a group or organisation or by another individual. A memorandum signed by a government minister, for example, may actually have been produced by one or more of the civil servants responsible for handling ministerial correspondence.

More complex difficulties arise where there has been a fraudulent attempt to pass off a forged or false document as the work of the named author. On rare occasions fraudulent entries have been discovered in parish registers, and there are a number of well-known forged documents. Famous forgeries of the past have included the eighth-century 'Donation of Constantine', aimed at enhancing the power of the papacy, and the 'Vinland' map, which was exposed as a forgery in 1794. Daniel Defoe produced two diaries, *Memories of a Cavalier* and *A Journal of a Plague Year*, which purported to be the genuine products of specific individuals but were, in fact, fictional accounts. Perhaps the most notorious example of forgery in recent years has been that of a set of diaries and their ascription to Adolf Hitler, a fraudulent claim that, for a time, was authenticated by a leading British historian.[4] Further problems of doubtful authorship arise in the case of satire, where a document ostensibly written by a named individual or espousing a particular idea is in fact written with the purpose of ridiculing the person or idea.

As in the case of assessing the soundness of a document, the authentication of authorship involves the use of both internal and external evidence. Internal evidence of vocabulary and literary style can be used to assess the coherence and consistency of a document and so to provide prima facie evidence of authorship, but this will generally have to be supplemented by such external evidence as chemical tests on the paper and ink, and examination of the handwriting, the relation of factual claims in the document to already established facts, and the plausibility of the content as an expression of the author's known views. Of particular importance in the detection of forgeries will be tests on the age and type of materials used and searches into the document's 'known provenance'.[5] Has, for example, a particularly startling and unexpected letter or diary suddenly been discovered in unusual circumstances rather than in a known and trusted archive, and are the materials used of a kind which were available to the supposed author?

In identifying satires with misleading attributions or doubtful claims to authorship it will often be necessary for the researcher to relate the document in question to what is known about the conditions surrounding its production: to assess, for example, whether its form and content are compatible with the procedures known to have been used by the individual or agency ostensibly responsible for it. Yet it should not be assumed that only authentic documents may be used in social research: as Platt points out, 'An inauthentic document may still be of much interest, but it cannot be fully or correctly understood unless one knows that it is not authentic'.[6]

Credibility: sincerity and accuracy

Assessing the credibility of a document involves an appraisal of how distorted its contents are likely to be. All accounts of social events are of course 'distorted', as there is always an element of selective accentuation in the attempt to describe social reality. The question of credibility concerns the extent to which an observer is sincere in the choice of a point of view and in the attempt to record an accurate account from that chosen standpoint. Langlois and Seignobos, in their discussion of this problem, advocate a stance of 'methodical distrust': the researcher should distrust everything that is found in the documents unless there are good reasons to believe them.[7] 'The value of an author's statement depends solely on the conditions under which he [*sic*] performed certain mental operations',[8] and so the task of the researcher is to undertake a critical scrutiny of these conditions in order to discover what reasons there might be for believing the author of the documents. For this to be carried out, it is necessary for the researcher to have an understanding of the circumstances which may lead people to be insincere or inaccurate.

The question of 'sincerity', therefore, is the question of whether the author of the document actually believed what he or she recorded, and involves an assessment of why the author chose to produce the document. In the case of official documents, the author may have little choice or discretion, as production of the documents may be a requirement of the official position held – though this is not to say that the official will always be required to be sincere in producing the document. Similarly, personal documents may be produced for a whole variety of reasons ranging from self-justification and exhibitionism to the intellectual search for the meaning of life.[9]

One of the most important considerations in assessing sincerity is the material interest that the author has in the contents of the document, the extent to which he or she seeks some practical advantage which might involve deceiving his or her readers. Many official documents are based on a political interest in presenting one view rather than another, in transforming propaganda into apparently sincere 'information' or in justifying a particular choice of action. Individual politicians and officials may also feel it is in their interests to engage in propaganda for their own actions and so may add to the insincerity of the documents they produce. Of equal importance are the pecuniary interests which individuals may have in the dishonest representation of events: to what extent, for example, does the need to sell newspapers determine the way in which 'news' is reported, or what financial inducements have been offered to those who supply the newspaper with stories. Above all, bribery and corruption are clearly conditions conducive to the production of insincere documents.

In the case of personal documents the researcher must try to uncover any prejudices which may have led the author to adopt a sympathetic or antipathetic stance towards the people and events reported. An individual may, for example, try to present matters in a favourable or unfavourable light in order to enhance the standing or espouse the beliefs of a group to which he or she belongs or is committed. Perhaps the author tends to present an overdramatised account so as to enhance the nature of his or her participation, or is unduly deferential to the prevailing morality or fashion in order to secure wider public acceptance. The researcher must always ask what individual or collective interest may have been felt by the authors of the documents which he or she studies.

Even where an author can be presumed to have acted sincerely, it is possible for the accuracy of the account to be questioned. As has been seen in the previous chapter, the accuracy of any report – scientific or otherwise – can never be known with any degree of certainty. But it is possible to identify conditions which might lead a sincere observer (or an insincere one) to report events inaccurately. These conditions concern the situation of the author at the time the report was compiled, and, in particular, the degree of proximity to the events in question.[10]

The historian's traditional preference for 'primary' sources rests on the belief that reports which are gathered by people actually involved in the events – first hand, eye-witness accounts – are more likely to be accurate, other things being equal, than the 'secondary' sources of non-participants who use second-hand information. The basis of this belief is the idea that the quality of first-hand information is, in general, higher than second-hand information because of the superior conditions under which the former is gathered. These conditions are essentially those of the spatial and temporal proximity of the author to the events, without which the accuracy of the report may be affected by lapses of memory, inadequate records, or ignorance of the conditions under which the original observers acquired their information. Record-keeping is a special problem, as it is not always feasible for participants to record events as they take place. Although shorthand was invented in the seventeenth century, mechanical recording devices were not feasible until well into the twentieth century. Therefore a researcher must attempt to discern the time-lapse between the events reported and the production of the report, the degree of participation of the author in the events, such expertise that the author may have had in handling the original data, the ways in which observations were recorded, and the extent to which the author seems to generalise beyond the scope of the original information.[11]

Even the 'primary' observer may be influenced by illusions, hallucinations, or simple mis-observation into believing that something happened which in fact has not. And both a 'primary' and a 'secondary' observer are liable to negligence and indifference in the reporting of observations and the handling of evidence. For these reasons the distinction between primary and secondary sources should not be equated with that between 'accurate' and 'inaccurate' sources; the probable accuracy of a document must always be assessed independently of its status as a primary or secondary source.

As with inauthentic documents, however, inaccurate sources have their uses in research, so long as they are recognised as being inaccurate. While the researcher may regard a document as being technically inaccurate with respect to the events in question, it *may* nevertheless be regarded as a credible (because sincere) account of the author's perceptions and experiences; and such a document may provide essential evidence of the attitudes and experiences of the author and those who share his or her situation.

Representativeness: survival and availability

The intelligent use of documents involves a judgement as to whether the documents consulted are representative of the totality of relevant documents. This is not to say that good research cannot be carried out with an unrepresentative selection; but the user must know to what extent and in what respects those documents are unrepresentative. An investigator of government decision-making using cabinet papers, for example, would have to know whether the papers he or she is able to consult are a complete or at least representative collection of *all* cabinet papers produced in the relevant period.

The question of representativeness involves the two aspects of 'survival' and 'availability'. In order to survive, documents must be 'deposited'. This may be through publication in a form which is itself capable of survival, or by way of storage in a public or private archive or more prosaically in a cardboard box in an attic. Not all documents are deposited in a place in which they are likely to survive, some (e.g. official papers) are destroyed in an incinerator or shredder, others (e.g. personal documents and 'ephemera') may be thrown away, and all are susceptible to accidental destruction or loss. Sometimes deposit is a deliberate, systematic and selective process which results in the survival of an unrepresentative selection: letters published by the editor of a newspaper, for example, are generally a small selection from the letters received – though how small is generally not known, and may vary over time – and so those published may well be unrepresentative of the letters actually written.[12]

Even where deposition occurs, the number surviving diminishes as time goes by. The mere physical process of ageing will, in the absence of attempts at preservation, result in deterioration and decay. Paper, especially modern acid-based paper, is a fragile medium unless stored under appropriate conditions of temperature and humidity, and can soon be reduced to a form in which it is digestible by rodents and insects. Marx and Engels are not the only writers whose unpublished manuscripts have been subjected to 'the gnawing criticism of the mice'.[13]

Documents which are protected from this fate may, even so, be destroyed by accident when someone unfamiliar with their value 'sorts out' a public or private store of them: for instance, many personal documents of potential value to social historians disappear on the death of their owners, when overzealous relatives consign the accumulation of a lifetime to the dustbin. Destruction such as this is merely misguided; but we have also to consider deliberate destruction or removal when documents are regarded as 'sensitive' or of particular importance. Official papers are subject to 'weeding' within their originating departments, a process in which the weeders are required to decide not only which documents are likely to be of value to historians but also whether any are too politically sensitive to be released into a public archive: some may contain confidential data about individuals or information which it is felt should not be disclosed. All the state papers of James II relating to 'Bloody' Judge Jeffreys, for example, are reputed to have been destroyed.[14] A great many documents are destroyed specifically in order to prevent their survival and entry to the public sphere.

A final aspect of the question of survival is simple disappearance through accidental misfiling or deliberate hiding. For example, a document may appear not to have survived because it is not in the place in an archive where it should be: e.g. the cabinet minutes for a particular day may not be in the relevant file. In such circumstances a document has, to all intents and purposes, failed to survive, though deliberately hidden documents may remain hidden only for as long as it is in the interests of the authorities to keep their existence obscured, and accidentally misfiled documents may subsequently come to light. The latter may happen with deliberately hidden documents if the official responsible is succeeded in office by someone who is unaware of his or her actions. Thus documents thought not to have survived may suddenly and unexpectedly be discovered, just as 'lost' or 'stolen' library books may eventually be discovered shelved in the wrong section of a library. In all such cases of unexpected discovery, however, the researcher must be clear about the authenticity of the discovered documents.

The question of survival is only half of the problem of representative-ness, as not all surviving documents may be available to the researcher. The various forms of openness and closure of access to documents discussed in the previous chapter affect availability: public documents of the central government in Britain, for example, are generally covered by a 'thirty-year rule', under which they become available for public inspection thirty years after their compilation.[15] Quite apart from the weeding of such documents to reduce their bulk and so to allow them to be stored until the thirty years have elapsed, they are weeded in order to ascertain which of them should remain closed to the public for a longer period or indefinitely. Thus, documents may be known to have survived, but they may not be accessible to the researcher.

Although this is clearly a considerable problem with official papers produced within the State, it is in some respects a greater problem in the private sphere, where there are few legal restrictions on the rights of individuals and organisations to destroy or restrict access to their records. Normally, such documents are required only to be available to the public when they have already entered the public sphere and become stored in public archives. Company records which make up the legally required annual return, for example, are retained for public inspection at a government office, and a company itself has little or no legal responsibility for ensuring the survival or availability of any other records. Where such private records have survived and are available they may be unrepresentative of business records as a whole – if for no other reason than that the enterprise itself has been successful enough to survive and is, hence, unrepresentative of unsuccessful enterprises.

In order to arrive at a judgement about the representativeness of a particular collection of documents the researcher must of course have some idea of the number and type of relevant documents that might have been produced in the first place, and this information is not always easy to obtain. Ideally the researcher requires a catalogue, index or calendar of the documents in which he or she is interested,[16] and preferably one which is contemporary with the documents rather than one produced at a later stage by an archivist. Many collections of documents have not been catalogued, and their very existence may be unknown to researchers. Those catalogues which have been produced are in varying states of quality and completeness.[17] Furthermore, there is neither an exhaustive list of catalogues nor an exhaustive list of collections, and in the very nature of things these can never be achieved. In Britain the establishment of the county record offices and various private archive collections, on the model of the earlier Public Record Office, has done much to improve the situation, as have improvements in the archival skills of libraries and museums, but little progress has been made outside the sphere of government documents. For this reason, the initial task of the researcher may be what the early German historians called 'heuristic' – a search for the sources by the researcher, and an attempt to understand the principles on which the various archives have been constructed, in order to compile a listing of the relevant documents.[18]

This heuristic task will generally form part of any strategy of sampling which the researcher pursues, as it is hardly ever appropriate or possible to consult all surviving documents of relevance. Indeed, a properly constructed sample – one which is a theoretically and empirically meaningful selection of documents – may be able to rectify some of the unrepresentativeness of the collection from which the sample is drawn. Sampling methods can sometimes be used, when no listing of documents exists, as a way of achieving a representative selection of the available documents. In their study of English local government, for example, the Webbs discovered that there was no central index or register of the records of the parish vestries and statutory authorities in which they were interested and that the records had been described only perfunctorily by others.[19] They decided that it would be virtually impossible to compile such a list for themselves and that the only adequate alternative was to base their work on Acts of Parliament, for which an adequate official list did exist. By taking a sample of years over the period they were studying they were able to examine all local Acts for those years, on the assumption that legal forms were nationally uniform and fairly stable over the short term.

While all scientific research involves the 'construction' of facts, the use of documents whose representativeness is unknown involves the possibility that the 'facts' constructed from the documents may be *purely* functions of the bias inherent in selective survival and availability. 'A single reference to a phenomenon may indicate the start of a trend, or the existence of a pattern, but it may be just historially idiosyncratic.'[20] A lack of information about the representativeness of documents may make it impossible to choose between these alternatives.

Meaning: literal and interpretative understanding

The ultimate purpose of examining documents, the point to which all the preceding issues have been leading, is to arrive at an understanding of the meaning and significance of what the document contains. This problem of meaning arises at two levels, the literal and the interpretative. The problem of literal understanding is summarised by Langlois and Seignobos as follows: 'Let us suppose we have before us a written document. What use can we make of it if we cannot read it?'[21] That is to say, it is necessary to decipher the script and translate the language into the linguistic forms current in the community of researchers of which the investigator is a part.

Langlois and Seignobos emphasise the importance of the technical skills of palaeography and philology which are required in reading historical documents on the grounds that the meaning of an indecipherable text, or one written in an unfamiliar language, will necessarily escape us.[22] British manuscript documents from the seventeenth century or earlier are generally written in a handwriting unfamiliar to those who are used to the italic styles of recent centuries, and many of the earliest such documents are written in Latin, or 'dog' Latin, which must be translated. All documents, as noted in the discussion of 'authenticity', may be liable to technical imperfections of printing and reproduction which make them difficult to read, and may contain unfamiliar argot or slang expressions. Even modern printed documents may contain technical terms, for example legal phraseology, which the researcher must be able to translate into more familiar words.

Occupational titles, for example, may be difficult to understand when the title, or even the occupation, has fallen into disuse. A nineteenth-century census return which records a man as a 'whitster', for example, is using a term which is not in current usage and which, even at the time, had two separate meanings. A whitster could be either a textile bleacher or a metal finisher, and the researcher will have to come to a decision about which is the most likely meaning for the person in question. The use of documents invariably involves such decisions – for instance, as to the literal meaning of terms like 'affeeror', 'forfang', 'chimin', 'smoot', 'lairstal', 'reamer', 'keeker', and 'finder'; and the precise meaning of even such commonplace words as 'clerk' or 'engineer' may not be obvious. The achievement of a literal reading of the words that appear in a text therefore involves deciding what the words designate and translating them into a more precise contemporary usage.[23]

Particular problems of literal meaning arise in the dating of documents, even given written dates, as calendar systems and ways of recording dates vary. The present Gregorian calendar was not introduced in official documents in Britain and British North America until 1752, before which time the Julian calendar was used. The change had already been made in Italy, France, Spain and Portugal in 1582, and it was adopted shortly after that in Prussia, Switzerland, Holland and Flanders. The Protestant states of Germany, the Netherlands, Denmark and Sweden made the change in the early eighteenth century. The change was not made until 1872 in Japan and 1917 in the Soviet Union.

In the Julian system the new year began on Lady Day, 25 March, and so dates from 1 January to 24 March were in the same year as the preceding December: a date shown as, say, 21 February 1750 corresponds to what would now be designated 21 February 1751. Documents other than official and legal documents often reckoned years according to the historical year, beginning 1 January, and dates would sometimes be rendered in both styles as, say 21 February 1722/3. With the introduction of the new calendar the two systems became known as 'Old Style' and 'New Style'. The importance of this change is that unless it is known in which style the date is recorded, it is not possible to work out accurately the lapse of time between two documents: 21 February 1750 and 21 February 1751 might appear to be one year apart until it is realised that the former date is recorded in 'Old Style' and that the two dates are, therefore, the same.[24]

Many British legal documents have, since 1066, been dated according to 'regnal years' rather than calendar years, each regnal year beginning on the anniversary of the current sovereign's accession to the throne. Thus, an Act of Parliament dated, for example, '25 Elizabeth II' would come from the 25th year of the reign. This is the period from 6 February 1976 to 5 February 1977, as Elizabeth II acceded to the throne on 6 February 1952.[25]

These are the main dating problems in British official documents, but similar problems arise with dated private documents: Masonic documents, for example, date years according to the 'Anno Lucius',[26] the

Eastern Orthodox churches retained the Julian calendar until well into the twentieth century, and some Jewish documents will be dated from a base line of 3760 BC, with the Jewish new year beginning during September of the Gregorian calendar.

The achievement of a literal understanding, however, is only the first step towards an interpretative understanding. It is all very well to decide that the literal meaning of 'whitster' is textile bleacher, but what do we know about the type of work involved, the conditions under which it was carried out, the level of skill and social standing that it involved, its remuneration, and so on? In short, the literal meanings of the words in a document give only its 'face value' meaning; they are the raw materials from which its real significance must be reconstructed. Interpretative understanding is the end-product of a hermeneutic process in which the researcher relates the literal meanings to the contexts in which they were produced in order to assess the meaning of the text as a whole.[27] The hermeneutic approach to the reading of texts evolved from the Kantian and Hegelian traditions in German philosophy and received its classic formulation in Dilthey's elaboration of Ranke's approach to historical sources.[28] Cultural phenomena are to be understood, argued Dilthey, by grasping them as 'totalities', by discovering the inner connections of the meanings 'objectivated' in them.

At its simplest, interpretation requires an understanding of the particular definitions and recording practices adopted and of the genre and stylisation employed in the text. The particular way in which a concept was defined and applied in practice changes over time and from place to place, and the researcher must discover as much as possible about these changes. While the incidence of crime has been measured in official documents over a number of years, the practical operationalisation of this concept has varied considerably. An attempt to use information on crime for two or more periods and places must take account of any variation in usage. Similarly, the measured rate of unemployment can rise or fall according to the ways in which the authorities choose to define and record the information they collect. The definitions adopted will depend in part upon the genre of the document. 'Genre' refers to the varying conventions governing a particular type of document: the stylistic differences between, for example, a government report, a party manifesto, and a personal diary. The same event observed from the same standpoint may be reported very differently in each of these three genres, and the variations can tell the researcher much about both the event and the observers.[29] 'Stylisation' involves the conscious or unconscious use of varying literary forms and embellishments within the conventions of a particular genre, and if this involves the use of allusion, allegory and irony the researcher must be aware that such stylisation has been employed if he or she is to understand the meaning of the document.

The hermeneutic process of interpretation, moreover, goes beyond these important and necessary preliminaries. The hermeneutic task involves interpretative understanding of individual concepts, appreciation of the social and cultural context through which the various concepts are related in a particular discourse, and a judgement on the meaning and significance of the text as a whole. The first step is to elucidate the underlying selective point of view from which the account or report is constructed. This is the standpoint from which the individual concepts acquire their relevance. But grasping this frame of meaning is no easy task, for no researcher can escape the concepts and assumptions of his or her own frame of meaning. One frame of meaning can only ever be understood from the standpoint of another. There can be no presuppositionless knowledge, and so the investigator must, in effect, enter into a dialogue with the author of the documents being studied.[30] Of course, direct personal dialogue will rarely be possible, and the hermeneutic notion of dialogue is, in any case, much wider than this. The researcher must seek to discover as much as possible about the conditions under which the text was produced, and must relate the use of individual concepts to this context. The ultimate interpretation of the meaning of the text will derive from the researcher's judgement that this interpretation 'makes sense', given his or her understanding of the author's situation and intentions.

Textual analysis involves mediation between the frames of reference of the researcher and those who produced the text. The aim of this dialogue is to move within the 'hermeneutic circle' in which we comprehend a text by understanding the frame of reference from which it was produced, and appreciate that frame of reference by understanding the text. The researcher's own frame of reference becomes the springboard from which the circle is entered, and so the circle reaches back to encompass the dialogue between the researcher and the text.

In recent years, a number of competing approaches to the hermeneutic task of textual analysis have arisen, though not all of them are rooted in the tradition of hermeneutic philosophy itself. A particularly influential approach has been that which draws upon the 'semiotic' tradition. The origins of the semiotic approach to textual analysis are to be found in Saussure's structural linguistics, with Barthes being a key figure in the translation of these ideas into textual analysis.[31] Barthes argued that the message of the text is embodied not in the individual words and phrases but in the system of 'rules' that structures the text as a whole. Semiotics, the science of signs, has the task of discovering these rules and of using them to decode the underlying, hidden meaning that is carried by the text.[32] This basic idea is present also in the works of Althusserian and post-Althusserian writers such as Foucault and Derrida, though they differ in many important ways.[33]

An older tradition of interpretative understanding, working from very different principles, is 'content analysis'. In this approach, quantitative techniques are used to assess the significance of particular items within a text. The number of times a particular idea is used and the number of contexts in which it appears, are taken as measures of the importance of this idea to the author of the document.

A great difficulty with all approaches to interpretative understanding is the question of how readings of texts are to be validated: on what grounds do we accept one reading as 'correct' and another as 'incorrect'? Content analysis attempts to ground its interpretations in rigorous criteria of enumeration, drawing upon an implicit theory of meaning according to which the significance of textual items derives from their frequency of appearance in a document. But 'frequency' is not the same as 'significance', and it is necessary for researchers to justify, in each case, *why* a frequency measure of significance is appropriate. It may be that a single striking word or phrase conveys a meaning out of all proportion to its frequency; and a non-quantitative approach may be better able to grasp the significance of such isolated references. The content analyst must engage in an act of qualitative synthesis when attempting to summarise the overall meaning of the text and its impact on a reader.

But the main non-quantitative approaches have also failed to provide solutions to this problem. For Barthes, the validity of a reading of a text is demonstrated by the coherence of the interpretation that the analyst discloses, though this position faces the obvious objection that an underlying meaning itself may not actually be coherent: the criterion of coherence is simply an ungrounded assumption of Barthes's methodology. For Althusser, on the other hand, validity is guaranteed by the use of appropriate 'scientific' tools and methods. Scientific textual analysis works on the surface concepts of a text to disclose an underlying structure, whereas 'ideological' analyses remain at the level of the superficial message of the text. For Althusser, however, 'science' is more an invocation than a rigorous method, and the specific tools and methods involved are neither spelled out nor justified. The semiotic tradition has failed to produce rigorous methodological criteria for choosing between alternative readings of a text.

This failure to provide a firm basis for choosing between alternative readings of a text has led writers to resort to various devices to validate their interpretations. One such attempt was that of Mannheim, whose materialist reconstruction of hermeneutics held that, because frames of meaning are rooted in social conditions, objectivity is guaranteed by the relative freedom from social determination that characterises the intelligentsia. Intellectuals are relatively detached from social interests and so can mediate rival positions and achieve an objective understanding of cultural phenomena.[34] But even if Mannheim's general position on the sociology of knowledge is accepted, no compelling grounds are offered for showing why intellectuals should be privileged in this way – indeed no criteria are given for identifying the intelligentsia and distinguishing them from mere ideologues and party propagandists.

This problem is non-existent for some writers who deny that there can be any link between a piece of analysis and the actual text itself. Saussure was concerned with the link between the conventional 'signs' used in a text and the 'ideas' they signify; he was not concerned with the link between either of these and the 'real world'. Giddens has correctly concluded that for Saussure 'how ideas or concepts achieve any capability of referring to objects or events in the world is completely unexplicated'.[35] This failure enabled such writers as Althusser to stress the distinction between 'thought objects' and 'real objects' and to claim that there is no way of establishing a link between the two; to attempt to make such a link would be to commit the error of 'empiricism'.[36] The relativistic implications of theories of interpretation have therefore seemed avoidable only by recourse to dogmatism: a particular interpretation is validated by virtue of arbitrarily imposed criteria such as coherence or frequency, or on the grounds of its production by a privileged social group or through privileged 'scientific' methods.

I wish to draw on Giddens's discussion of this problem in order to propose a workable basis for the interpretation of meaning.[37] Giddens shows that philosophical discussions of the hermeneutic problem have involved the separation of the text from its author and its audience. Textual analysts have attempted to elucidate the 'objective' meaning of the text itself, arguing that its cultural significance depends on what messages it actually contains and not on what its author may have intended. Giddens argues that this is a search for a chimera. Although a text does indeed 'escape' from its author and achieve a reception that was not intended, the message an audience takes from a text will not necessarily be that which content analysts or semioticians have discovered within it. The text as an objective cultural entity, therefore, is ephemeral and must be reunited with the intentions of its author and the perspectives of its audiences. Texts must be studied as socially situated products.

The disjuction between the intentions of the author and the message received by the audience is, in part, due to the author's use of 'rules' of which he or she may be only partially aware. A native speaker of English, for example, will not normally be consciously aware of the grammatical rules which structure speech. Speakers therefore produce statements whose meaning is ambiguous and whose reception cannot be predicted. This can be illustrated through the old chestnut of English grammar: 'The piano was sold to the lady with carved wooden legs'. The author of this sentence may have meant that the lady who bought the piano was a disabled person with carved wooden legs, even though his or her readers understood that the piano had carved wooden legs when it was sold to the lady.

Authors of texts employ not only grammatical rules, but also conventions of definition, genre and stylisation. These are less precise and less well known than the grammatical rules of subject and object, and so the possibility of variations in interpretation between author and audience, and within the audience, are that much greater.[38]

Moreover, a complex social process intervenes between the author and the audience. The author of a novel, for example, will find the text dealt with by agents, literary editors, copy-editors, and compositors, and will have little control over the 'packaging' and conditions under which it is sold to the public. The reader will, in turn, approach the novel on the basis of advertising hype, reviews, personal recommendations from family and friends, or simply by discovering the book in a public library. All of the factors that intervene between author, text, and audience – and the novel is used simply as an example– will transform the meanings that are found in the text.

I wish to argue that we must recognise three aspects of the meaning of a text – three 'moments' in the movement of the text from author to audience. The *intended content* of a text is the meaning which the author of the text intended to produce, while the *received content* is the meaning constructed by its audience. Both author and audience may be socially differentiated entities, and so there may be numerous intended and received meanings for the same text. Intervening between the intended and the received meanings is the transient and ephemeral *internal meaning* that semioticians and content analysts have tried to identify. But this internal meaning cannot be known independently of its reception by an audience. As soon as a researcher approaches a text to interpret its meaning, he or she becomes a part of its audience. The most that can be achieved by a researcher is an analysis which shows how the inferred internal meaning of the text opens up some possibilities for interpretation by its audience and closes off others. The researcher cannot adopt the stance of Mannheim's free floating intelligentsia and produce an absolutely valid reading of the 'objective meaning' of the text. The interpretation of a text which is offered by the researcher must pay close attention to the perspectives and interests of its various potential audiences.

It follows from this, therefore, that the interpretation of a text cannot be separated from the questions of its production and its effects. The reading of a text is validated by relating it to the intentions of the author, and by taking account of the fact that its 'objective meaning' goes beyond these intentions, and also by relating the text to its audience.

The four criteria of authenticity, credibility, representativeness and meaning should not be regarded as distinct stages in assessing the quality of documentary sources. It should be clear from my discussion that they are interdependent and that the researcher cannot adequately apply one criterion without simultaneously invoking the conclusions derived from applying the other three. In this sense, quality appraisal is a never-ending process, as any conclusions arrived at can be used to push the appraisal a little further. The interpretative meaning of the document which the researcher aims to produce therefore is, in a very real sense, a tentative and provisional judgement which must be constantly in need of revision as new discoveries and new problems force the researcher to reappraise the evidence. For this reason, the criteria must not be applied in a rigid and formalistic way. Although the four criteria will be systematically applied at a number of points in this book, this is for purposes of explication only, and it should not be assumed that professional researchers approach their evidence with such a check-list. Once understood and acquired, the assessment criteria become part of the professional expertise of the researcher and are applied in more subtle and informed ways. In the following chapter I shall use examples of documentary research to show how these taken-for-granted criteria can be made explicit in order to assess the validity of research reports.

3 The Use of Documents in Social Research

I have discussed the place of documents in the whole range of sources available to the social researcher, and I have reviewed the criteria used to assess the quality of documentary sources. It is now necessary to explore more fully how documents are actually used in social research. The simplest use, of course, is consulting them as references for a particular piece of information. The researcher may look up a biographical reference book, for example, in order to discover what school was attended by a person, or may consult the published criminal statistics in order to discover the number of people convicted of housebreaking in a particular year. This use is analogous to the everyday use of such documents as a personal diary and a bus timetable to enable an appointment to be kept on a particular day. In this type of work, the social researcher is using documentary sources as adjuncts to a larger research process. It is therefore necessary to go beyond this rudimentary level to documentary research *per se*, where documents are used systematically as material for research.

Systematic documentary research may involve one of two interdependent focuses of interest: documents can be used as *resources* or as *topics*. To pursue the previous examples, the use of documents as *resources* might involve the use of biographical reference books to compile a comprehensive set of data on a particular sample of individuals regarded as members of an elite, or the use of criminal statistics to compile data on trends in housebreaking over a fifty-year period in a number of different cities. In such research the quality of the documents is appraised in terms of their value in constructing valid descriptive statements about the things to which they refer: the researcher is interested in what they denote about the world. When documents are used as *topics*, on the other hand, the researcher's main concern is to explain the nature of the documents themselves: they are regarded as social products and are treated as the objects of sociological analysis. The aim is to elucidate the social processes through which they were produced in order to explain their form and content and perhaps something about their authors and the circumstances in which they were living. For instance, biographical reference books may be regarded as devices used by privileged and powerful people to legitimate their advantages; they may be seen as social registers, arbiters of acceptance in privileged social circles. In investigating this, the researcher must address such matters as the social background of the editors and publishers, the criteria which they employ in deciding who to include in their pages, and the matters on which they choose to record – or not to record – information. The form and content of the book will reflect such judgements, interests, and conditions.

There is a very real sense in which reading books by other researchers is documentary research. A systematic reading of Marx's works, for example, can be undertaken in order to learn something about how capitalism works or in order to understand how Marx came to write those particular texts. An attempt to understand 'what Marx really meant', for instance, involves questions of authorship, error, and so forth. The reader must assess, say, to what extent it is possible to distinguish the contribution of Marx from that of Engels in the jointly authored *Communist Manifesto* and the posthumously published volumes of *Capital*, whether translators have correctly inferred the original meaning when they employ a single word such as 'alienation' to cover a variety of German words, and indeed whether the words originally used were intended to reflect nuances of meaning and emphasis or simply to introduce stylistic variation. The latter issues cannot be considered without asking what mistakes in writing Marx may have made and whether further errors were introduced in editing and printing the various editions of the work. The succession of editions of a particular work of Marx must be understood in the overall context of the genealogy of his texts: to what extent are the *Economic and Philosophical Manuscripts* the original sources from which the *Grundrisse* was later constructed and from which, in turn, the volumes of *Capital* and *Theories of Surplus Value* were compiled? Does the genealogy of the texts, for example, disclose an epistemological break?

These considerations point to the common features involved in handling documentary sources, regardless of the purpose of the research. My main concern in this book, however, is with those types of documents reviewed in the previous chapter: documents produced outside the context of social research itself. It is these source materials for which questions of authenticity, credibility, representativeness and meaning are especially acute, and the remainder of this book will be devoted to their consideration.

I have claimed that the two focuses of interest – documents as resources and documents as topics – are interdependent, and that any researcher will inevitably be forced to consider the documents he or she uses from both points of view. Just as it is not possible to assess the quality of documents as resources without paying attention to the social conditions under which they were produced, so also it is not possible to explain documents as the outcome of a system of social production without some consideration of how they relate to the events they ostensibly describe. But this point cannot simply be asserted. It is necessary to demonstrate it through a consideration of some actual examples of documentary research. How is documentary research undertaken? Historians have accumulated a particular expertise in handling documentary sources, and so I shall examine some cases of historical research before turning to a classic piece of sociological research.

The search for King Arthur

The first case of documentary research I shall examine is the attempt by Lesley Alcock[1] to establish the existence of 'King Arthur'. Alcock uses documentary sources and archaeological evidence to assess the extent to which the conventional view of Arthur and his life can be considered as an accurate historical record. While concerned with documents of the pre-modern period, the very paucity of sources highlights with unusual clarity the mechanics of documentary research. Alcock's exemplary piece of work shows how popular history and literature can be assessed as historical evidence, and how this assessment involves an appraisal of the quality of alternative sources of evidence.

The story of King Arthur and the knights of the round table has been a subject for children's play over generations and has been told and retold in a great many picture books, poems and novels. It has been performed on stage, television and film. The life of Arthur is first known to have been given literary expression by the early medieval monk Geoffrey of Monmouth, who recorded as fact the existence of Arthur, King of the Britons, in the sixth century and dramatised his struggles against the Saxon invaders. Geoffrey peopled his tale with such characters as Queen Guinevere, the knights Gawain, Mordred, Bedevere, Cador and Kay, and Merlin the magician, and he recounted the stories of Arthur's sword Caliburn (and his less well-known spear called Ron), his mortal injury at the battle of Camlann, and the taking of his body to the Isle of Avalon. Geoffrey's account of Arthur ends with his report of the legend that Arthur will eventually rise from his rest on Avalon to fulfil Merlin's prophecy that the Britons will overthrow the Saxon yoke and will once again be ruled by a British king.[2] Geoffrey's story, written in about 1136, was the basis for many subsequent English and French writers who elaborated on the Arthurian story, the best known of their works being Sir Thomas Malory's *Morte d'Arthur*, the anonymous *Sir Gawain and the Green Knight*, and Tennyson's *Idylls of the King*. These and other sources added many elements to Geoffrey's original story: the round table, Sir Lancelot, and the quest for the Holy Grail being the best known.

The task which Alcock set for himself was to decide what credibility could be attached to the story reported by Geoffrey. Later literary accretions having no basis in any surviving documentary or archaeological evidence could be discarded, but how much truth was contained in the original account? Geoffrey is known to have used certain surviving historical documents and is believed to have drawn on contemporary oral tradition, a tradition which persisted for 600 years after the events in question. But he also claimed to have used a book which is unknown to any later writer. It is not possible, of course, for any historian to arrive at a complete and accurate picture of Arthur and his life, but it is possible to say which parts of Geoffrey's story can be supported by independent evidence. This is the task that Alcock set himself: to discern the irreducible minimum of historical truth, if any, concerning Arthur.

The bald historical narrative presented by Geoffrey himself, disregarding all elements peripheral to the realm of ascertainable fact, begins with Vortigern, who plotted to seize the throne of Britain by securing the crown for Constans and then engineering his death.[3] Constans's brothers, Ambrosius and Uther, fled to Brittany, while Vortigern buttressed his hold on the throne by building alliances with Hengist and his Saxon troops. The Saxons, however, betrayed Vortigern and conquered Britain; then Ambrosius landed in Britain, killed Vortigern, and went on to defeat the Saxons. Intermittent warfare with the Saxons continued, and Ambrosius was poisoned by a Saxon spy. He was succeeded as king by his brother Uther, who was eventually succeeded by his son, Arthur. Arthur appears on the British historical scene at a time when the throne was still insecure, because of continuing waves of Saxon invasion; and he is depicted by Geoffrey as the defender of Christian Britain. While Arthur was away fighting the Romans, as a member of an international crusading force, his cousin Mordred usurped the throne and entered into an alliance with the Saxons. A series of battles between Arthur and Mordred ensued, culminating in that of Camlann in 542 AD. It was in this battle that Mordred was killed and Arthur mortally wounded.

This historical narrative reflects the values and concerns of the period in which it was written, and contains many elements which were to encourage later writers to elaborate on it in terms of *their* values and concerns. Alcock's intention was to test the narrative against the available evidence in order to assess its credibility. The most detailed source of evidence on the events of the period is a manuscript known to historians as the *British Historical Miscellany*, and other important sources include Gildas's *De excidio et conquestu Britanniae* and the *Anglo-Saxon Chronicle*. The latter two sources formed the basis of Bede's *Ecclesiastical History of the English People*. The *Miscellany* is a Latin compendium of source material which was acquired by the British Museum in 1729. Nothing is known of its ownership and location prior to the British Museum acquisition, but it appears to be a complete though unfinished document: the text is complete, but the initial letters, illuminations, title-page and so on are missing. From the annotated Easter tables (calendars used in calculating and recording the dates of Easter) and the royal genealogies that it contains, Alcock estimated that the manuscript was a twelfth-century copy of tenth-century originals, and internal evidence suggested that the copying was carried out at the St David's scriptorium.[4]

The part of the *Miscellany* that specifically concerns Arthur has for a long time been imputed to the original authorship of Nennius, and is known to have been used by Geoffrey himself, as was Gildas's *De excidio et conquestu Britanniae* (the ruin and conquest of Britain). The latter is a sixth-century Latin text which was principally concerned with denouncing the state of religion in Britain, but which also recounted a great deal of supposedly factual information. The earliest surviving copy of Gildas's text, however, dates from the eleventh century – indeed, extremely few manuscripts at all have survived from the sixth century. This same problem applies to the ninth-century *Anglo-Saxon Chronicle*, compiled from earlier manuscripts, which exists now only in later copies and extensions.[5] The *Chronicle* does, however, appear to draw on original sources unavailable to either Nennius or Gildas.

It is impossible here to relate the whole of Alcock's long and detailed argument, and I propose to concentrate on his discussion of two elements in the Arthurian narrative: the existence of Arthur, and the location of one of his major battle victories. The battle of Mount Badon is described in each of the historical texts as a major British victory, yet the question of when and where it took place can be resolved only from the agreement between *independent* sources of evidence. A single text cannot be accepted on its own authority, and a statement in one text which simply repeats what is found in another cannot be regarded as giving independent corroboration. While Gildas mentions a battle, he does not give the name of the British commander. Nennius does, however, mention Arthur in this context, and is independently supported by some surviving historical annals which were not themselves used by Nennius. The independent evidence leads Alcock to conclude that 'the battle of Mount Badon was certainly a historical event and that Arthur's connection with it is also probably authentic.'[6] But where did it take place?

The obvious way to attempt to locate Badon would be to postulate that such a name derived from a personal name such as Badda and that it would have been transformed by the Saxons into a name something like Baddanbyrig or Baddanbury. The modern form of such a Saxon name would be Badbury, and five places with this name can be found from Dorset to Lincoln. There is, however, a flaw in this argument. The British pronunciation of the 'd' in Badon would, in fact, have been closer to the modern 'th' sound, and so would not be likely to result in the Saxon forms postulated. Alcock argues therefore that there may be some truth in a Welsh tradition which identifies Badon with the Aquae Sulis of the Romans. The Saxon settlers, on discovering the Roman baths assimilated the root of Baðon (pronounced 'Bathon') to their own word for 'bath', thus giving the form Badon. This interpretation is supported by surviving references to Baðanceaster and Baðum in the *Chronicle*. Alcock concludes, therefore, that the battle took place on a hill (or mount) outside Bath.[7]

Calculation of the date of the battle from Easter tables printed in the *Miscellany* suggests a date of 518 AD, but this leads to internal contradictions and so suggests an error. Gildas adds to the problem by claiming that it was in the same year as his own birth, about which there is considerable disagreement. Alcock attempts to resolve the problem by identifying a source of error which would allow the various statements to be reconciled. Specifically, he postulates that the errors resulted from a confusion between two different systems of dating. The earliest Christian system of dating related years to the *death* of Christ, and it was not until the fifth century that the Dionysiac (AD) system of dating events from his birth was invented. The latter system reached Britain only in the seventh century. It is, therefore, not always clear which system a particular author used, and a scribe translating dates could easily make a mistake of 28 years (the supposed length of Christ's life). If it is assumed that there was such an error in the calculation of the date 518 AD, a new date of 490 AD can be computed. This restores some consistency to the texts and is supported by Gildas's placing of Badon close in time to a victory of Ambrosius known to have taken place in 475 AD.[8]

In the surviving copies of Dark Age sources, only a handful of named individuals appear with any certainty. Two of these, Ambrosius and Arthur, are depicted as great battle leaders. The *Miscellany* claims that Arthur fought twelve battles with the British kings against the Saxons, but it does not describe Arthur himself as a king. These battles were spread across the country, the final one being Mount Badon. Gildas, however, describes Badon as a crucial victory of the Britons over the Saxons in which the British general was called Ambrosius. But Gildas's text is full of ambiguities and its meaning is far from clear: leadership by Arthur at Badon would certainly not be incompatible with it. The basis of the discussion in the *Miscellany* is a Welsh battle poem which introduces Arthur and ascribes victory at Badon to him. Most importantly, Arthur is described as 'dux bellorum' fighting alongside the kings of the Britons.

These sources suggest, Alcock argues, that both Arthur and Ambrosius were battle commanders leading troops drawn from several of the British kingdoms. There is no evidence that either of them was himself a king, and although there is no evidence to the contrary it would seem likely that they would have been described as kings if that were in fact the case. The kingship of Arthur seems a later fictional accretion. Arthur emerges from Alcock's discussion as a general working on behalf of the dominant king in the British confederation. This king is described in Latin as 'superbus tyrannus', supreme ruler, and the British equivalent of this phrase is 'vortigern'. Thus Vortigern may be a recognisable British supreme ruler, or simply a misunderstanding of the generic term for the holder of such a position.

Alcock concludes that Arthur, a general commanding about 1,000 troops, was the victor of Mount Badon in about 490 AD, and that the battle was fought on a hill outside Bath. From additional researches he adds that Arthur also fought in Scotland, at Caerleon or Chester, and in eastern England. He died in about 510 AD in the battle of Camlann (site unknown), an internecine struggle among the British troops.[9] Further than this the sources will not allow us to go. This is the core of truth from which Geoffrey's story was constructed, though it is not impossible that some of his additions may have been based on reliable sources which have not survived.

Who wrote the Zinoviev letter?

I have taken the case of the investigation of Arthur as an example of historical practice in which a single historian, building on the work of earlier researchers, explored the contradictions and inconsistencies between particular texts as well as those within each of them. It was possible to follow Alcock's reasoning in assessing the quality of his evidence and balancing it against the conlusions of other researchers. Despite the emphasis on the importance of sources that is found in writings of historical method, such explicit and transparent accounts of the use of documents in historical research are rare. Yet it is possible to pursue the issue of the historian's · se of documents in another way, by examining what happens when writers disagree with one another over the quality of a particular source. In such a situation, historians are forced to make explicit their assessments of quality, which are normally taken for granted in their work. In examining such a case, it will become apparent that the construction of historical facts from documentary evidence is a social process in which collective decisions must be made. If there is no consensus among the researchers over the quality of the evidence, it is impossible to use that evidence in constructing indisputable factual statements.

The case I propose to examine is the 'Zinoviev letter', the publication of which, in 1924, has been blamed for the electoral failure of the first Labour government in Britain.[10] In October 1924, following a series of hints and rumours in the press, the national newspapers published the text of a letter signed by Grigori Zinoviev, the President of the Third Communist International, and addressed to the British Communist Party. The letter was published just four days before the Labour government was to face the country in a general election, and it was widely felt to have fuelled a 'Red scare' which effectively destroyed the Labour Party's chances of winning a second term in office. The letter exhorted the Communist Party to make greater efforts in agitation and organisation among the troops and munition workers, and particularly it required Communist Party activists to mobilise support for an Anglo–Soviet trade treaty which was being negotiated by the Government. Publication of the letter not only damaged Labour's chances in the elections, but also helped to prevent ratification of the treaty.

The text of the letter had been released by the Labour government itself, following veiled threats from the *Daily Mail* and the *Morning Post* that they would publish copies in their possession unless the Government made it public. Along with the text of the letter the Government released the text of a protest note from the Prime Minister, Ramsay MacDonald, to the Soviet chargé d'affaires in London, the intention being to show that the Government was unwilling to countenance Soviet activities which were incompatible with the growing diplomatic relations between the two countries. A copy of the letter had apparently been obtained by the British Foreign Office, and the Government had immediately taken resolute action.

The *Daily Herald*, a paper supporting the Labour Party, was alone in denouncing the letter as a forgery, though both the *Manchester Guardian* and the *Sunday Express* had voiced some doubts about its authenticity. MacDonald claimed that he, too, had certain reservations about the letter, and he claimed that the protest note, which assumed it to be genuine, had been drafted and sent by the Foreign Office without his final approval. The Russian authorities also denounced the letter as a forgery and criticised the Government for having failed to check its authenticity before releasing it for publication. Austen Chamberlain, for the incoming Conservative government, and most of the national press continued to act on the assumption that the letter was genuine.

So, the problem was set in starkly practical terms: was the letter that damaged Labour's electoral opportunities authentic, and, if not, who was its author? The case has been used by politicians to draw conclusions about Soviet intentions, anti-Labour conspiracies in the establishment, the weakness of the Labour Party, and so on; but unless the fundamental question about its authenticity is answered, the letter itself cannot be used as evidence for any of these conclusions. A number of official inquiries did little to resolve the issue, and it was not until forty years later that the letter came under the close scrutiny of historical researchers.

Louis Chester and two other journalists working for the *Sunday Times* reopened the case in 1967, claiming that the results of their inquiries would allow historians to see that the letter was, in fact, a forgery. They argued that the letter ruined the Anglo–Soviet treaty proposal and that it is unlikely that even the revolutionary Zinoviev would have acted in a way that would have endangered this central plank of Soviet foreign policy.[11]

The journalists interviewed an elderly woman, the widow of Alexis Bellegarde, who claimed that her husband and Alexander Gumansky, both Russian *émigrés*, had forged the Zinoviev letter in Berlin using genuine, but stolen, notepaper. The forgers had used published texts and speeches to ensure the correct style and language, and had copied the signature from a Comintern circular. The forgery had, apparently, been instigated by the Polish secret service, and the Polish authorities had undertaken the job of transmitting the letter to London. Chester and his colleagues claim that Mme Bellegarde's story is consistent with other known facts and can, therefore, be accepted as truthful, though it is not impossible that their informant actually sought to construct a fictional account which fitted the known facts. Their conclusions do not, however, rest entirely on Mme Bellegarde's testimony, but concern also the surviving copies of the letter itself.

Their account involves a reconstruction of the number of copies which ought to exist if the letter were genuine. The British Secret Intelligence Service (SIS) received a Russian text of the letter, apparently through routine interceptions of the mail, believing this to be a copy of the original version drawn up in Moscow. A letter to the British Communist Party, however, would have to be written in English, and the SIS assumed that the Russian original would have been translated in Moscow and then sent to London. There would, therefore, be two 'originals': a Russian text (retained in Moscow) and an English text (held by the CP in London). The version of the letter published in the press in 1924 was a translation of the SIS copy of the Russian document. As the Communist Party and the Soviet government consistently claimed the letter to be a forgery and had not opened their archives to the public, and the Foreign Office file covering SIS documents for 1924 had not been released to the Public Record Office, the letter was known to historians only through the published English version. It was clearly important, therefore, to discover the provenance of the SIS copy and the accuracy of the published versions.

The Chester account claims that SIS were not too concerned with the provenance of the letter, as its leadership had a vested interest in guaranteeing its authenticity. There was a fear within the organisation that the Labour government intended to abolish it, and publication of a letter damaging to Labour could not help but strengthen the SIS.[12] As far as the Foreign Office was concerned, the fact that the letter arrived in their hands from the SIS was sufficient to convince officials that it was genuine. The fact that the letter was believed to be genuine, however, was hardly likely to lead a Labour government to publish it four days before a general election. The letter was damaging to the Government's reputation, and if the SIS wished to see it published they would have to engineer 'informed leaks' to the press in order to put pressure on the Government.

Chester and his colleagues, however, accepted Mme Bellegarde's story of the forgery, and so they sought to show that those responsible for the forgery manipulated officials and encouraged their efforts to secure publication. The key piece of evidence which the journalists produce to support their interpretation is the 1920s diary of Conrad im Thurn, an obscure London businessman and former M.I.5 official who retained close contact with his former colleagues in the security service. The Chester account reports that although the original of the diary is unknown, a typed copy has been discovered which is authentic 'beyond doubt'.[13] The diary's provenance was known and this the researchers regarded as sufficient evidence for its authenticity, though they published no information about its provenance. In this diary im Thurn recorded that a friend had told him of the existence of the letter and that he at once contacted associates in M.I.5, Scotland Yard, and the Conservative Party. It was im Thurn and his contacts who were responsible for the first intimations of the letter's existence in the press and, ultimately, for its publication. Crucial to the case proposed by the Chester account is the claim that im Thurn had, in fact, been duped by his friend: the latter was not informing him of the existence of a genuine letter but was part of the Polish conspiracy seeking to ensure the publication of its forgery.[14]

The conclusion of Chester and his associates therefore is that the letter is a forgery and that the efforts of the Polish and anti-Russian elements to secure its acceptance and publication were helped along by the anti-labour feelings of the British establishment and the fears of the Secret Service. However, it is not difficult to see how insecure this conclusion is. If Mme Bellegarde's testimony is discounted, all the known facts are compatible with the letter being genuine, and no independent reasons are produced for accepting what Mme Bellegarde claimed.

The difficulty in resolving this issue is not helped by the fact that the Russian copy of the letter supposedly held by the SIS has never been made public. Since Chester and his colleagues published their book, the relevant Foreign Office files have been released to the Public Record Office, but they do not contain the letter. All that survive in the files are later copies of that copy, and without the 'original' copy it is impossible to carry out any physical tests for forgery. As it is unlikely that such an important document would be accidentally lost or destroyed, the only plausible explanations might seem to be that it has been withheld or purposefully destroyed, because it was discovered to be a forgery, or that it never existed in the first place and the whole thing was manufactured by the SIS to secure the downfall of the Labour government. It is not impossible, however, that the letter was genuine, as officials have claimed all along, but that it was nevertheless felt to be too 'sensitive' to disclose in a public archive.

This uncertainty has allowed historians to question the conclusions of Chester and his associates. Recent discussion of the secret intelligence services, for example show Nigel West[15] supporting their claims and Christopher Andrew rejecting them. Andrew recognises the extent of their reliance on the testimony of Mme Bellegarde – pointing to the numerous other known forgers who have at various times claimed responsibility for the Zinoviev letter;[16] and he further adds that the Secret Service was particularly vigilant for Soviet forgeries as a result of having been misled by forgeries in 1921. For these reasons, he turns to the evidence offered by the style and content of the letter itself, and by their relationship to the style and content of documents known to be genuine.

Andrew's argument is that the letter must have caused little surprise in either the SIS or the Foreign Office, as it is perfectly compatible with known Soviet aims and with the known actions and views of Zinoviev. Similar official pronouncements were well known, and previous intercepts of Comintern mail showed a similar line. 'If the Zinoviev letter was not genuine, its contents at least reflected genuine Comintern policy.'[17] Further, the Prime Minister and senior Foreign Office officials were expecting soon to intercept such a letter and had planned to make an official protest as soon as evidence was to hand. MacDonald sought to check the authenticity of the letter and to draft a note of protest as soon as he was aware that it had been intercepted, and fully intended to publish both the letter and his protest, but delays and confusions during the election campaign led Foreign Office officials to authorise publication before MacDonald had been personally convinced of its authenticity. The Foreign Office, however, was convinced, and the newly elected Conservative government strongly maintained the line that the letter was genuine – a claim that is supported by other intelligence documents lodged at the PRO.

Andrew concludes that it is very unlikely that the letter was a completely unfounded forgery, as it accords so well with known Soviet views. It was either genuine or is a forged version based on one or more very similar letters. For historians interested in Soviet policy and intentions and in the British understanding of these, the letter in itself adds nothing new. Acceptance or rejection of it by historians, whether correct or not, would not cause any need to revise the accepted view. In other areas, however, the issue of authenticity is crucial. If the letter is a forgery, important questions arise about who forged it, why they did so, and how they placed it with the SIS. If the letter is genuine, then it is necessary to explain why it has not been released into the public archive. The failure of historians to resolve the question of the authenticity of the

Zinoviev letter thus poses major problems for those investigating the secret intelligence system.

The social meanings of suicide

Two different cases of historical investigation using documentary sources have been examined in order to gain some idea of the nature of documentary research, and it is now possible to move to a classic case of sociological research which illustrates how similar questions arise when the researcher is interested in the general rather than the particular. Whereas Alcock's study of Arthur and the dispute over the Zinoviev letter were concerned with the existence of particular persons and the occurrence of particular events, Durkheim's study of suicide[18] aimed to abstract from the unique characteristics of individual cases of suicide in order to explore the social conditions responsible for high or low rates of suicide. He was, further, rather more interested in these social conditions than he was in suicide *per se*: suicide was used as a topic that would illuminate some of the general conditions of social life. It is this concern which has led sociologists to regard Durkheim's book as a central theoretical text as well as an exemplary piece of empirical research.[19] I propose to consider the way in which Durkheim approached the use of documents and to show how subsequent critical discussion of this has raised the very same issues that historians face in using documents relating to particular people and events.

Durkheim's theoretical framework was worked out in his thesis, *The Division of Labour in Society*, and elaborated in his *Rules of the Sociological Method*.[20] It was this theoretical framework that was further explored in *Suicide*; and these three books, published within a few years of one another, can be regarded as a single expression of Durkheim's thought at a particular stage in his career. In the *Division of Labour* Durkheim had already expounded the idea that societies could be classified by their level and form of 'social solidarity', and he uses this insight to develop a typology of the social conditions that should be expected to generate high rates of suicide. Solidarity involves the integration of individuals into groups and the regulation of their behaviour by social norms. Excessive – or 'pathological' – levels of suicide are to be expected whenever the levels of integration and regulation approach their extreme positive or negative values.[21] Thus Durkheim identifies four social conditions responsible for high levels of suicide: 'egoism' (insufficient integration), 'altruism' (excessive integration), 'anomie' (insufficient regulation), and 'fatalism' (excessive regulation). The two states that he regards as being of greatest theoretical and empirical importance – egoism and anomie – serve to illustrate the structure of his argument.

Egoism is generated by the same social conditions that are responsible for individualism. The latter exists where there is a reduction in the size of the domestic group and where religions encourage free inquiry rather than providing authoritative answers. Egoism is, however, a distorted expression of the emergence of individualism, and it occurs where the conditions responsible for individualism have progressed so far that people are left totally unanchored in social groups. In such conditions people experience a meaninglessness in their lives. The social problem of meaning can no longer be resolved by commonly accepted group ideas, but must be grappled with anew by each individual. In such circumstances people are easily prone to despair and so are more likely to perceive suicide as a solution.

If egoism is a form of meaninglessness which is expressed in depression and apathy, anomie, resulting from a failure of social regulation, on the other hand, generates uncontrolled passions which are expressed in irritation and anger. In a situation of anomie, peoples' wants are unrestrained and so are impossible to fulfil. The situation to which Durkheim gives greatest attention is that in which economic change opens up or closes off opportunities, and where people's goals are not regulated in line with their changed circumstances.[22] In situations of rapid change, therefore, anomie arises from a failure to establish adequate norms of behaviour for the new social conditions. Goals become unachievable, unhappiness results, and frustration is more likely to be expressed in suicide. Egoism and anomie are closely linked conditions, resulting from the interdependence of integration and regulation. They were seen by Durkheim as two aspects – the intellectual and the emotional – of the same process of 'hyper-civilis-ation' that results in the failure of a rapidly changing society to establish mechanisms of organic solidarity.

Durkheim used statistical data to try to demonstrate associations between indicators of egoistic and anomic tendencies and rates of recorded suicides. A correlation between these two measures is taken as a confirmation of the theory. The statistics used by Durkheim are of three different types. First, his nephew, Marcel Mauss, was permitted to study the unpublished official records of 'some 26,000 suicides' in France over the period 1889–91, classifying them by 'their age, sex, marital status, and the presence or absence of children'. These data were obtained directly 'from documents of the Ministry of Justice not appearing in the annual reports' and were compiled by Mauss into two large tables, which Durkheim regarded as being central to his study.[23] Second, Durkheim employed published compilations of official statistics, though his actual sources were not always shown. For example, the very first table in his book is used to demonstrate the stability in rates of suicide over time in six selected countries, but no source is shown.[24] This practice is followed in the remaining tables of the Introduction and at numerous points throughout the text. The only indication as to where the statistics might originate is the final footnote to his Introduction, where he lists a number of publications 'forming our principal sources'.[25] These are generally the annual statistical abstracts and census reports of various countries and states: Austria, Belgium, Baden, Bavaria, Oldenburg, Prussia, Württemberg, France, Italy and the United States are all mentioned. Third, he uses secondary sources which were themselves based on published and unpublished official statistics – material on Austria, England and Spain is obtained in this way – and he makes reference also to the data compiled by earlier researchers into suicide.

Durkheim's tables seem to draw on all three sets of source materials in varying combinations. Of particular importance in assessing Durkheim's work, therefore, are the assessments he made concerning the quality of the published and unpublished statistics available to him. But it would be no exaggeration to say that he appears to take over these sources in a totally uncritical way. Rarely does he consider the problems they pose. These problems must therefore be broached through the work of his critics, who have often pointed to the difficulties involved in handling such data. While I am not here concerned with their judgements on the validity of his theory, it is important to examine the issues involved in appraising the evidence on which such judgements are made. I shall consider these discussions in terms of the four quality control criteria of authenticity, credibility, representativeness and meaning.

The problem of authenticity is not generally considered by Durkheim or by his commentators, the presumption being that they regarded the official statistics as authentic beyond reasonable doubt. But the fact that authenticity is taken for granted poses particular problems for anyone wishing to use Durkheim's data for secondary analysis, as Durkheim fails to give specific sources for his tables. He does not seem to have considered whether his sources were sound (were there, for example, any printing mistakes in the official tabulations?), and it is virtually impossible for anyone to go back to the original sources and check.

Durkheim does recognize, however, the problem of representativeness. Mauss was asked to compile his tabulations from unpublished sources precisely because Durkheim recognized that the representativeness of the published data could be called into question. But he does not seem to have considered the wider question of the representativeness of the whole set of data that he compiled. In so far as he was concerned with the *general* issue of suicide, we must ask whether the countries for which data were available comprised an adequate sample of all the societies to which he expected his theory to apply. He had, for example, no east European source material, nothing on Sweden and the Netherlands, and only a very limited amount of material on Britain and the United States. In fact, the bulk of his statistics came from France and the German states, and this may not warrant his large-scale generalisations.

The problems of authenticity and representativeness that might be raised in relation to Durkheim's use of official statistics, however, are greatly overshadowed by the chronic problems of credibility and meaning that he faced. It is on these issues that his critics have concentrated, and it is in considering their arguments that we learn most about social research using official statistics.

Writers before Durkheim recognized the problem of the credibility of published suicide statistics. They noted inaccuracies such as those which resulted from falsification: for example, when families of suicide victims obscured the circumstances surrounding the deaths because of their fear of public shame. They also pointed to inaccuracies which arose in the official process of investigation itself – inaccuracies which were consequences of the inadequate information available to coroners and from which judgements on motivation had to be made. Indeed, there was a concern that the level of medical knowledge was inadequate for any accurate assessment of the physical causes of deaths to be made.[26]

Despite this, one of the most important of these early writers, Morselli, held that any such errors occurred at random and that, for this reason, aggregate rates of suicide were credible indicators of the actual rates.[27] But there is no reason to expect errors to be generated randomly rather than systematically. Stability in recorded rates of suicide may more appropriately be seen as the systematic outcome of stable systems of recording and decision-making. The stable rates cannot be taken as indicators of stability in suicidal behaviour itself. Durkheim glimpses this problem in his analysis of the ways in which officials record the motivation that they assume to lie behind suicidal acts; but his theoretical conceptions lead him to miss the crucial point. Discussing the tabulation of such records, he concludes that the stability in the rates of suicide cannot be taken as an indicator of stable patterns of motivation.[28] Rather, he argues, it is to be seen as a reflection of the underlying social causes. Thus, Durkheim's determination to replace psychological, motivational theories with a theory of social conditions leads him to ignore the possible inference that the stabilities in his tables result from stable decision-making systems operating in terms of particular taken-for-granted assumptions about the motivation of suicidal acts.

The significance of this omission in Durkheim's research is that he fails to see that the classification of a particular death as a case of suicide is never straightforward. It is always necessary for officials to arrive at a decision that a particular case does or does not meet the relevant criteria used to distinguish 'suicide' from other types of death.[29] Officials employ specific identification criteria and search procedures in making their decisions, and it is variations in these which are responsible for some of the variation in recorded rates. Doctors, coroners and police employ considerations of background, motivation and circumstance in identifying suicides. For some officials, a death may be regarded as a suicide only when a note is present; they take the note as a necessary condition for the death to be treated as suicide. For other officials, the absence of a note is relatively unimportant, and evidence on the person's state of mind over the preceding days may be more important. In so far as officials differ in the criteria they employ, there will be variations in the ways in which they would classify the same death. Moreover, whatever criteria are employed, officials will also vary in the procedures they use to test for those criteria. Such procedures include a search for witnesses, searches for notes or other relevant physical evidence, investigations into the character of the deceased, and so on, and they will vary in terms of the methods employed and the tenacity with which they are pursued.[30]

Durkheim's critics have argued, then, that doctors, coroners and the police, no matter how sincere they may be, are always involved in the making of decisions which involve not simply the possibility of error, but the actual *creation* of data. Far from generating random errors, the administrative routines and situated decisions of officials operate systematically to produce rates of recorded suicide which reflect the operating assumptions of the recording system as much as they do the actual levels of suicidal behaviour.

This recognition of the centrality of recording systems to the credibility of official accounts appears again when the question of the meaning of the statistics is raised. The crucial problems for Durkheim's research were not those of the literal meaning of the statistics, but were questions to do with their interpretation. The statistics were ostensibly concerned with suicidal behaviour, but what did officials mean by 'suicide'? Did Durkheim and the officials mean the same thing when they used the word 'suicide'?

Despite his doubts about the possibility of identifying subjective states of mind, Durkheim defines suicide as death which results from actions whose consequences were known by the individual to be likely to result in his or her death. But Douglas correctly points out that this definition rapidly became irrelevant to Durkheim's research as he took over, without questioning them, the definitions embodied in the official statistics. These definitions, furthermore, varied from time to time and from place to place, and any assessment of Durkheim's work must ask what each particular set of suicide statistics signifies. 'What were the meanings of suicide among the many different subcultures of Europe on the common-sense level of thought at which most of the doctors, coroners, official statisticians, families of victims, etc., worked in deciding whether or not a death was a suicide?'[31] Since neither Durkheim nor those on whom he relied had asked this question, there was no evidence available on what different officials meant by 'suicide'. Douglas concludes that 'It is, then, a completely open question as to whether the official statistics labelled "suicide" statistics are measures of the same phenomena'.[32]

It is inappropriate to assume, without evidence, that there is an adquate level of consistency among the various common-sense definitions and between these and a sociological definition.[33] Researchers must investigate directly the actual meanings and definitions employed in different areas and periods. Coroners, for example, play a key role in determining and reaffirming what is officially to be regarded as suicide, and so they have a major impact on the meaning of the term 'suicide' in everyday life. They are central to the social construction of reality so far as certain types of death are concerned, and it is impossible to study suicide without studying the social meanings constructed by coroners.[34] Increasing or decreasing rates of suicide, or variations in rates between social groups, reflect the workings of the official mind and serve as part of the construction of 'moral panics' about social problems.

The discussion of Durkheim's account of suicide thus leads to the conclusion that his explanation cannot be accepted because the evidence from which he constructed his data is of uncertain quality. The problems of credibility and meaning that he failed to confront must be reduced to the point at which it is possible to state with some certainty what were the actual rates of suicide. Only then is it possible to even begin to address Durkheim's question of how those rates are to be explained.

Social research and the relativity of accounts

The case studies I have discussed have shown various levels of uncertainty in their conclusions. Indeed, I have deliberately introduced more problems with each case. Alcock was convinced that Arthur existed and that he was a major battle leader, but he was uncertain of the location of many battles and of Arthur's status as a member of a ruling family. Those discussing the Zinoviev letter have little doubt about its relationship to Soviet policy in the 1920s, but there is no certainty at all about its authenticity. Finally, the discussion of suicide has shown a move away from Durkheim's certainty about the link between suicide and social solidarity to a situation where some writers have claimed that it is not possible to come to any definite conclusions on the aetiology of suicide. For some of Durkheim's critics the very idea of an objective rate of suicidal behaviour to which officially recorded rates relate has been rejected as a misunderstanding of the relationship between social actions and the definitions and constructions that are placed upon them.[35]

The discussion of Durkheim's work, in particular, has shown that the question of meaning is fundamental to the whole enterprise of social research. Historians and sociologists strive to construct their explanations on the basis of a firm bedrock of factual data, and I have argued that the status of the 'facts' available to them has to be constantly assessed through the four quality control criteria. A critical awareness of the quality of the evidence that has been used allows them to gauge the uncertainty they should attach to the factual basis of their research. What is involved here is the nature of historical 'facts' and of the 'objectivity' of social research. Facts are not raw perceptions but are theoretically constructed observations.[36] The establishment of the facts about Arthur, the Zinoviev letter, or suicide is a hermeneutical process. This can be illustrated by considering such an apparently simple factual statement as 'the battle of Waterloo took place on Sunday, 18 June 1815' – a statement clearly dependent upon certain theoretical conventions of dating which have come to be accepted by researchers. At its simplest level it depends on the Dionysiac system of calculating years, and this system is now so widely accepted that it is not generally thought necessary to qualify the date as '1815 AD'. Such dating conventions are not unimportant in historical research – as the discussion of the battle at Mount Badon indicated – but they pose few fundamental problems of objectivity for historians, so long as their dating conventions are convertible. A historian who chose to say that the battle of Waterloo took place in 4676 in the Jewish calendar and a historian who said that it happened in 55 George II could nevertheless agree that their statements referred to the same event.

Conventions of calendrical dating are mutually convertible only when their fundamental theoretical assumptions are held in common. The conventions in general use today rest upon certain specific physical theories of the universe. All calendrical systems assume that days are of equal length, years are of equal length, and so on. In the modern calendars, a day is defined as the time taken for the earth to rotate on its axis through one complete rotation. Similarly, a year is the time taken for the earth to rotate around the sun. Modern calendrical calculation assumes each of these speeds of rotation to be constant, and it is only on this assumption that calendar years can be treated as units of equal length. Unless the speed of the universe is constant, time cannot be measured on a cardinal scale. If this speed were not constant, it would not have been possible, say, in 1987 to state that the battle of Waterloo occurred 172 years ago and the battle of Chalgrave (1643) 172 years before that. Without such an assumption in our accepted systems of dating, we could say only that the battle of Waterloo occurred before the Great Reform Act and after the battle of Trafalgar – we could say nothing about the lapse of time between these events.

There is, of course, no strong evidence that there is anything fundamentally wrong with the physical theory upon which existing conventions of calendrical dating depend,[37] but it is not impossible that physicists will, one day, produce a new theory of the universe which would undermine existing calendrical calculations. The Dionysiac system survived the change from the geocentric to the heliocentric theory of the universe, but there can be no certainty that this would be the case in any future change in scientific knowledge.

Such a possibility is, perhaps, of minor relevance to the calendrical calculations made by modern historians, but the dependence on theory of systems of dating is of crucial importance to students of prehistory. The post-war period saw the invention of radio-carbon dating, which enabled estimates to be made of the absolute age of bones, rocks and artefacts. This technique depended upon a theory of the rate of decay of carbon 14 and was widely accepted as providing a firm basis for non-calendrical dating. However, it has recently been argued that this technique leads to apparent underestimates of age as compared with those produced by other techniques. Those who argue this position have claimed that radio-carbon dates should be recalibrated to improve their accuracy.[38] What is involved here, then, is a clash of theories which makes it impossible to derive a generally accepted dating of events in the prehistoric period.

Even if it is accepted that theoretical disputes over dating are of minor importance in reporting the facts of modern history, other theoretical issues cannot be disregarded in this way. This is especially likely to be the case when researchers do not aim simply to report on the facts but to describe them in some way. Description necessarily involves the use of concepts. The statement that 'the battle of Waterloo took place on Sunday, 18 June 1815' depends, for example, upon a conceptualisation of the difference between a battle, a war, and other forms of conflict, just as a statement about the rate of suicide for women would depend upon a conceptualisation of both suicide and women.[39] The intrusion of theoretical concerns into factual description marks no real difference, of course, between social science and history on the one hand and natural science on the other. The choice of concepts in social research is, however, inherently involved in the hermeneutic problem of meaning: the meanings that social researchers employ must be related to the meanings already created by those who are being studied. Social or cultural phenomena are intrinsically meaningful in a way that is not the case with natural phenomena.

I showed in the previous chapter that the attempt to understand the actions of another, as reported in a text, involves a dialogue between the researcher and the author of the text. In this dialogue there is a confrontation between two frames of meaning, as the researcher can only achieve an interpretation from the standpoint of his or her cultural assumptions. The theories that researchers construct to explain their facts, and therefore the concepts they employ to describe those facts, are integral parts of their frames of meaning.

The implications of this have been most forcefully explored by Weber, who shows that social research involves the interdependence of sources of evidence, theoretical arguments, and cultural values. Weber's discussion of the objectivity of social and historical research was presented by him simply as an attempt to outline the editorial policy of a journal which he, Sombart and Jaffé had taken over, but his arguments range far beyond this parochial concern and are rightly regarded as the foundation of virtually all the major discussions of sociological theorisation.[40] Weber's central idea is that of the 'cultural significance' of the phenomena of the social world. Social scientists, like physical scientists, must select and organise the phenomena of the external world from the standpoint of the theoretical framework they employ. But the concepts employed in the social sciences reflect judgements about the cultural significance of the phenomena in question.[41] Something is 'significant' because it is relevant to values, and social scientific description is, implicitly or explicitly, an attempt to relate social phenomena to cultural values.

Weber's usage of the notion of 'value' has been widely criticised for its ambiguity, and it is certainly the case that he uses the term in a number of different senses.[42] He uses the term in this context, however, to refer to the sentiments and cultural assumptions of an audience, including both the members of a scientific community and the wider public. The work of the social scientist achieves its significance by making contact with the sentiments and understandings of others; s/he interprets the past by relating it to cultural assumptions from the present. The distinctiveness of social science, therefore, is to be found in the value relatedness of its concepts. Any description of the meaning of an action involves a choice between concepts which differ in their connotations, and this choice cannot be resolved on the basis of theoretically neutral observations. Argument over concepts therefore plays a far more central role in social science than it does in the natural sciences: a diversity of points of view and continuing conceptual controversy are endemic features of the social scientific enterprise.

Weber is at pains to stress that his position does not involve the replacement of scientific judgement by value judgement. Objectivity in the social sciences consists in producing arguments which are technically valid within the context of the particular value-relevant point of view adopted. Marxist and liberal accounts of the same events, for example, may be equally valid, despite their use of different concepts. What matters, so far as the question of objectivity is concerned, is that they should observe the technical requirements of empirical research: that they should be honest and scrupulous in handling their evidence, that the data they construct should be of the highest possible quality, and that their arguments follow the canons of logic. It is when researchers disregard these criteria that their research ceases to be objective and value relatedness gives way to mere relativism. If social researchers abandon objectivity and come to believe that any account is as good as any other, the way is open for the intrusion of value judgements into scientific practice.

The entry of value judgements into social research is therefore not a necessary feature of social research itself. Whether the social scientist should, as an individual, 'take sides' and express a judgement on the rights and wrongs of the phenomena studied has been much debated,[43] but the question of whether or not to take sides is an ethical and political question which cannot be resolved from within scientific discourse itself. In the world of practical politics the scientist, as citizen or politician, may choose to advocate or act upon one theory rather than another purely on the grounds of his or her value preferences. But Weber was surely correct to argue that the scientist should not seek to legitimate such advocacy under the guise of science.

Few areas of social science have been successful in producing a firm bedrock of evidence acceptable to rival theoreticians. Feminists, Marxists, liberals, and so on, construct different facts and have frequently been both unable and unwilling to establish conventions for translating statements from one framework into another. Indeed, it is sometimes argued that each theoretical position occupies a completely enclosed cultural world and that mututal intelligibility is impossible.[44] The interpretation of scientific activity that has been outlined above requires a rejection of this view. If the social sciences have failed to advance to the same extent as the physical sciences, this is due to the greater difficulty in establishing factual statements and to the confusion of value relevance with value judgement. Descriptions and explanations are continually refined in the light of new evidence or the reassessment of existing evidence. This reassessment is analogous to what occurs in the natural sciences, and there is every reason to expect 'progress' in our factual knowledge to be the result.[45]

But it is also important to recognise that there is a sense in which history must be constantly rewritten. Changing cultural values lead to changing conceptions of the historical significance of particular events. For this reason it is far more difficult to speak of the development of knowledge in the social sciences than it is in natural science. The history written by one school of thought or one generation may be judged as factually more reliable than that of another, but it cannot be seen as superior, *tout court*. Positions which are equally objective and based on an equally reliable factual basis may be simply different.

In this discussion of scientific method in social research I have attempted to outline a framework for using documents as sources of evidence. Many of the features of documentary research, I have argued, are features of social research in general, though they have particular implications and involve distinct techniques when research involves documents rather than, say, participant observation. It is now possible to consider how the use of each of the types of document identified in chapter 1 involves specific issues within the general framework of documentary research. I shall begin this task in the following chapter with a consideration of official documents.

4 The Official Realm: Public and Private

The single most important category of documentary sources used in social research consists of the administrative papers produced by governmental and private agencies. Though often subject to closed or restricted access, many such documents are published, and even more are available in public archives. Historians have typically made extensive use of political and diplomatic records, while sociologists have paid greatest attention to official statistics, but the range of possible sources is immense.

Official documents are shaped by the structure and activities of the State, both directly and indirectly. Public documents are most obviously shaped in this way, as they are often the by-products of policy and administration and, as the creations of public bodies, they reflect the organisation and interests of state agencies. Many of the most important public documents form a part of the systems of surveillance and social control that have become such an integral part of bureaucratic nation states. While private official records are structured by the legal and organisational forms of the bodies producing them, they too are indirectly shaped by systems of regulation and monitoring established by nation states and, increasingly, by international agencies. Many private administrative documents simply would not be produced – certainly not in their existing form – if it were not for the need to meet legally imposed requirements.

In this and the next chapter I shall show how public and private documents have come to develop in this way, and I shall consider some of the features that they share. These general features concern the administrative routines and situated decisions that are central aspects of formal organisation and that lead to the production of such documents. In chapter 6 I shall examine a number of studies which have used these sources and will demonstrate how an understanding of the processes through which they are produced is essential for all social researchers.

The State, surveillance and secrecy

Public and private administrative records are shaped by the structure and activities of the particular national state within which they arise, but behind this diversity are certain features common to all nation states. All modern nation states exhibit enlarged systems of surveillance, first established in the Europe of the eighteenth and nineteenth centuries as states adopted more bureaucratic forms of administration. Central to such systems were practices of 'moral accounting', whereby a state initiated a system for monitoring the activities of its members through the policing of the population. As a system of social control, such policing was aimed at the identification of those perceived as 'deviants'. This was at its clearest in the establishment of police forces concerned with the enforcement of the criminal law and in the institutions evolved for the treatment and confinement of the insane,[1] but it is apparent throughout the expanded system of surveillance. The census, vital registration and the system of poor law administration, for example, were concerned, among other things, with identifying actual and potential claimants for public support, and the nineteenth-century framework of company law was aimed at the prevention of fraudulent business practices.

Administrative records therefore are not, and never were, merely neutral reports of events. They are shaped by the political context in which they are produced and by the cultural and ideological assumptions that lie behind it. They are most obviously shaped by general cultural assumptions with specific manifestations in such ideas as 'individual responsibility' and 'the sanctity of life', and widely accepted sexist, patriarchal and racist values. In the West, Protestant religious values have had a major impact in shaping official documents. The Protestant ethic and the capitalist spirit which Weber held that it encouraged were associated with wider systems of 'rational', calculative action.[2] The rational policy orientation of nation states was expressed in the attention given to the calculation of the effects of official action in relation to policy goals, and this had important consequences for the ways in which deviance was perceived. These systems of surveillance rested upon an absolutist view of moral categories, as actions had to be seen independently of their particular contexts if they were to be rationally processed: a murder is a murder is a murder. It was only through the adoption of such an absolutist perspective that early forms of quantification and statistical analysis became possible.

Thus moral values and legal procedures are integrally connected in the systems of surveillance and social control that are responsible for official record-keeping. For example, what appears in the criminal statistics depends upon what has come to be defined as a crime through the legal processes of the State. It has been emphasised by the so-called labelling theorists that 'the legal definitions of crimes are constructed primarily by those few groups who control the political power of the state legislature and who purposefully use the criminal laws to try to control those forms of activities which they find detrimental to their own interests'.[3] Becker, for example, makes the general point that 'social groups create deviance by making the rules whose infraction constitutes deviance, and by applying those rules to particular people and labelling them as outsiders',[4] and he follows this with a discussion of the 'moral entrepreneurs' who create and enforce social rules. Those with a vested interest or moral concern are often able to initiate a 'moral crusade' aimed at changing the law or at introducing new regulations, and may become institutionalised as pressure groups or state agencies with a strong vested interest in the rules they have created.[5] What are to count as instances of theft, poverty, or immigration, for example, depend upon the pressures imposed by moral entrepreneurs.

This is true even where the State is not itself responsible for the label. In an area such as health and illness, for example, medical categories are rarely derived directly from the law: the category of 'measles', for example, does not depend upon legal enactment but upon medical diagnosis. But the activities of the State are relevant in determining the legally sanctioned processes through which such labelling is officially regulated or monitored. The interests of the State in the compilation of medical statistics and in planning the materials and personnel of the health services constrain the ways in which medical diagnoses are presented in official records. Such constraints go much further when legal categories enter directly into medical diagnoses – as in the case of psychiatric committals and the determination of suicide.

This emphasis on the role of moral entrepreneurs and agents of control should not, however, lead us to ignore the structure of the State itself. As Taylor, Walton and Young have argued, 'the social reaction theorists . . . fail to lay bare the structured inequalities in power and interest which underpin the processes whereby the laws are created and enforced'.[6] Labelling theorists have been predisposed towards a pluralist perspective on political power which ignores the political economy of state activities. For this reason, they have not dealt with 'the larger processes which form the governing framework for the smaller processes and transactions'.[7] A consideration of the historical transformation of national states must, therefore, complement any discussion of the rule of moral entrepreneurs within particular states.

It is within the State itself, and within bureaucratically structured private organisations, that categories and concepts are evolved for measuring and monitoring the actions of those who are the object of surveillance. The relevant authorities must in addition devise methods for collecting and analysing the information they seek. These concepts and methods reflect the cultural underpinnings of state and private action, but they must be translated into specific administrative procedures before they can be applied. Information collection must become built into the regular routines of official action, and these administrative routines reflect the particular patterns taken by state and private activities.

From the standpoint of the researcher, a particularly important question concerns the kind of access which may be had to official documents. For if the production of the documents is a politically and bureaucratically structured process, so too is access to the documents produced. Not all official documents are published, and those unpublished documents that become available to researchers in open archives are but a selection of all the documents produced. Researchers must frequently negotiate with those who act as custodians of the documents, as they are the gatekeepers to the information produced. Nowhere is this more apparent than in the sphere of official secrecy.

Conceptions of official secrecy in Britain arose as the State became more bureaucratic and democratic. Robertson has argued that as elected politicians acquired greater responsibility for state actions in Britain, so they sought tighter control over official information. In a liberal context of responsible government, official information was no longer regarded as politically neutral.[8] Concern for official secrecy in Britain emerged in parallel with the introduction of the democratic reforms of the nineteenth century. Between 1832 and 1870 parliamentary control over public appointments was gradually increased and a body of civil servants, permanent officials divorced from day-to-day party politics, was established.[9] Parliamentary control over these officials was enhanced by the notion of official secrecy, which served to weaken the power of the appointed administrators. Decisions on the release of documents and information were to be made by politicians on political grounds, and so officials had to be prevented from making their own decisions about access to official information.

Initial attempts to prevent civil servants from taking such decisions involved procedures for control over diaries and memoirs as well as the attempt to prevent 'leaks' of official papers. This involved an emphasis on the idea of government property rights in official documents. A Treasury minute of 1873, however, established the modern idea of official secrecy by setting out an ethic of public service and trust for civil servants and making the unauthorised disclosure of information sufficient grounds for dismissal. Only in 1889 did this become codified in an Official Secrets Act, which embodied Admiralty concern that the sale of official secrets to foreign powers should carry a greater penalty than mere dismissal. German spy fever hastened the passing of a new Act in 1911,[10] but the main impetus behind this Act seems to have been the continuing attempt of government to eliminate civil service leaks.[11] Though the 1911 Act has been amended at various times, regulation of the conditions of public access to official reports is still governed by its general principles.

Private organisations are not constrained by the Official Secrets Act unless they are working on government defence contracts, but equally there are few rights of public or research access to private documents. Those government documents that are not regarded as too sensitive to disclose are made available to the Public Record Office and certain other archives, but they are generally weeded before being deposited. The most obvious reason for this is to reduce the bulk of the documents, as it is physically impossible to store all the paper produced by government departments. The researcher, however, has very little control over the weeding process and will often be unclear about the criteria of selection employed.

Official documents in the State

The written records and results of political rule, maintained in archives and employed in the formulation and implementation of government policy, are very much a product of the emergence of the modern state. Such records, it is true, are as old as the literacy that allowed political events to be recorded, but the earliest records are erratic and unsystematic before the formation of centralised state administration laid the foundations for systematic surveillance and record-keeping. French government finance was organised through the Knights Templar for a long period and so no separate exchequer was established until late in the thirteenth century. The earliest systematic records in Britain date from the twelfth century, when Exchequer records of government finance and taxation and Chancery records of charters, grants of land,

and public appointments began to be kept on a routine basis. This systematic record-keeping reflected the importance of written precedent in the legal and administrative procedures of the medieval Anglo-Norman state.[12]

The basis for much later record-keeping, however, was provided by an early inquiry instigated by William I in the wake of his conquest of England. Although Charlemagne had envisaged an inquiry into the extent and value of his lands, little survives of this, and none of the eleventh-century surveys in France and Germany matched the scope of William's inquiry. In 1085 he ordered an investigation into the extent of the various landholdings in England in order to establish a secure basis of information for his fiscal policies. Commissioners were sent into every shire to uncover the information from local officials and to undertake their own investigations, and they presented their report to the Treasury in 1086. This report – the so-called Domesday Book – became the indisputable legal basis for all subsequent changes in land ownership.[13] The Domesday inquiry took as its survey unit the manor, a unit of administration which was closely associated with later parochial administration, and information was collected on such variables as the size of landholdings, the names of owners, land use, population, location of markets, and the value of the land. These data were displayed in a county-by-county text, with the holdings grouped according to the various categories of landowner – the king, religious bodies, tenants-in-chief, and so on. The importance of the Domesday inquiry from the present point of view is not only that it provided baseline information for later administrators, but also that it established a model of investigation which was taken up once more in the nineteenth century and became the characteristic form of official research. William's use of commissioners to collect information was the precedent for the later Royal Commissions and similar bodies that investigated factory and mine conditions, schools, poor law administration, and other aspects of nineteenth-century society.[14]

In the period between the eleventh and nineteenth centuries, however, such commissions were rare, and the surviving official documents are mainly the routinely maintained results of the regular operations of government administration. The number and range of official documents expanded with the bureaucratisation under the Tudors. The administrative revolution of Henry VIII and Thomas Cromwell sharpened the separation of the State from the private affairs of the Royal Household and created a number of new departments of state and official positions.[15] The most important documents to date from this period are the State Papers of the Privy Council, the monarch's central executive body, and the diplomatic papers produced by ambassadors and foreign secretaries. As ensuing administrations expanded the number and range of such documents, the need to maintain them in adequate archives became obvious. This was not because of their possible value to researchers, however, but because of their continuing relevance to decision-making.

A State Paper Office was set up at the beginning of the seventeenth century, but this had limited success in organising material until late in the eighteenth century and it was not until the Public Record Office was set up in 1838 that the records of all the various government departments began to be brought together into a central archive.[16] While the nineteenth century, sometimes glibly described as the 'Age of Reform', did indeed transform many features of national and local administration, many of these changes had their origins in the eighteenth century. They proved highly consequential for the nature and survival of county and parish documents, as the formation of the PRO to store national government documents stimulated a concern for the maintenance of local records. Such concern was limited and haphazard, however, and it was as late as 1963 that a legal requirement was enacted for the establishment of county record offices to store these documents.

Parliament, as it became an important source of power independent of the Crown, began to maintain its own records under its own control: House of Lords Papers date from 1492, and separate Commons Papers from 1834. The *Parliamentary History,* however, a 36-volume historical work containing summaries of parliamentary debates, did not begin until 1803, and was originally published as a private venture by William Cobbett. Its successor as the running record of Parliament, *Parliamentary Debates* ('Hansard'), was also a private venture of Cobbett, the Hansard family and, later, a syndicate headed by Horatio Bottomley; it was taken over by HMSO as an official record in 1909. From 1803 to the present, therefore, a continuous transcript of all parliamentary debates, verbatim since 1909, has been published and maintained.[17] This documentation of parliamentary debates, however, was based upon a synthesis of newspaper reports (themselves often highly imaginative) until Hansard established its own reporter in the Commons' gallery in 1878. Not until it became an official parliamentary record in 1909 did it publish verbatim transcripts.

By the late nineteenth-century, a great mass of political, constitutional and diplomatic records of government and parliamentary activities had survived, been stored in archives, and, in many cases, published. For researchers interested in discovering the past, these records were the most obvious and easily accessible sources of information. It is hardly surprising that the form of historical research which developed and became institutionalised during the nineteenth century was concerned with political, constitutional and diplomatic matters. History was 'political history' rather than 'economic history' or 'social history', because the documentary sources consulted by historians to discover the traces left by people in the past were the 'political' records of the State. But while such documents were the most obvious historical sources, they were neither the only official sources nor the most numerous.

The majority of the surviving official documents were widely dispersed throughout the country in the various organs of the established Church, which, for many purposes, provided an alternative and complementary structure of official administration to that of the State. Indeed, it is frequently impossible to separate Church and State in their administrative activies for much of English history. For most of the medieval period and into modern times the Church could be regarded as an integral part of official administration.[18] Church records cover all aspects of the operations of the Church, the earliest – dating from the thirteenth century – being the bishops' registers of the clergy, teachers, surgeons, midwives and others who had to obtain licences to practise their work, and the records of bishops' visitations of parishes. These documents were maintained in each diocese by the bishop's administrative staff, as were records of the land and property owned by the Church. In addition to its own episcopal and monastic records the Church maintained the records of the ecclesiastical courts, which had jurisdiction over such secular matters as the proving of wills and the regulation of interpersonal behaviour – matters which later became subject to the civil and criminal law. Until 1860 ecclesiastical courts in Canterbury and York supervised diocesan and archdeaconry courts, which provided a parallel structure to that of the civil courts.[19]

Local administration from the Norman period until the Tudor centralisation of the State was undertaken through the manor, the semi-autonomous legal unit based around the feudal relation of a local lord to his tenants and serfs. The lord of the manor, often a religious body, had absolute authority over many local matters, with only minimal supervision exercised by the county sheriff on behalf of the Crown. Surviving manorial records date from the thirteenth century and are of both a judicial and an administrative type, covering such things as landholding and disputes over territory as well as criminal matters.

The Tudors sought to assert a royal monopoly of social control, and were partially successful in transforming local administration into a delegated form of royal power. Their instruments for achieving this were the magistrates, crown appointees with judicial and administrative powers, who largely supplanted the old manorial system – though many magistrates were manorial lords. The official role of the magistrates centred on the quarter sessions for each county. Held in the chief towns, it was at quarter sessions that the magistrates would sit to deliberate as justices in court and to undertake the supervision of county administration. The surviving judicial records of the quarter sessions include records of petitions, licences, alehouse recognizances, crimes and offenders, prison administration, and the names of jurors and the magistrates themselves. Quarter session records also concern such administrative matters as the county accounts, tax assessments, enclosure awards, electoral registers, and poll books.[20]

Linked to the quarter session records were the records of the county lieutenancy, the Lord-Lieutenant of the county being responsible for the appointment of magistrates, from among whom the seniors were appointed as deputy lieutenants, and for the supervision and financing of the militia. The Lord-Lieutenant, through subordinate 'high constables', ensured that the constables in each parish arranged musters of the men eligible for military service. Thus, the lieutenancy records cover details on the men and resources of the militia, and the provisions made for training. While some records remain in the counties, many are to be found among the State Papers of the Privy Council, which supervised the Lieutenants.[21]

The power of the country magistrates existed in an ill-defined and uneasy balance with local parish authority.[22] The parish was a unit of Church administration, centred on a particular church and generally covering a village and its immediately surrounding area, and it became a unit of civil administration as local powers were devolved upon it.[23] As a result, civil and ecclesiastical matters became inextricably linked in the parish authorities, just as the State and the established Church were linked at the national level. Constables and churchwardens were appointed in each parish and were responsible for overseeing the election or appointment of other parish officials, and it was through such offices that many local activities were regulated.

The main documents of early parish administration were the churchwarden's accounts, which were later supplemented by the parish registers and the records of other parish officials. Parish meetings were generally held in the vestry of the church, and the term 'vestry' came to designate both the system of parish administration and the predecessor of the modern town hall. The minutes of the vestry meetings detail the involvement of the parish officials in the collection of local rates, poor relief, education, markets, housing, highways, sanitation and other parish affairs. Churchwardens maintained accounts of all receipts and payments on behalf of the parish church, and so their accounts cover such things as poor relief, church rates, pew fees, purchases of candles, bread and wine, and the maintenance of church buildings. Linked to poor relief were the charity accounts of the church, containing details of donations and payments, inventories ('terriers') of church property, and certain tithe records.

The separate accounts and records of the so-called petty constables concerned juries, the militia, and other aspects of the policing of the parish and county. The constables collected the main parish rate, but the establishment of the Poor Law system created new officials and a separate poor rate. Although parish provision for the relief of the poor had a long history, an Act of 1601 (made permanent in 1640) established a basic system of relief, and hence of documentary recording, which survived until the nineteenth century. Under these Poor Law regulations, churchwardens and substantial householders were appointed as overseers of the poor, whose job it was to raise money through local taxation in order to provide for the poor of the parish. This provision took the form of monetary relief for the sick and disabled, and compulsory work for those able to undertake it.

Poor Law accounts detail payments made and received by particular individuals and the purposes for which such payments were made, and include the predecessors of modern rating schedules – showing the owners and occupiers of all property in the parish. Because of the way in which the Poor Law was administered, everyone was required to have a place of settlement, a parish which was responsible for their support in time of need and to which anyone could be returned if found out of work in any other part of the country. Parish overseers frequently kept registers of the places of settlement of their residents, therefore, and all families were supposed to have certificates of settlement. The documents stored in the parish chest – initially a strong oak box which was legally required for the storage of the parish records – would include, in addition to the registers, copies of certificates of indenture for members of the parish apprenticed to a master craftsman, such certificates showing name, age, address, parentage of the apprentice, and the name of the master.[24]

Undoubtedly the most systematic and important of parish documents, however, are those concerned with vital registration. Thomas Cromwell, royal official of Henry VIII and Vicar-General of the Anglican Church, initiated the system of registering details of all the baptisms, marriages and burials carried out in each parish, his purpose being to secure systematic knowledge of the size and distribution of the population. Cromwell's concern for vital registration was a reflection of the growing concern of the English State for the surveillance of its population. The institutional separation of the State from what came to be called 'civil society' and the high level of intervention of the absolutist State in everyday life required higher levels of documentation by the State authorities. This documentation of society and of the State's activities enabled the accumulation of information which could be processed and analysed within the emergent bureaucratic departments of state and converted into the kind of intelligence that was usable in policy-making and so enhanced the power of the State. Surveillance through information collection and bureaucratic supervision thus became an integral feature of the nation state, and the scope of this surveillance became wider and more extensive with the development of industrial capitalism in the eighteenth century.[25]

Initially intending to begin the system of vital registration in 1535, the official mandate was eventually issued by Cromwell in 1538. The regulations were tightened up in 1598, under Elizabeth I, and it was required that regular entries be maintained in a special parchment volume (the parish register) and that annual transcripts of all entries should be sent to the diocesan registry.[26] This requirement for diocesan copies – the so-called Archdeacon's and Bishop's transcripts – was a compromise solution which emerged from the failure of Burghley, Elizabeth's Lord Treasurer, to set up a national register office. Thus, vital registration remained a purely local matter until the nineteenth century, and the records could not be used as the basis for an accurate count of the national population.[27]

Parish registration was also a phenomenon of the sixteenth century in other European countries, although some earlier experiments had been made. Parish clergy in parts of Italy had begun parish registration during the fourteenth century, and some bishops in France, Spain and Italy had attempted to establish registration in their sees during the fifteenth century. The main impetus towards national systems of parish registration, however, occurred in the sixteenth century under the impact of the Reformation: Switzerland took this step in 1520, anticipating the practice adopted by England in 1538 and Scotland in 1551. It was not always the case, however, that the formation of a national Church stimulated early parish registration, as registration was not established in the Netherlands until the seventeenth century, and the Catholic Church in France consolidated earlier attempts at registration in 1539.[28]

The system of quarter session and parish administration in Britain continued until the establishment of county councils in 1888, and the expanding sphere of activities of local authorities in the twentieth century led to the production and survival of many more documents than in the past: minutes and accounts of the county and borough councils themselves and of their subcommittees and of departments responsible for education, housing, social services, libraries, parks, etc. Particularly consequential for the main type of documents of interest to the sociologist and social historian, however, was a series of national reforms implemented in the 1820s and 1830s, when the growing involvement of the State in providing the conditions for capital accumulation made itself felt in a rash of statistical documentation on the size and distribution of the population and of national wealth and the reintroduction of commissions to inquire into the conditions of work and education of the work-force.

The systematic collection of numerical data relevant to political administration in the seventeenth and eighteenth centuries was geared to the acceptance of the mercantilist idea that quantitative social data would enhance the power of the nation state by making its decisions and actions more effective. This political arithmetic later came to be called 'statistics', reflecting its relevance to the 'statist' or politician. Political arithmetic had its earliest expression in the collation of trade figures in the late seventeenth century by the department of the Inspector-General of Imports and Exports, but little advance was made in other areas until the late eighteenth century.

Stimulated by a concern that the population had been falling during the course of the century – with possibly disastrous consequences for national wealth and military recruitment – a bill to establish a regular census of population was introduced into Parliament in 1753, followed by a bill for national vital registration in 1758. Neither of these bills reached the statute book, as the collection and centralization of such information was widely viewed as a costly exercise which would only serve as the basis for increased personal taxation. One MP opposed the 1753 bill as 'totally subversive of the last remains of English liberty'.[29] By the turn of the century, however, the old mercantilist beliefs had given way to a concern with the difficulties of feeding a large population and of providing for the poor, and a new bill for a national census was introduced in 1800. The enactment of this bill was undoubtedly stimulated not simply by an intellectual concern for the population problem (though the influence of Malthus's first *Essay on Population* of 1798 has often been overstated), but also by practical difficulties. There was a wide recognition that the forces of industrial capitalism were responsible for the growth in population and were creating new problems of urban concentration and social control, and this recognition was allied with a pressing need to have more systematic knowledge of national population and resources to aid military planning at the height of the Napoleonic wars.[30]

National civil registration of births, marriages and deaths did not begin until 1837 in England and Wales, and the General Register Office was set up at the same time to co-ordinate the census and vital registration.[31] Prior to this time the censuses – carried out in 1801, 1811, 1821, and 1831 – had been inefficient and ill thought-out exercises, but the bureaucratisation and professionalisation of data collection and processing did much to ensure the improved quality of the 1841 and succeeding decennial censuses. All censuses prior to 1921 were legalised by special Acts of Parliament, but a general empowering Census Act in 1920 established the population census as a regular requirement, and censuses have been undertaken virtually every ten years since then.[32] The sole exception was the wartime year of 1941, but this was anticipated and a 'National Register' was compiled in 1939 to provide the necessary information for rationing, civil defence and military recruitment which would otherwise have been provided by the census. National Registration had the advantage over the census, as far as the wartime authorities were concerned, of involving the issue of identity cards through which closer surveillance of individuals could be maintained.

The expansion of statistical data collection occurred simultaneously in Britain, France and Germany between 1770 and 1840, though each country showed a distinct 'national path to statistics'.[33] The peculiarities of State-formation in each country resulted in different structures of data-gathering and different forms of presentation, though there was a common concern to collect and collate statistics on wealth, trade, industry and population, and to relate these to topographical investigations.

Statistics developed in France in the second half of the eighteenth century, under State sponsorship and as an adjunct to the French State's physiocratic ideals of national and imperial expansion. Increasingly, a concern with population and health data supplemented earlier concerns with agriculture and commerce, and this was associated with the establishment of a Statistical Bureau in 1800.[34] While separate divisions within the Ministry of the Interior retained responsibility for non-demographic statistics, statistical data collection in France became far more centralised than in Britain. During the early part of the nineteenth century, the Statistical Bureau in France became concerned with statistics of criminal and police activities, education, religion and poverty, and it began to undertake public attitude and opinion surveys.

The French system initially centred around regional statistical accounts, in the form of the 'Grandes mémoires statistiques' of 1803 and after, which presented statistical data on a topographical basis. Gradually these regional accounts were supplemented by sectoral industrial accounts, though each of these was approached as a separate inquiry rather than being treated as part of a systematic national data-gathering exercise. Napoleon became dissatisfied with these studies and demanded statistics which were more limited in scope but more regular in appearance. To this end, the Statistical Bureau was abolished in 1812 and its work dispersed to other agencies. This aim of securing data for long-term monitoring continued after the Restoration of 1814.

National censuses and civil registration developed hand-in-hand from the middle of the eighteenth century, with official population censuses generally preceding the transfer of vital registration from Church to State. The earliest known censuses were in Scandinavia, as the Church in Sweden (with Finland) initiated a local, annual household census in 1628 as part of its existing system of parochial registration. In most other countries, parochial, district or national household listings were compiled mainly for fiscal or military purposes or as parts of *ad hoc* topographical surveys. In 1662, for example, a census of adult males was carried out in Norway as an aid to military recruitment. The most systematic of these early censuses was that of Japan, where, from 1726, there was a procedure for undertaking a family enumeration every six years, though families of both courtiers and paupers were excluded from this.

The hallmark of the modern census is the attempt at a complete and systematic coverage of the population under the aegis of the national state, the earliest example being the State take-over of the Swedish census in 1749.[35] This was followed by the Italian states of Tuscany, Parma and Sardinia in the 1760s and 1770s, Denmark and Spain in 1787, the United Stated in 1790, and Britain,[36] France and Portugal in 1801.[37] Sweden took the lead in civil registration when, in 1756, the State undertook responsibility for collating and publishing data collected through parochial registration. Although France initiated civil registration at the time of the Revolution in 1792, and introduced this into the annexed areas of Belgium and the Netherlands in 1796, this was highly localised at town or prefecture level. Most countries adopted civil registration in the nineteenth century: Belgium adopted an independent system in 1803, England and Wales in 1837, Scotland in 1855, Ireland in 1864, Australia in 1860, Italy in 1862, Spain and New Zealand in 1870, and Switzerland in 1874. German unification led to the introduction of a national system of civil registration in 1875, but, like the French system, this was highly decentralised. Austria began civil registration very late, following German annexation in 1938. Similarly, civil registration in North America was a twentieth-century phenomenon. Only in French Canada had there been any system of parochial registration, and while Massachusetts and Nova Scotia had early systems of civil registration, it was not until the 1920s that Canada and the United States adopted what had become international practice. In Canada civil registration began in 1926, and the full registration of births in the United States did not take place until 1929.[38]

A further area of statistical endeavour to emerge during the nineteenth century was the collection and collation of criminal statistics.[39] The publication of annual statistical returns in Britain began in 1805 with the presentation of county-by-county figures on the number of men and women committed for trial by jury, the data deriving from court records. Publication was started because of the beginnings of a debate on the death penalty which attached to many crimes at that time. During the 1820s and 1830s the fruits of this debate were the gradual removal of some of the more repressive features of the eighteenth-century 'bloody code': a reduction in the number of capital offences, the ending of transportation and an expansion in the number of prisons. This was, in turn, reflected in the publication from 1836 of a new series of criminal statistics showing the number of committals to prison and their distribution by age and sex. A regular police force emerged only slowly to replace the parish constables and to take over many of the domestic responsibilities of the militia. Peel's Metropolitan Police Act of 1829 was followed by similar plans for other cities in the 1830s and 1840s, and the establishment of county and city police forces became mandatory in 1856. Thus from 1857 statistics on indictable offences known to the police were collated and published for each police district and county, as were statistics on the number of committals to magistrates' courts.[40]

The development of the police and criminal statistics and the establishment of the census and civil registration were a response to public debate about 'overpopulation' and the 'dangerous classes' unleashed by agricultural change and industrialisation. These same concerns were also responsible for a growing documentation of poverty. Provision for the poor had become an increasingly costly element in parish finances during the eighteenth century as the practice of making monetary payments to the 'able-bodied', instead of applying the workhouse test, became widespread. In 1795 the magistrates at Speenhamland, near Newbury, began to relate the level of poor relief to the size of the family and the price of bread. As their example was followed in other parishes in the south of the country a virtual national scale of assistance was established, which led to the subsidisation of low wages out of the poor rates and a consequent large increase in the level of local rates. The increasing cost of poor relief led to pressure for reform, and following a House of Lords Committee report on maladministration in 1817, a Royal Commission was set up in 1832 to report on the working and reform of the Poor Law.

As a result of the Report of the Poor Law Commission, published in 1834, parish administration was replaced by Poor Law unions, groups of towns and parishes, each group governed by an elected Board of Guardians and supervised nationally by the Poor Law Commissioners. This new system of Poor Law administration survived until it was transferred to the county councils in 1929, and the system was eventually transferred to national government in 1948. Poor Law administration created numerous documents relating to the administration of poor relief and workhouses, including case reports, correspondence, accounts and minutes. The Royal Commission, in many ways an innovation of the nineteenth century, harked back to the Domesday inquiry of 1086, but was able to adopt more up-to-date methods of data collection.

One of the immediate models for the Royal Commission was the *Statistical Account of Scotland*, the result of a private inquiry undertaken by John Sinclair MP towards the end of the eighteenth century.[41] Sinclair sent questionnaires to ministers of the Church throughout Scotland, aiming to collect topographical information and statistics on such things as population, employment, poverty and crime. His methods of research were far ahead of those prevailing at the time, involving not only questionnaires and statistical tabulations, but also follow-up enquiries to non-respondents. Sinclair's results were published in 21 volumes between 1791 and 1799, arranged around the 938 parishes of Scotland, and the study was repeated in 1845 by the Church of Scotland itself in its *New Statistical Account of Scotland*.

When Sinclair became President of the Board of Agriculture he drew up a proposal for a similar, but official, account of England, but he was forced to drop this plan because of opposition from the Church of England authorities, who feared an attack on their tithes. His successor in this task, Sir Frederick Eden, was able, however, to carry out a much watered-down version of the study, publishing the results in 1797 as *The State of the Poor*.[42] The administrative machinery and research methods for large-scale Royal Commissions now existed, and the Royal Commission on the Poor Law was only the first in a series of investigations which produced statistical findings, textual reports, and proposals for reform. The Royal Commission on the Poor Law was, perhaps, the best known of the Commissions that produced documentary evidence; it led to the establishment of administrative boards and commissions which produced yet further sources of documentary evidence for researchers. The reports of factory inspectors, for example, were extensively used by Karl Marx in his research for *Capital*.[43]

The expansion of the State's role in surveillance was also felt in the increased attention given to the mapping of the British Isles, where official innovations were stimulated by military and economic requirements and resulted in a massive array of official documents. The earliest modern maps to be produced, all as private ventures, were products of attempts by the Tudor landowners to map out and establish the boundaries of their estates. This desire to determine estate boundaries was not, of course, new – it was the primary purpose of the Domesday inquiry,[44] and land charters outlining boundaries have survived from as early as the seventh century. Indeed, the whole of the medieval period was marked by the production of numerous legal investigations (variously termed 'inquisitions', 'terriers' and 'extents') into boundaries, topography and land use.[45] All these documents were textual accounts with little or no use made of pictorial representation, and it was not until the sixteenth century that map-making was revolutionised by a rash of international exploration by Europeans, by rediscovery of the work of Ptolemy, and by the development of surveying techniques. Of particular importance were cartographic developments in the Low Countries, in particular the work of Mercator.

Estate maps, under the impetus of the demands of capitalist agriculture, generally covered relatively small areas in great detail, but Elizabethan map-makers also began to take the administrative county as their unit and initiated a series of popular county maps.[46] Chief among these early map-makers were Saxton, Norden, and Speed, the main achievements being the production of William Camden's *Britannia* in 1607 and John Speed's atlas in 1611.[47] Maps of villages and urban areas were far less common, though a number of town plans (beginning with that of Norwich in 1559) were produced, often for use on the borders and periphery of the relevant county maps.[48]

State involvement in map-making was a relatively late phenomenon. In France the Academie de Sciences undertook a national triangulation in 1744, preceding similar work in Belgium and in Britain. Official map-making in Britain was stimulated by the logistical problems faced by the Duke of Cumberland in the course of his brutal pacification of the Scottish Highlands in the wake of the battle of Culloden (1746). These problems highlighted the military need for adequate maps, and 1747 saw the beginning of the mapping of the Highlands as the basis for the construction of new roads which would allow troops and equipment easier access to the area. This military survey of Scotland lasted for eight years, and its surveyor, William Roy, became the head of the Board of Ordnance's new military survey unit. Roy and his successors attempted to carry out a 'trigonometrical survey' of the whole of Britain from 1791, with political support for this endeavour coming from the fear of foreign invasion during the Napoleonic wars.

The first official map to be published was that of Kent, in 1801, and military needs led the Survey Unit to concentrate on the south coast in the first instance. These maps were produced at a scale of an inch to the mile (1:63,360), much larger in scale than the conventional county maps. By 1840 the whole of the country south of a line from Hull to Preston had been mapped at this scale, and the increased use of the maps for commercial purposes led to the activities of the Survey Unit being regulated under the Ordnance Survey Act of 1841. The Ordnance Survey, as the unit was henceforward called, was to be a branch of the military services producing maps which would meet the military and administrative requirements of the State and which could be sold on a commercial basis.

The basic commercial maps of the Ordnance Survey were the one inch series of county (or part-county) maps, which came to be known as the Old Series. These were produced between 1801 and 1873, with many revisions being made to take account of the expansion of the railways in this period, and they constitute a major source for the Victorian period. The Second Series of one-inch maps began publication in 1872, and further series followed.[49] The one-inch maps have now been converted to a metric basis with publication at the slightly larger scale of 1 : 50,000.

To meet the needs of land transfer, urban improvement, and local welfare administration in the nineteenth century, the Ordnance Survey began to produce much larger scale, specialist maps. From 1824 a six inches to the mile (1 : 10,560) series was produced, and from 1858 much of the country was covered in the 'County Series' at a scale of twenty-five inches to the mile (1:2,500).[50] These maps are highly detailed, showing the location and plans of individual houses, while the large-scale urban maps show such details as lampposts, pillar-boxes, and front-door steps. By 1896 the national large-scale survey was complete, and a number of subsequent revisions have been carried out.[51] Following the Second World War a series of maps intermediate between the one-inch and six-inch series was produced at a scale of two and a half inches to a mile (1:25,000).[52]

Some British military and naval mapping of North America was undertaken prior to the American War of Independence, and state-by-state mapping was well advanced by the early nineteenth century. An American coastal survey was begun in 1807 under what later became the United States Coast and Geodetic Survey, and surveying of the expanding western areas was incorporated into the United States Geological Survey. By the Second World War, however, less than a half of the United States had been comprehensively mapped.[53]

The current and earlier Ordnance Survey maps in Britain provide a record of topography and boundares which usefully supplement textual accounts, statistics and unpublished maps. Landownership and land use in the eighteenth and nineteenth centuries can be discovered from such unpublished maps as those produced for enclosure awards and tithe commutation. In those areas of the country subject to the enclosure of agricultural land, lists of the names and property of all people affected were produced alongside maps showing the awards of land that were to be made, and numerous such maps were produced in the late eighteenth and early nineteenth centuries. The Tithe Commutation Act of 1836 converted payments in kind to cash payments, and required the holding of village meetings to discuss the terms of the commutation. Not only have many of the minute books of these meetings survived, and are generally now in the county record offices, but large-scale maps (generally around twenty-five inches to the mile) had to be produced to show each property together with the name of the property owners and the tithe payable. As these maps show the type of property (house, farm, etc.), the owner and the occupier, and the acreage involved, they allow the construction of a comprehensive picture of landownership as it was in the 1830s and 1840s. Documents relating to enclosure and commutation were often combined in one process, with the rector being awarded land in lieu of a tithe, but separate enclosure documents of an earlier date have often survived – especially where enclosure was brought about through a private Act of Parliament.

Tithe and enclosure documents can be complemented by land-tax registers from 1780 to 1832.[54] These were produced by local magistrates and show the names of the owners and occupiers of property, the nature of their property, and the amount of tax payable. Land-tax registers were no longer maintained after 1832, though some similar data are contained in the modern rating registers and, of course, the actual title-deeds relating to the conveyance of land, mortgages and leases. The current Register of Title, maintained by the Land Registry, is intended soon to cover the whole of Britain and to detail property and property ownership with an index map. But access is highly restricted, as the Register is currently available only to those with a legal interest in the land they intend to investigate. Although open access has been proposed by the Law Commission, there is no facility for public or research access at the moment.

Official records in the private sphere

In the earliest periods for which documents survive, the distinction between the public, the private and the personal was not at all sharply marked. As has been seen, many of the earliest public documents in fact had their origin not in the State *per se*, but in the Church. Similarly, those documents which would today be regarded as private were formerly an integral part of the personal records of families. It was only very gradually, for example, that the management of landed estates became separated from the normal day-to-day activities of the families that owned the land, and hence many of the earliest records of such undertakings are contained in household account books and personal correspondence.[55] Where the families concerned were actively involved in public office, their papers were often of the quasi-official kind already discussed. Just as bureaucratisation of the State brought about a sharper separation of the public and the personal activities of the family, so the creation of the legal trust and the family settlements encouraged a distinction between their personal affairs and their private estate matters. In the sphere of business, the legal concept of the partnership allowed a partial separation of family affairs from commercial and manufacturing enterprises, but only with the creation of the joint-stock company in the nineteenth century did this division become either marked or permanent.

In the Western world today there is a sharp differentiation of the personal from the official sphere, and most private official documents are produced from within bureaucratic organisations similar to those of the State. This similarity of organisational form results in a similarity in the internal records which are maintained. Although certain of these records are the basis of publications by private bodies, there is no real private sector equivalent to the publication of official statistics by the State. Nevertheless, the framework of law established by the State has resulted in the creation of systems of regulation and disclosure which compel private organisations to publish some classes of records or to deposit them in open public archives. In this section I concentrate on those private official documents that are unpublished or available only in public archives. Private documents produced specifically for publication in a printed form, and generally without reference to any governmental requirements, involve certain distinct problems and will be discussed in chapter 7.

The role of State regulation in the production of private records is clear in the development in Britain of company records, which were among the earliest of private records to be regulated in this way. The creation of the legal form of the joint-stock company allowed a business undertaking to have a legal existence separate from that of the individual or family that ran the concern, and the establishment of limited liability finalised this separation. The legal recognition of 'corporate' bodies was largely restricted to the business sphere, where there were considerable obstacles to the formation of a joint-stock company until late in the century, but some precursors and parallel entities were to be found in the turnpike trusts, school boards, and Poor Law unions that were established in the eighteenth and nineteenth centuries. Corporate organisation for workers in trade unions was difficult for much of this period and was explicitly made illegal in the 1799 and 1800 Combination Acts. Though some corporate rights for trade unions were established in 1824, their legal status remained uncertain until 1876.

All of the corporate bodies that evolved in the nineteenth and, more rapidly, in the twentieth century were producers of both routine and *ad hoc* records, yet they vary in the extent to which they have been required to disclose or maintain such records. In most cases the legal requirement for record-keeping extends only to the annual budget and the obligation, perhaps, to file these reports with a State official for scrutiny and safe-keeping. The majority of corporate bodies have maintained their own working archives of records. Schools and hospitals, for example, maintain personnel records on their staff as well as having records of the progress and treatment of their pupils and patients. Such records, especially those of hospitals, have to be stored for long periods so that they can be consulted whenever decisions about individual cases have to be made. Trade unions keep records of staff and membership, and of the particular firms and organisations with which they deal, and all corporate bodies tend to maintain minutes of meetings, copies of correspondence, and routine financial records.[56] I shall illustrate the growth and range of private records by considering the documents produced by corporate businesses and educational organisations.

Joint-stock legislation in England and Wales, beginning with the Companies Act of 1844, allowed business undertakings to be organised as corporate bodies with a minimum of formality by registering as a company with the Registrar of Companies.[57] The legislation established what was, in effect, a model constitution for companies, with boards of directors, annual general meetings of shareholders, and audited accounts. Limited liability was added in 1856. This constitution created the need for specific classes of document linked to the financial control of corporate affairs, these affairs being regulated through a framework of public disclosure of key documents. These documents were the registers of directors and shareholders and the audited balance sheet and profit / loss account which had to be kept up to date and deposited annually with the Registrar. The register of shareholders, for example, shows the name and address of each shareholder in the company, together with the number of shares held and any purchases or sales of shares during the course of the year. The requirement for its public disclosure was initially designed to allow those entering into a contract with a company to see who was behind its affairs. The requirement for audited and disclosed accounts was designed initially to protect the financial situation of the shareholders themselves, who were in danger of being misled by directors, and to give a reasonably secure basis upon which potential shareholders could decide whether to invest.[58]

Legal regulation of companies in the United States was a local, state matter until well into the twentieth century. Massachusetts established a framework of regulation for railways, utilities and investment companies in 1852, and this example was followed by a number of other statess. Such legislation, however, was concerned with creating distinct regulations for each specific type of company, and not until after the turn of the century was there any move towards general company laws applicable to all joint-stock companies – 'corporations' in American law. This early general legislation, the so-called 'Blue Sky' laws, was concerned with the prevention of fraud, and there was little in the way of a legal framework for normal, routine business activities. The Federal Trade Commission (FTC) and the Clayton Antitrust Act were the first moves by the federal government to establish this kind of general regulation, and the final outcome was the Securities Act of 1933, which gave considerably greater power to the central authorities through its establishment of the Securities and Exchange Commission (SEC) in 1934. The documents required for disclosure by law are similar to those in Britain, with the important exception of the register of shareholders. Although large shareholdings must be disclosed to the SEC, there is no requirement for the deposit of a full register.[59]

The purely internal records of private bodies developed in tandem with the frameworks of public regulation. The formalisation of bureaucratic surveillance within industry and commerce, for example, resulted in the multiplication of internal documents as massive filing systems became the mainsprings of the emerging managerial hierarchies.[60] The mass of memos, correspondence, notes, reminders and diary entries were processed by the bureaucratic machinery to produce formal minutes, registers and reports with increasingly standardised formats. Formalisation and standardisation became the hallmark of the *genre*. These qualities were crucial to the attempt to expunge personal considerations from public and private administration.[61]

Developments in corporate business were rapidly matched in other areas of private administration. Education, like health and welfare somewhat ambiguously located between the public and the private sphere, illustrates this clearly. Many of the personnel and financial records of bodies in these areas were analogous to those of corporate business, but important records and files were also established in their central operating areas.

The earliest educational records in the United States were the school registers of Massachusetts and Connecticut which were begun in the 1820s and 1830s. These recorded information on the number of pupils and their attendance, and had their origins in local concern about absenteeism and truancy.[62] Allied to attendance records were records of examination entry and the general 'character' and behaviour of pupils. The adoption of a standardised book-keeping system for pupil records by Massachusetts in 1838 was rapidly copied by other states. From the 1870s, secondary school records became more closely geared to the needs of college entry. They outlined pupil attainment in particular subjects and, from 1900, psychological testing became a routine practice. Broader, holistic assessments of pupils became more typical in the 1940s, as the concerns of educational ideology changed, and school records became a formalised codification of the subjective assessments made by teachers. The lack of standardisation at a national level, overcoming divergent state and local requirements, was a feature of the post-war period, and the guidelines on 'pupil accounting' were issued in 1964 by the US Office of Education.

Colleges and universities adopted systematic record-keeping for courses, grades and credits because of the requirement for certification in the American system of mass education, and this became even more extensive with the drift towards 'credentialism'.[63] In those universities involved in training for medicine, law and engineering, internal documents and certification became increasingly geared to the external requirements of professional qualifying associations and the federal State.[64]

In Britain as elsewhere, the official records of public and private bodies have played an increasingly important part in the personal lives of individuals as the surveillance role of the State has expanded. People have come to depend more and more on the personal possession of certified copies or extracts of official documents which guarantee their rights with respect to benefits, privileges and opportunities. Civil registration, probate and other areas of State activity led to the early multiplication of official certificates, licences and grants which were held by individuals. Such certificates – as they may generically be termed – came to be seen by their possessors as 'personal' documents, though they are distinct from documents produced exclusively within the personal sphere itself. Private bodies rapidly contributed to this burgeoning of official certificates. Share certificates, certificates of insurance, bonds for mortgages and loans, pay slips, school attendance certificates, diplomas, school reports, medical cards and National Savings Certificates typify the range of such documents, each depending on the existence of bureaucratic filing systems with standardised register volumes.[65] Many such certificates are required for the normal day-to-day operations of an organisation or in order to meet its commitments to customers and clients, while others are required by the expanding system of State monitoring and surveillance which has been imposed upon an increasing number of private bodies.

In this chapter I have looked at the administrative documents produced by government and private agencies, perhaps the most important of the various types of document available to the social researcher. I have shown how these public and private records are shaped by the structure and activities of the State and other organisations. In the next chapter I shall look in more detail at the impact of administrative routines and decision-making on the statistics and reports that are produced.

5 Administrative Routines and Situated Decisions

All official records are produced in a particular administrative context involving everyday routines which are established in order to meet the requirements of the agency or organisation concerned. The routines operating in a government ministry may differ from those employed in a private company, and each may vary its routines according to the task in hand. Behind these variations are certain organisational uniformities. Adapting the argument of Hakim, it is possible to identify three typical administrative routines for record-making: recurrent, regular, and special.[1]

Recurrent administrative routines are those that produce records which are 'an expected and necessary part of the work of administrators'[2] and so form a central part of the bureaucratic operations of an organisation. Whether produced for statutory purposes, to aid the service operations of an organisation or for statistical purposes, recurrent records are an integral part of normal operating procedures and are, therefore, deeply embedded in organisational routines and practices. Peter Blau has shown how the records of a government employment agency were shaped by the formal and informal organisation of the agency and how, for this reason, the categories employed in the records departed from the general statutory requirements that had been laid down.[3] Although an organisation is generally required to produce knowledge in a particular form, it may have to adapt these requirements to the needs of its efficient day-to-day operations. The actual categories and rules adopted by its members may well differ from those required by its supervisors, and so the administrative records will have to be reconstructed when they are presented in official reports to outside bodies.[4] The publication of recurrent administrative records, therefore, involves the 'translation' of the operating categories into the officially required categories.

While the aim behind recurrent records is that they should be comprehensive, continuous and reliable, *regular* records may depart from these criteria in certain respects. Regular organisational routines produce records on a continuing basis, but do not form an integral or central part of the organisation's operations. The records are produced purely for external purposes – such as to meet a statutory requirement of disclosure – and therefore tend to be regarded by members of the organisation as of less importance than its own recurrent records. Regular records may require the establishment of separate and distinct administrative routines in order to ensure that they are correctly produced, and if they are produced from within the existing routines then those practices may have to be modified. Finally, *special* records are those *ad hoc* surveys and exercises that must, from time to time, be carried out alongside the production of recurrent and regular records.

These analytically distinct classes of document are not always produced by specific departments, sections or routines, and most organisations produce all three. The Department of Employment in Britain, for example, maintains recurrent records on the number of people registered as unemployed, has produced regular reports on the ethnic background of those registered, and undertakes occasional special surveys of the unemployed. Clearly, the administrative routines involved in the processing of incoming data related to the Department's operations in job centres will differ from those established in its research branch when it undertakes a sample survey. In many cases, however, existing routines will be adapted to permit the production of whatever records are necessary, with consequent implications for the form and content of the records.

Conceptual instruments and administrative routines

Records and reports of all kinds involve adaptation of the concepts and methods of information-gathering and analysis to the administrative routines of the department or organisation responsible for producing the documents. Official documents are not impartial and autonomous intellectual accounts; rather they are integral elements of policy and administration. Hindess has usefully discussed this shaping of documents in terms of the impact of organisational exigencies on what he terms the conceptual and technical instruments of information-gathering.[5]

'Conceptual instruments' comprise the framework of categories used in producing a report: the specific definitions of, for example, 'wealth', 'suicide', 'region', 'unemployment', 'homeless'. These concepts may rarely be thought through in a systematic theoretical way, but are necessary features of any data-gathering exercise. 'Unemployment' as measured in the Department of Employment statistics may not correspond to any of the concepts used by sociologists, and it may not correspond either to the way in which 'unemployment' is understood by politicians or ordinary citizens, but nevertheless it is based on a specific concept which can be uncovered through critical examination of the reports and the processes through which they are produced. In order to assess the meaning of published official statistics on unemployment, this particular conceptual instrument must be understood. The conceptual instruments employed by any particular department or organisation result from the specific way in which its requirements for information-collecting are shaped by general cultural understandings and by the structure of the organisation and its location in the wider society.

By 'technical instruments' Hindess means the specific methods by which the necessary information is collected and processed. Tax returns, questionnaires and occupational classifications, for example, are all used as technical instruments, and their particular forms depend upon the way in which they are embedded in censuses, Royal Commissions, and other means of collection and analysis. The methods and techniques depend upon, and help to define, the conceptual instruments that are employed. The conceptualisation and measurement of 'unemployment' by the Department of Employment, for example, is influenced by the fact that the Department operates the job centres through which people must pass in order to claim unemployment benefit. The procedure of registration becomes a technical instrument of data collection which, in turn, shapes official conceptions of what it is to be 'unemployed'.

The ways in which conceptual and technical instruments impinge upon administrative records can best be illustrated through an extended example, and I propose to do this by considering the definitions and measurements of social class that have been used in the census and in vital registration in Britain. The General Register Office (GRO) and Office of Population, Censuses and Surveys (OPCS) have devised and modified various classifications of work, industry and employment for use in their published statistics, the best known of their technical instruments being related to a specific conceptualisation of social class.

Despite many criticisms, the Registrar-General's 'Classification of Occupations' remains one of the most widely used measures of social class in social research. It was some time, however, before the concept of social class achieved any influence within the GRO. The earliest form of social classification used was a simple geographical one, though the

1801 census had required informants to classify the population intuitively into 'agriculture', 'trade', and 'manufacture'. This *ad hoc* approach was refined somewhat in 1821 and 1831, when a list of nine broad industrial sectors was devised for use by the enumerators. These categories were specified in very general terms as 'employed in manufacture or manufacturing machinery', 'capitalists, bankers, professionals and other educated men', and so on.[6] With the introduction of household schedules in 1841 it was possible to devise a more complex schema for use by the census officials in classifying the individual information recorded by the enumerators. The classification employed, however, was simply an alphabetical list of 877 occupational groups, constructed *post hoc* from the recorded occupational titles, and it was widely recognised as inadequate.

Davies has argued that it was not until the middle of the nineteenth century that the notion of a personal occupation became at all meaningful to most people, as this idea depended upon the establishment both of a more-or-less complete separation of the domestic sphere of the 'home' from the sphere of gainful employment outside the home and of the growing rate of individual mobility from one area of employment to another.[7] Because such practices had only partially evolved in the first half of the nineteenth century, social classification in the early censuses involved an attempt to group whole families by their sphere of economic activity. Neither the census office nor the enumerators could devise or apply a scheme of *occupational* classification.

It was, therefore, not until William Farr and his fellow statisticians in the GRO devised a more adequate procedure for classifying the occupational titles recorded in censuses that any significant advances were made. Their classification was devised to take account of the sector of employment and aspects of what today would be called the 'work situation' (level of skill and type of technology), though it gave greatest attention to the sector of employment.[8] The classification involved 17 industrial orders, divided into 91 sub-orders, the number of orders being increased to 18 in 1871 and 24 in 1881, and the basic schema remained unaltered until the report on the 1911 census. In the report for that year the classification was explicitly recognised as the *industrial* classification that it undoubtedly was, and various refinements were made in following years which eventuated in the 24-order Standard Industrial Classification (SIC) of 1948.[9]

The official system of occupational classification – now generally referred to as the 'Registrar-General's Classification' – has its origins in nineteenth-century debates between the advocates of the 'environmentalist' and 'hereditarian' explanations of health and intelligence.

The prevailing view within the GRO in its early days was the environmentalism of the medical statisticians and public health specialists, who held that mortality rates, for example, had to be related to such environmental conditions as the level of urbanisation and family employment patterns (especially the employment of mothers).[10] Such an approach was compatible with the professional role and interests of the local medical officers of health, who often served as registrars, in the health and sanitation policies of the towns and cities in the latter half of the nineteenth century. 'For these exponents of public health and for their allies at the GRO, the principal political purpose of a social classification scheme would be to promote the policy of preventive sanitation, predicated on the strongly environmentalist understanding of the causes of poverty which these members of the medical profession held.'[11]

This environmentalism was shared by Charles Booth, a private social researcher who combined census and interview materials to produce an influential study of poverty in which each street of London was classified according to the social class of its residents.[12] In opposition to this position were the Darwinist writings of Sir Francis Galton, who formulated an hereditarian, or eugenic, argument. Despite their contrasting theoretical assumptions, Galton and Booth shared the view that social classes should be regarded as hierarchically structured occupational groups with differing life chances and experiences. Galton argued that the class structure described by Booth was to be explained by the distribution of innate ability or 'generic worth' in the population, and he attempted to map Booth's class schema on to the normal curve that he held measured the distribution of intelligence.[13]

In 1887 the Assistant Registrar-General argued for the adoption of a social class schema for the analysis of census and registration data, but only when eugenics appeared as a stronger threat to the environmentalist assumptions and professional interests of the medical statisticians at the GRO did the suggestion receive any real support. An official inquiry into 'national efficiency' heard from leading advocates of eugenics that a decline in national physique and intellect had been brought about by public health measures which had interfered with the process of natural selection. Sanitation and other improvements had allowed the 'weak' to survive and so threaten those who were naturally most 'fit', and this decline in physical and intellectual standards was claimed to be directly responsible for Britain's political and military failures in the second Boer War.

Public health officials and GRO administrators sought to counter this argument by showing that it was not supported by the evidence of the census, and to demonstrate this they had to devise a satisfactory social class scheme. T. H. C. Stevenson, a medical statistician at the GRO, constructed a system of five social classes, defined on the basis of occupation. This was to be used for analysing data on infant mortality, with children being allocated to classes by their parent's occupation.[14] This schema, first used in 1911, became the basis of all succeeding official analyses of social class.

Stevenson's argument was that the occupation of the head of a household was an indicator of the level occupied by that household in the social hierarchy.[15] Whereas the hereditarians held that innate differences were reflected in the skills and abilities required for different kinds of employment, Stevenson sought to show that occupational differences were expressions of those environmental conditions that were the causes of differences in skill, ability, health and mortality. In the Registrar-General's Classification a social class is a group of family households whose members share similar residential and working conditions, and the relative social standing of the classes is expressed in the differences of income and culture (their life-style and status) that their environmental conditions produce.

Two possible, and conflicting, lines of argument follow from this basic position. The first holds that environmental conditions generate a continuous scale of stratification, with social class boundaries being arbitrary divisions along this scale, which, nevertheless, accords closely with conventional, everyday images of class and with broad differences in life chances. The alternative argument is that environmental conditions create sharp divisions between classes, and that these real boundaries are partially masked by those everyday conceptions that postulate a degree of continuity in the class hierarchy. Stevenson himself equivocated between these two positions, and they have been basic causes of divergence among those who have tried to build on his work.

The Registrar-General's social class schema seems to have been constructed in a largely implicit and unsystematic way, and it is a testimony to the robustness and empirical power of the schema that, despite its inadequacies, it has lasted so long. Although little is known about how the schema originated, it seems likely likely that Stevenson's common-sense knowledge as a member of the middle class in British society enabled him easily to devise a plausible set of classes from debates current between environmentalists and hereditarians. But this was only the first step, as it was necessary then to devise a reliable way of allocating occupations to one – and only one – of these classes. The next step must therefore have been to identify what he felt to be the occupations comprising the core of each class. These core occupations could then be used to identify others which could be related to them in terms of skill, qualifications, and life-style. The result would be sets of equivalent occupations each corresponding to one of the social class labels, defined in some kind of code book or 'dictionary'. The task of classifying individuals from census and registration returns thus became a simple one of looking up their occupations in the dictionary and from it recording their social class.

The dictionary used by the GRO was derived from earlier occupational coding schemes and was eventually published under the title *Classification of Occupations*. The elements of the coding scheme are the occupational groups into which each job can be classified and which, since the 1970s, have been directly translatable into the five social classes of the Registrar-General's Classification and also the more complex CODOT (Classification of Occupations and Directory of Occupational Titles) occupational schema used by the Department of Employment.[16] The Registrar-General's Classification has been periodically revised to reflect what are felt to have been the changing fortunes of particular occupations, and the 1970 edition states that the allocation of occupations to the five social classes has varied 'in accordance with changes in economic conditions and with the intention of presenting a gradient rather than literal continuity'.[17] In the same way, some social historians have suggested modifications to the coding scheme which would allow the Registrar-General's Classification to be used with nineteenth-century data.[18]

Stevenson's 1911 schema centred on a sharp differentiation of three core classes: (I) the upper and middle classes, (III) skilled workmen and (V) unskilled labourers. These comprised, respectively, the 'top', 'middle' and 'bottom' layers of the stratification system, and the differentiation was modified by the inclusion of a number of other social classes which cut across the main axis of class division: 'intermediate occupations' (II) and 'partly skilled occupations' (IV) were diverse and amorphous social classes between the main ones, while agricultural, textile and mining workers were each extracted from the main skilled and unskilled classes (III and V) for separate attention.[19] During the 1920s the latter industrial groups were merged with the main classes to leave the basic five-class model that has largely survived to the present.

A major innovation to the Classification was the introduction, made during the 1960s, of manual/non-manual and industrial/agrarian divisions within the intermediate, skilled and unskilled social classes. This combination of a social class schema with a sectoral and employment status division followed the introduction in 1951 of a similar classification of occupations into 'economic classes'. The basic

Figure 5.1   *The Registrar-General's classifications*

Social class	Economic class
I Professional, etc.	I Professional
II Intermediate	II Employers and managers
III (n) Skilled non-manual	III Intermediate
III (m) Skilled manual	IV Skilled manual and self-employed
IV Partly skilled	V Semi-skilled and personal service
V Unskilled manual	VI Unskilled manual

occupational groups were combined with indicators of employment status (employed, self-employed, employee, and level of supervisory responsibility) and industry to produce seventeen socio-economic groups (SEGs),[20] which have been collapsed by OPCS into a six-category schema of 'economic classes'.[21] The six economic classes bear a striking similarity to the five 'social classes' (see figure 5.1), though the hybrid nature of the schema means that there is no one-to-one correspondence. Indeed it has been claimed that the socio-economic groups 'cross cut [social classes] in rather a curious way and it is not easy to see any systematic criteria in their composition'.[22] There has been little interest in the SEGs and economic classes by social researchers, and their main purpose for OPCS seems to have been to complement the SIC as a way of ensuring international comparability of official data.

Situated decisions

The conceptual and technical instruments implied by statutory definitions and administrative routines leave considerable ambiguity about their application in particular cases. No matter how precise the concept and no matter how systematic the method, those responsible for applying it to particular cases will always have a high degree of discretion in the decisions they make. It is never possible for a general rule to be unproblematically applied to particular cases: an official must decide that in *this* situation, under *these* circumstances, the rule will be applied. It is always necessary for agents to construct concrete interpretations of the rules under which they operate and which they see as relevant in the situations with which they are faced.[23]

If it is known, for example, that the occupation of clerk is to be allocated to Registrar-General's social class III(n), it is still necessary for registrars and OPCS clerks to decide whether this particular person's work history warrants his or her designation as a clerk. Similarly, police and doctors investigating suicide search for information relevant to the criteria that they regard as specifying legal and medical definitions. This may involve a search for evidence of character, intention and motivation from the external signs of dress and presence or absence of a note. What is observed may itself be interpreted in the light of the ways in which the person has been typified by others. As shown in the discussion of Durkheim's work in chapter 3, official reports are reconstructed accounts which translate the outcomes of situational decisions into general rules. To assume an unproblematic relationship between the creation of a general rule and the official reports on its application is to ignore the mediating factors of administrative routines and situated decisions.

The relevance of situated decisions can best be seen in the discussions which have ensued over criminal statistics. A long-standing debate over the use and value of criminal statistics has explored the consequences of administrative routines and situated decisions for investigations into deviance and control. It has been argued that the 'dark figure' of crime which does not get recorded in the official statistics undermines the ability of researchers to generalise from recorded crime. Criminal acts which become recorded in official reports and statistics are simply a sample of the whole range of criminal behaviour and, like any sample, may be subject to bias: that is to say, officially recorded crime may be unrepresentative of the nature of all crime and may considerably understate the amount of crime. As Box has argued, 'crimes officially known to the police must be an *unknown* and *unknowable* proportion of the total number of crimes committed. That is, since the 'real' volume of crime remains *unmeasured* . . . there is no possible method of estimating accurately the proportion that is officially recorded.'[24]

It has been argued, however, that a knowledge of the processes through which criminal statistics are produced can enable researchers to come to an informed opinion of the main sources of bias and inaccuracy and, therefore, to correct the official statistics. The problems of bias and inaccuracy are technical problems which can be overcome by the researcher.[25] Whether a particular crime gets into the official statistics depends upon whether it is recorded in the police files from which the statistics ultimately derive,[26] and this depends upon a series of decisions made by members of the public and by the police themselves. The main types of decision which have been identified are those relating to the *reportability*, *visibility* and *recordability* of crimes.

As criminals do not usually report their own offences to the police, it is necessary for the victim or some other person to bring it to their attention. A major factor in determining whether this will happen is the perceived seriousness of the crime, as many crimes which are 'victimless' or are regarded as trivial will tend not to be reported. This is true for such offences as the dropping of litter and also for such things as the 'fiddling' of expenses. The latter may simply not be regarded, by those involved, as a 'real' crime. But even when a crime is regarded as being serious, it may go unreported because its seriousness does not outweigh the practical difficulties involved in making a report. There may be no police in the vicinity, a telephone may not be available, it may be a long walk to the police station, or the person involved may simply wish to avoid spending time at a police station making a statement. Such decisions are especially likely to be made when people believe that the police themselves would be unlikely to take the offence seriously or be unable to do anything about it.

But in many situations where all participants recognise the severity of an offence there may still be an unwillingness to report it to the police. This may be because the behaviour is regarded as a private matter to be settled personally or within the confines of an organisation – a particularly common response in such situations as street fights between rival gangs or theft by employees from their employers. Of particular importance, however, are those situations where the victim of a crime fears embarrassment or intimidation by the police and the courts or fears public disclosure of the offence. It has been argued that many cases of rape go unrecorded for precisely these reasons, and that most victims of blackmail prefer victimisation to disclosure.[27] In those cases where the 'victim' is a willing participant in the offence, reporting is especially unlikely.

The issue of the visibility of an offence is closely related to its perceived seriousness, as many offences which are regarded as trivial may become virtually invisible: people may fail to see litter-mongers and traffic offenders. In many situations, especially where the victim is an organisation or an abstract category (such as 'the public'), there may be no recognition at all that an offence has been committed. Embezzlement, for example, may be all but undetectable by those who work alongside the embezzler. In this case, as in many others, it may only be the unsuccessful criminal who becomes visible and so likely to be reported.

The final category of situated decision concerns whether those crimes that are both visible and reported actually come to be recorded in police files by the police themselves. It is at this point that the various decisions which have been discussed so far come into direct contact with the administrative routines of the police. The law is necessarily enforced in a discretionary way, and the police must make decisions about where to concentrate their limited resources. Such decisions become embedded in administrative routines concerning the districts that they will police and the types of crime which they will seek to uncover. Police districts will differ in terms of the proportion of police resources allocated to traffic offences, drug offences, burglary, and so on, and this means that published national statistics will mask substantial regional variations in patterns of policing. Once established, administrative routines constrain the decisions that the police make about crimes which are reported to them: they may decide not to record the offence, or to record a complex act involving a number of offences under only the most serious category.

Once a crime enters the system of official social control it comes to be influenced by a further series of administrative routines and situated decisions which determine whether it appears in particular sets of official statistics. There is a progressive 'funnelling' of criminality which results in imprisoned criminals, for example, accounting for an extremely small sample of even the number of recorded crimes.

The organisation of the police will determine how successful they are in detection and, therefore, the number of arrests they make. It is for this reason that the clear-up rate is sometimes taken as a measure of police efficiency. Both the arrest rate and the subsequent charge rate will depend upon such organisational constraints as the perceived need for arrests in a particular area and grants of immunity, and on such situational factors as the appearance, demeanour, gender and class of the offender – all of which may be regarded as indicators of the seriousness of the offence or the likelihood of its being repeated. Only some of those who are charged will be convicted by a court, and court proceedings may result in a decision not only that a particular defendant was not, after all, a criminal but also that no crime was committed in any case – the person arrested and charged with drunken driving, for example, may be found not to have been intoxicated at all.[28] Such outcomes throw further doubt on the accuracy of the statistics on reported crimes, though they rarely lead to any official revision of the figures.

The final stage in the 'funnelling' of criminal behaviour occurs as a result of sentencing variations, where the routines followed by particular courts, the establishment of informal 'tariffs', and individual case-by-case variations lead to differences over time and space in the number of people receiving particular sentences for similar offences.

Thus criminal statistics include only a proportion of the actual number of crimes and criminals, together with an unknown number of people who are wrongfully detected or convicted. They are an insecure basis for generalisation about criminality because of the administrative routines and situated decisions that shape their production. The conventional response to this by criminologists has been that a knowledge of these decisions and routines allows us to correct the statistics and to improve their validity. It should be apparent, however, that this is by no means straightforward. A major implication of the work of ethnomethodologists and others is that the very idea of an 'actual' or 'real' rate of crime must be thrown into question. Indeed, the very categories of 'criminal', 'offence', and 'crime' have been seen as social definitions which arise within the system of official control rather than as objective descriptions of behaviour outside the routines and decisions of the system.

Ethnomethodologists have made the radical claim that there can be no correspondence between statistical rates and behaviour in 'the real world'. Because official statistics are the outcome of the situated application of rules in a variety of ways by a variety of observers, 'the mere aggregation of different observers' reports must produce a meaningless jumble of figures'.[29] Official statistics have no meaning except as devices used by the police and others to account for, and hence to legitimate, their own actions. The criminal statistics may be taken as a *topic* of research, but they do not comprise a *resource* for research.

The problems inherent in such a conclusion have frequently been pointed out: the denial of a direct correspondence between 'labels' and 'behaviour' shades over into a more extreme position which denies the existence of the behaviour itself. Becker's statement of the labelling theory involved an acceptance of the idea that acts capable of falling foul of the criminal law actually took place,[30] though they may subsequently become misdescribed through the labelling process. For the ethnomethodologists, however, no such acts can exist – or if they do exist we can never know anything about them. Gatrell has forcibly argued that this step must be resisted: 'Whether perceived and reacted against or not, a murder, a burglary, a wounding or a theft remains a discrete act, defined as clearly as possible in law on the premise that it is a discrete act; and a specific number of these acts is committed.'[31] This is to say, the criminal statistics are imperfect records of these acts but are nevertheless corrigible indicators of real rates of behaviour. When assessed, as all documentary sources must be assessed, for their authenticity, credibility, representativenesss and meaning, official statistics may serve as useful evidence on social behaviour. 'What criminal statistics record . . . is not a direct transcription of the social reality of crime, but a refraction of that reality through the various processes involved in the collection and recording of data.'[32]

A knowledge of these processes allows the researcher to utilise statistical sources of evidence. The researcher must uncover the conceptual and technical instruments employed by social statisticians and agents of social control and must assess whether the administrative routines and situated decisions that result in the statistics produce knowledge which is valid *from the standpoint of the officially defined categories.*[33] It is then possible to proceed from this question of the 'internal validity' of the statistics to the question of their adequacy in relation to the theoretical framework of the researcher. The closer the correspondence between the researcher's concepts and those of the official statisticians, the easier this step becomes. The further removed these concepts are from one another, the more corrections and adjustments will be required and the greater will be the degree of uncertainty in the researcher's results. This uncertainty, however, is very different from the total agnosticism about 'the real world' which many sociologists have drawn from the ethnomethodologists' position.

6 Explorations in Official Documents

In the previous chapters I have outlined the development of documentary reports and accounts in the official sphere of public action, examining both State and private documentary sources. I have tried to show how these documents are shaped by the structure and activities of the departments and organisations responsible for them and by the overarching structure of State policy and surveillance. I wish now to draw on this discussion to illustrate the uses that can be made of official documents in social research. My discussion rests upon the argument that it makes sense to use these sources in research only when the researcher is sensitive to their conditions of production and storage. Only then is the researcher aware of the problems of quality control that inhere in this source of evidence.

To this end, I shall look at how official categories and measures, based on particular conceptual and technical instruments, can be adapted to meet the rigorous requirements of social research. I shall illustrate my argument through the documents of class, welfare and industrial relations. The argument of the chapter is cumulative, with each section building on the points already made. I shall use the discussion of class to raise each of the quality control criteria in a systematic way. The discussions of welfare and industrial relations make further explorations into the problem of meaning and examine some of the additional questions of authenticity, credibility and representativeness that must be raised.

Occupation, class and inequality

The published data compiled by OPCS from the census and vital registration have been widely used by sociologists interested in charting the changing class structure of British society, while social historians have additionally made use of the original census and registration evidence. Users of this kind of material can take much for granted about its quality for research purposes – the question of the authorship of official statistics, for example, needs rarely to be raised. A researcher who is well versed in assessing the quality of documentary sources may take the general quality of such data on trust and raise only those problems specific to her or his study. Particular investigations need not systematically rehearse the various questions of authenticity, credibility, representativeness and meaning. In this section, however, I shall make explicit what is taken for granted by most researchers in order to highlight just how much work has been done, on our behalf, by earlier researchers. Newcomers and novices in the use of census and registration data need to have this established background of taken-for-granted assumptions made explicit for them. I shall, therefore, review this source material in terms of each of the four quality control criteria and, in the following section, illustrate how it may be used in social research.

Vital registration – the systematic collection of information on the major demographic events in the life cycle – was established in sixteenth-century Britain with the minimal requirement that ministers of the established Church should record the details of every baptism, marriage and burial at which they officiated.[1] The recording of this information was uneven and haphazard, with the parochial clergy showing considerable variation in both enthusiasm and diligence, and many parishes were late to begin their registration. Early registration took various forms, often involving the use of loose sheets of paper, and the requirement to maintain a proper parish register in a parchment volume was not introduced until 1598; and it was not until that year that many of the earlier records were transcribed into the new registers. From this same date annual copies of the parish registers had to be made for storage at the diocesan registry, and these so-called 'bishop's transcripts' opened up numerous possibilities for errors in copying: missing entries and items, gaps in the run of events, misspellings, and so on. It is often difficult for the researcher using such data to know whether a particular document is an original or a copy, as the so-called 'transcripts' seem often to have been the original rough notes from which the actual register was compiled.

Until the middle of the seventeenth century, vital registration remained at this rather basic level. It was not until 1644–5, for example, that there was any attempt to ensure either the recording of the names of the parents of baptised children or the recording of dates of birth and death alongside those of baptism and burial. These items were not a compulsory requirement until the nineteenth-century reform of vital registration. Parish registration was disrupted during the period of the Commonwealth, when the partial separation of Church from State and the abolition of bishops led to an attempt to transfer registration to civil registrars. Many of the parochial clergy, however, continued to record baptisms, burials and marriages throughout the period 1653–60, and there was some attempt to maintain the diocesan returns. The period from 1538 to 1836 can, in general, be regarded as one in which parochial registration and diocesan returns provide the main sources of information on the vital statistics of individuals, communities and the population as a whole.

From 1836 the recording requirements for parish registers were tightened, registration by Nonconformist ministers was permitted, and local registration offices were introduced to undertake civil, non-parochial registration. The superintendent registrars in the Poor Law districts became the responsible officers for the compulsory civil registration of births and deaths, with the clergy continuing to record the baptisms, burials and marriages that they undertook. The system was further centralised when, in 1837, parochial and civil registrars were required to submit quarterly returns of copies of their registers to the newly established General Register Office in London.[2] This system was initially limited to England and Wales, with civil registration being introduced to Scotland in 1855 and Ireland in 1864.[3] Under the new system of national registration the local officials, whether clergy or civil registrars, had to maintain separate volumes for births/baptisms, death/burials and marriages,[4] these volumes being supplied to them as printed books of blank forms,[5] and had to send a copy of the relevant registers to the GRO each quarter. Since 1837 the GRO has been responsible for maintaining a national index of births, deaths and marriages,[6] and for ensuring that the indexes, though not the copy registers, are accessible to the public and to social researchers.[7] Both local registrars and the GRO are required to provide, for a fee, certified copies of register entries – commonly termed birth, death and marriage 'certificates' – to anyone requiring them.

The information available in registers and their copies has, since 1836, been standardised throughout England and Wales, with rather more detailed information being recorded in Scotland. A record of birth contains the child's name, sex, place and date of birth, the names of both parents, the maiden name of any mother taking her husband's name,[8] the occupation of the father, and the name and address of the informant (usually one of the parents). In the case of a marriage, the register shows the date of the marriage, the names, ages and occupations of the bride and groom, and the names and occupations of their fathers, as well as the 'condition' (bachelor, spinster, widow, etc.) and residence of the two parties, and the names of the witnesses. An entry in the register of deaths is the least informative, giving the name, age, sex and occupation of the deceased, the cause and place of death, and the name and address of the informant. In the case of all three registers, the entries will show the name of the registrar, the date of registration, and the registration district, with marriage registers adding the place of marriage. Certified copies of register entries contain all these items of information, as well as the date on which the copy was made and the name of the registrar responsible.[9]

The census of 1801 was, like its immediate successors in 1811, 1821, and 1831, a rather haphazard exercise in which the methods both of data collection and of data analysis were untried and, in many respects, unsuccessful. Most of the information collected in the census was derived from returns completed by the overseers of the poor and other parish officials, with local collection being supervised by the magistrates. Local officials simply collected information on the number of houses in their area, the occupants of these houses, and their form of employment: these early censuses were mere headcounts, with no personal data on individuals collected. Ambiguity over the wording of the questions which were to be answered by the census officials and a lack of guidance on the methods to be used resulted in great problems of reliability and validity. These problems were only half-heartedly considered in the following censuses, and the information on anything other than the mere totals of population in various areas must be treated with the greatest caution. Fortunately, the information collected by parish officials was supplemented by the evidence that bishops were required to collect from their parochial clergy. The latter were to extract from their parish registers the numbers of baptisms and burials in each decade of the eighteenth century and in each of the ten years preceding the census, so giving a check on the 1801 census totals and a time series of comparable estimates. The clergy were also required to record the numbers of marriages in the years 1754–1800.[10]

The changes made in the system of Poor Law administration in 1834, and the introduction of civil registration two years later, proved consequential for the 1841 census. The superintendent registrars became the responsible local officials for the census, subject to the supervision of the Registrar-General in the new GRO in London. Each local registrar was to appoint census enumerators for each area within the registration district,[11] and each enumerator distributed self-completion census forms to the occupants of all the houses in the area for which he or she was responsible. Such 'enumeration districts' were supposed to average 100 households, but in practice they varied widely in size. The prime task of the enumerator was to collect the completed forms and exercise some degree of quality control over their completion and initial processing. The census forms recorded the name, age, place of birth, and occupation of each member of a household, and in later censuses also recorded their marital status and relationship to the head of household – as wife, son, or servant, for example. The information contained on each form was transcribed by the enumerator into a book ruled into columns, and these enumerators' books comprised the primary data set on which later analysis by the registrars and their clerks was based.

All subsequent censuses have followed this model, though techniques of data processing and the number and range of questions on the form has been altered over the years. With two exceptions censuses have been decennial, the two exceptions being the failure to hold a census in 1941 (though wartime national registration was undertaken in 1939) and the inclusion of an additional census of a 10 per cent sample of the population in 1966. Though seen as the first in a series of inter-census investigations, the innovation of a sample census has never been followed. Indeed, the census has, since 1971, been slimmed down in its coverage of topics and has increasingly come to be regarded as providing regular fixed bench-marks for the more frequent household sample surveys carried out by OPCS.

The types of census data available have multiplied over the years. The main sources for many researchers are the statistical summaries published in book form since 1801 as a series of national and county reports covering such topics as housing, household composition, car ownership, language, pensions and migration. Separate censuses of religion and education were carried out in 1851, collecting information on the number and type of schools and churches together with details on the numbers of those attending. Neither of these exercises has ever been repeated.[12] Since 1971, there have also been 'small area statistics', which are unpublished but available on demand. These statistics are based around the separate enumeration districts and aggregations of such districts, and are often available in customised form on computer tape and microfilm as well as on printed sheets.[13] Certain standard unpublished tables, including general statistics for political areas (such as constituencies), travel-to-work tables and migration tables, are also routinely produced and are available to researchers.

Of great importance to social researchers as a source comparable with civil registration data are the original census forms and enumerators' books which are available, after 100 years, at the Public Record Office. Prior to 1841 there were no household forms and the local officials collected only summary data, and so the survival of anything other than aggregate data is rather patchy. The enumerators' books from 1841 to 1881 are available to researchers, generally on microfilm. Thus, at the beginning of 1992 it should be possible for researchers to consult the enumerators' books for 1891. Owing to the destruction in 1904 of virtually all the original schedules, up to and including 1901, it will not be possible for researchers to use any of the self-completion forms until 2012, when those for 1911 will become public. Indeed, 1911 was the first year in which the census office dispensed with enumerators' books and produced coded data on punched cards directly from the household schedules. For this reason it is, in general, impossible to compare enumerators' books and household schedules for the same year: with a very few exceptions, where local records have survived, there is no census year for which both types of 'raw' data now survive.

There is no consistent international practice on the compilation of census and registration data, though certain similarities exist. The United States Federal Census has been carried out every ten years since 1790, with enumeration in the early years being the responsibility of the US marshals and their assistants.[14] Printed schedules were first introduced in 1830, but not until 1850 was information recorded on individuals – following the British practice of nine years earlier. British practice was followed again in 1880 when census enumeration was reorganised along district lines, each district being subordinated to a census office within the Department of the Interior.[15] Fire almost completely destroyed the returns for 1890, making a gap in the run of original data, and a decision was made in 1956 to retain only microfilm copies of the returns from 1900 to 1940. Thereafter, the returns from each census have been destroyed after microfilming, and the microfims themselves remain subject to closed access for a period of 72 years. Thus, open archival access is possible for a much later period than in Britain, but this access is only to the surviving microfilm copies. In France, neither the census records nor the vital registers are stored centrally. Census enumerators' books are retained within each department, while civil registers remain at the level of each *arrondissement*. As in Britain, a 100-year rule of confidentiality is observed.[16]

While the British situation – like any other – is unique, there are sufficient similarities in the form of the data and access to them to make an understanding of the British material a useful basis for understanding that of any other country. This understanding can best be approached through considering each of the four quality control criteria discussed in chapter 2.

Authenticity

Parish and civil registers are official documents produced by ministers and registrars and their staff, and are generally regarded as having a high degree of authenticity. There are no known cases of registrars making fraudulent entires or copies from the civil registers, though registration certificates have undoubtedly been as subject to fraud, forgery and alteration as any other official document, and entries in parish registers are known to have been altered. Forged and fraudulent census returns are even less likely to occur, as there is little advantage to be gained from such practices, though there may well be many cases where someone other than the householder has completed the householder's schedule or where an enumerator has fraudulently completed a schedule or enumeration book. In general, however, such cases seem to be rare, and any problems can best be dealt with in connection with the question of 'credibility'.

More important problems of authenticity concern the soundness of the documents being handled. Copy registers, certificates, and indexes can be mistranscribed, producing misprints or incomplete entries, and in some cases the entry in the original register may be a mistranscription from rough notes. This is a particular problem for those researching the post-1837 period, as the absence of any public right to search the civil registers in England and Wales means that the researcher will always be working from copies or from indexes. The only alternative to this is to use post-1837 parish registers – the originals of which are open to the public – although these became far less comprehensive after the introduction of civil registration.

A certificate issued by the GRO will have been the result of two distinct transcription processes, each involving its own sources of error, and the GRO indexes to births, marriages and deaths are themselves compiled from copy registers. Local indexes and certificates supplied by local registrars are normally compiled from the original registers and so involve fewer opportunities for errors and omissions.[17] It is clear that numerous registrations fail to get indexed and that mistakes, such as the copying of 'Edward' for 'Edmund' or 'Barclay' for 'Berkeley', are far from infrequent. Copies of parish registers, especially those produced by amateurs or for commercial publication in the past, are known to involve even greater problems of authenticity. More recent commercial and private copies, including those made for the genealogical archive of the Mormon Church, have been found to involve fewer such problems than earlier transcripts and extracts.[18]

Census material also must be assessed for its authenticity, even though problems of fraud and forgery may be regarded as rare. Of particular importance is the routine copying and editing procedures to which the original returns have been subjected. Census officials must constantly make situated decisions as part of their continuous administrative routines. The census enumerators compiled their books from the original household schedules that they distributed and, in many cases, helped to complete. Illiteracy in the population during the nineteenth century meant that the enumerators frequently had to 'correct' some responses on the schedules and convert them into 'normal', standardised responses. While this undoubtedly reduced the possibilities of error in the subsequent writing of the enumerators' books, the practice throws into question the authenticity of the original schedules. However, the absence of surviving schedules from the nineteenth-century censuses means that it is impossible to compare the contents of schedules with the information contained in enumerators' books.[19]

Once the schedules had been copied into enumerators' books they were edited by registrars and their clerks, under instruction, in order to check them against the schedules and to assess the internal consistency of the responses. The aim of the registrars was to see whether the information in the books looked 'right' and to convert it into what they felt to be authentic responses. The purpose of this editing, therefore, was to reduce the number of copying errors introduced by the enumerators, though it introduced the possibility of editing errors on the part of the registrars. Although later twentieth-century censuses have dispensed with the enumerator's book, moving directly from schedule to coded data, there is still an internal process of appraisal and editing in the census offices, with consequent problems of authenticity.[20] These problems have been compounded by the recent practice of microfilming those enumerators' books which are available for public search. Although the original books can be consulted on request, access is normally to the microfilms. The researcher must ensure that these films are complete copies of the originals, though even the latter may be incomplete through damage or loss of pages with the passage of time.

Credibility

Census and registration information is recorded and, in some cases, classified by the enumerators and by the registration staff. In assessing the credibility of census data, therefore, an important issue is that of how reliable these people can be regarded as observers and reporters on what they were told. Did they sincerely and accurately record their observations? In answering this question it is necessary to come to some conclusion about whether the person recording the information had it directly from the person concerned or from a third party, or was, perhaps, guessing or relying on his or her own knowledge. Official forms and registers may have been completed from memory or from notes, despite this practice being illegal.

Little is known about the early census enumerators and of what qualities were looked for by those who recruited them. Some were paid workers, while others were unpaid volunteers; and it was not until the 1841 census that there was any central regulation of their recruitment. It has been found that the motives of enumerators varied considerably, suggesting possible sources of variation in the credibility of their returns. Drake has reported that mid-century enumerators ranged from clergy seeking to discover more about the poor of their parish, to members of a Volunteer Regiment seeking to raise regimental funds from their fees.[21] By 1881 there was still considerable concern in the GRO about the literacy and general quality of the enumerators employed. For the nineteenth century, Drake concludes that 'one ought to approach the enumerators' returns with all one's critical faculties fully alerted',[22] Even in the twentieth century, when greater care has been employed in the recruitment of enumerators, they have generally been given little more than a few hours training by officers with full-time responsibilities for civil registration.

Registration information must also be regarded as variable in quality. In general it may be correct to presume that birth and death registrations are more credible than those for marriages, though the recorded age at death is notoriously unreliable. Recording accurate and useful information on occupations and addresses requires certain skills which have to be acquired by professional registrars: when to probe for further details, what to ask in order to clarify responses, and so on. Where a marriage takes place in a church the officiating minister may not possess these skills, and may not even appreciate the need for accurate and detailed occupational data. When the registration is carried out in the course of the marriage ceremony, the participants may have other things on their minds, and there is little incentive for the minister to seek details of, for example, exactly what kind of 'engineer' the bride's father was.

Frequent inaccuracies in parish registration, civil registration and census enumeration have been discovered in respect of ages, kinship and employment. Age information, for example, has always involved some degree of estimation, even when the information has been supplied directly by the person concerned. For much of the nineteenth century there were large numbers of people who did not know their true age, and even today people will 'round up' or 'round down' their age to that which they feel happy stating. Such problems are exacerbated when ages are recorded in age-bands, rather than as exact numbers of years, or when registrars record those over 21 as 'of full age'.[23] Information on parentage in parish and civil registers must be regarded as possibly inaccurate in the case of illegitimate births, as it was not until the late nineteenth century that there was any real control over who was named by an unmarried woman as the father of her child. Employment and occupational data are especially susceptible to inaccuracy, and this is particularly important if industrial or social class schema are to be used. In the early censuses the numerous women and children who were employed part time or seasonally, especially in agriculture, would not have been described as 'labourers' but would have been allocated to the 'residual' category,[24] and the nineteenth-century censuses included no questions on part-time work.[25]

When the original information is processed by registrars to produce summaries and tabulations, the researcher must ask how credible the codings and allocations are.[26] For example, is the information in the registers and returns comprehensive enough for accurate allocations to be made, and are the procedures used both valid and reliable? Some of the issues raised here are more appropriately considered under the heading of 'meaning', but one of the questions at issue is, for example, whether the categories used discriminate equally well for all types of work. For instance, are different types of manual work distinguished as finely as the various types of professional work, and are the categories used in one year the same as those used in others? The general problem is that while the procedures employed have become clearer and more public over time, there is very little solid evidence about the procedures and routines followed by officials in the early years of the census and civil registration.

Representativeness

The coverage of parish and civil registration and of the census is fairly good. Although baptism was far from universal and some Nonconformist marriages were not recorded in the parish registers, burial was almost unavoidable, and most parish ministers and churchwardens seem to have attempted to keep full records once the practice of registration became established. Whereas the civil registration of births involved under-recording in the years up to the 1880s, few problems of representative coverage have been found for later years.[27] Particular problems arise in the census, where it is not unknown for the enumerator to miss a household, or even a complete street: the whole of Grosvenor Square in Central London, for example, was missed in the 1851 census.[28] It has also been reported that very young children were sometimes missed off the household returns, and that some householders would not co-operate with the enumerator. In the early years of the census, the fear that it was the prelude to conscription or taxation led some people to refuse specific items of information.[29]

More difficult problems of representativeness, however, arise when researchers attempt to study particular localities. If the aim is to study a whole community, or a sample drawn from that community, the researcher cannot be sure that the relevant records were complete: people normally resident in one parish or district may have been temporarily absent on census night, or may have married or been confined in a parish other than that in which they normally lived. It may also be difficult to ensure that the records are representative of all the events that occurred in a specified period, as civil records are arranged and indexed by the period in which they were registered rather than by the date of the event itself.[30]

Even if these problems can be resolved, and the researcher is confident in his or her judgement of the representativeness of the original material, it cannot be assumed that all this material has actually survived to the present. Many parish registers have been destroyed, stolen or simply lost over the years, as have the bulk of the original nineteenth-century census documents. The civil registers, on the other hand, have not suffered in this way and are believed to survive intact.[31]

Access is often granted only to copies of the original documents, especially where the latter are in poor condition, and inadequate copying may limit the representativeness of the sources available to the researcher. This is further exacerbated by specific legal restrictions on access, such as the non-availability of census returns for 100 years and the severe restrictions on access to the birth registration data of adopted persons. Most parish registers prior to 1836, and many for periods since then, have now been transferred to county record offices or, in Scotland, to New Register House; and since 1979 there has been a legal requirement for ministers to ensure that this is the case if stringent conditions on storage cannot be met.[32] In addition to the public archives of the GRO and county record offices, many copies and extracts from parish registers have been made by private organisations, and the libraries of the Society of Genealogists and the Mormon Church are now the most important private archives to which researchers may gain access.

Even the public indexes to civil registration, the only point of access to these records for researchers, are far from complete, and the many other indexes and calendars which have been produced by amateurs and volunteers cannot be relied upon with any certainty.[33] Indexes are especially important in constructing a sample for study, as registration districts rarely coincide with the area in which the researcher is interested. Enumeration districts may have to be split and combined to reconstitute them into useful areas, and in urban areas a good street index is essential for this task. Not all areas are street indexed, however, and the only other census indexes that have been produced, generally unofficially, are the surname indexes of the family historians. A researcher interested in a sample of people engaged in a particular occupation, for example, will not generally find the available indexes of much value and will have to spend a great deal of time constructing a sample.[34]

Meaning

The immediate problem in handling census and registration material is to achieve a literal understanding: to decipher texts in 'secretary' or 'court' hand, to translate from Latin, to resolve difficulties in Old Style and New Style dating, to discern correctly the names, addresses and occupations given in the documents, and so on. But this is a prelude to the more difficult task of interpretative understanding, where the researcher aims to infer the denotation and connotation of the recorded items of information. This task can be seen most clearly in the handling of occupational evidence, where three distinct aspects of interpretation arise: the *specification*, *linkage* and *classification* of items.

The key issue in the specification of occupational items is to determine what kind of work is, or was, actually implied by the occupational title given. Does the researcher know, for example, what work was carried out by a 'horn worker', a 'hugger-off', a 'knobbler' or a 'worm boy'?[35] Even such straightforward terms as 'engineer' and 'clerk' may be difficult to specify unless further information is supplied; and when occupation is shown as 'unemployed', 'retired' or 'student' it may be difficult to obtain any useful data. It will not always be known whether people supplying information were currently in employment. They may, for example, have sought to avoid the designation unemployed by reporting their last occupation. Similar problems arise with part-time work. Registrars generally aim to record only full-time employment, but the meaning of 'full time' is far from clear. For this reason, people in part-time employment, which may involve a large number of hours of work, may fail to have their occupation recorded: they may appear as being without employment. This is particularly problematic for those involved in casual work or outwork.[36]

Occupational titles may be specified incorrectly by the researcher when the nature of the work has changed. The occupation of 'clerk', for example, had quasi-managerial status and authority in the nineteenth century, and was a predominantly male occupation, whereas today it has been femininised and has been transformed into a largely routine non-managerial job. Thus, a person recorded as a clerk in 1861 may have been carrying out a fundamentally different task to one so classified in 1961.[37] Davies has shown how the occupation of 'nurse' was transformed from that of a domestic servant into that of a medical subordinate, and she argues that the constancy of terminology masked a complex series of changes and that 'built into these changes was a constant ambivalence about nursing, domestic work, and women'.[38]

For all these reasons, therefore, it may be difficult to specify from an occupational title exactly what work a person carried out. But even where these problems can be resolved, specification of the significance of this work for a person's life may be extremely difficult to gauge. The primary reason for this is that official registration is blind to the career, life cycle and gender relevance of occupational evidence. Recorded occupations are generally the current or, in the case of the retired, unemployed and deceased, the last occupation held. People's occupations change, however, as a part of normal job mobility and as they pass through the life cycle. A person recorded as an agricultural labourer on the night of a particular census, may have recently entered that occupation and may have moved on to another occupation shortly after the census. Moreover, the 'snapshot' picture provided by a census may give a poor indication of the actual work carried out by an individual. When the researcher compares people at different stages of the life cycle – comparing an unmarried person of 20 with a married person of 50 – their sharing of the same occupational title may be of little significance.[39]

Such life-cycle changes are especially important in the case of women, whose occupational specification is further compounded by their heavy involvement in part-time employment and unpaid work, and by their entry into occupations whose status and work content has been radically altered over the past hundred years. Recent discussions have centred on the practice of the census authorities of assuming the existence of a 'head of household', generally assumed to be male, to whom all information about other household members is related. Thus, a woman who is married to a farmer and engages in domestic work, unpaid farm labour and the letting of holiday accommodation, may be shown simply as 'farmer's wife'. The general tendency in civil registration is to record more details about a woman's husband and father than about the woman herself, a fact which creates particular problems for occupational classification.[40]

Once a researcher has specified the meaning of an item of occupational information, he or she may wish to try to link this with other items of information. The linkage of items has received much attention recently in studies of family and community reconstitution.[41] Parish registers and civil registration documents, unlike the later censuses, generally contain information about individuals, with only partial indications of the other individuals to whom they are related. The researcher who is interested in studying families and households therefore has the task of using the methods of the genealogist and family historian to reconstruct families from evidence at the individual level.[42] To achieve this, it is necessary for the researcher to arrive at a decision on whether two records containing the same name can be assumed to refer to the same person. Only if such a decision can be made may the contents of the two documents be linked.

Winchester has pointed out that such decisions are often based on an inadequate empiricist view of knowledge in which it is assumed that there is an unproblematic correspondence between a name in a record and a real person.[43] In fact, people in the past can only be known through the records that survive, and so there is no possibility of recourse to external evidence about the person. Even for those who are our contemporaries, scientific knowledge can be gained only through the technical and conceptual instruments of interviewing, observation and questionnairing. Any judgement about the identity of individuals named in various records, therefore, must be based purely upon the internal evidence of the records themselves. In pursuing this task of what has been called 'nominal record linkage', the researcher is assessing the consistency in the recorded evidence.

The important question, therefore, concerns how that consistency is to be assessed. Although there have been attempts to evolve pragmatic rules which can be applied in a computer program,[44] this assessment will always involve some judgement of the balance of probability in each particular case. The guidelines employed in making this judgement will involve such considerations as consistency in age calculations between two dates, the order of listing in an enumeration book as an indicator of kinship and birth order, and the rarity of the names and occupations shown. Assessing whether two records referring to the name John Smith concern the same person is a difficult task because Smith is a very common name, but the linkage can be strengthened if ages, addresses and occupations correspond. Be that as it may, the ultimate uncertainty involved in this judgement should be clear from the fact that addresses and occupations change, often unpredictably, over the course of a person's life. It is possible therefore for John Smith, greengrocer, to be the same person as John Smith, cab proprietor, if the records are separated in time.

In order to minimise this uncertainty, the researcher may draw upon the techniques of conjectural emendation used in assessing the soundness of a document. If the likely sources of error can be identified, discrepancies between documents may be resolved. Winchester gives the case of one record referring to G. J. Berkeley, a tailor born in 1676 in Ireland, and another record referring to J. G. Barclay, a sailor born in 1667 in Dublin. No single item of information corresponds between records, yet it is not implausible that they refer to the same person. The researcher may legitimately link the two records if it seems likely that errors of transposition and spelling ('1676' for '1667', 'G. J.' for 'J. G.', 'Berkeley' for 'Barclay', 'sailor' for 'tailor') and the use of generic terms ('Ireland' to include 'Dublin') are typical for this class of document. In this case, the researcher may conclude that the two records refer to the same person but will not know the actual name and identity of that person. There is no way of choosing between the two alternative descriptions of the same person.[45]

There is a paradox in this conception of record linkage: the greater the certainty in making a link, the less the information that will be obtained. If two documents, each containing a large number of items, prove to have a perfect consistency, then there will be a very strong certainty that they refer to the same person. But in this case the documents will be, to all intents and purposes, identical, and no additional information will have been produced from using a second document. In order to achieve additional information, the second document must differ from the first in theoretically and empirically relevant respects; and where the documents differ, the certainty of any linkage will be lower. The paradox is that the acquisition of information requires uncertainty in the linkage of records.

An alternative to the 'relational' approach of nominal record linkage is the 'aggregative' approach employed in many census and OPCS publications. In this approach the aim is to examine summary totals of rates over time, and the key problem will be that of the classification of items rather than their linkage.[46] As has been emphasised at a number of points in this book, classification is necessarily a theoretical task. Anyone undertaking their own classification or using a scheme of classification devised by others must be concerned with the principles underlying the classification employed. In her discussion of the published census commentaries, Hakim has correctly argued that they 'reveal the subjectivity, historical relativity, and cultural relativity that often lie behind the statistical facts presented in the published census reports'.[47] This is most obviously the case when the Registrar-General's Classification of occupations is employed.

Class schemas and the problem of meaning

The Registrar-General's Classification, whose origins were discussed in the previous chapter, has been widely used in official publications and in the works of historians and sociologists; even so, academic users have also tried to evolve alternative, and more adequate, class schemas. The Registrar-General's Classification, it will be recalled, was based on the assumption that occupational titles were valid and reliable indicators of class position, where the latter was defined in terms of the environmental conditions of housing and work. Among those who have attempted to improve upon the Classification, there has, in many cases, been an implicit rejection of this concept of class. Instead of occupation serving as an indicator of class, it is sometimes regarded as a determinant of it. Class has been re-defined, for example, as the outcome of popular evaluations of occupational 'prestige'; but this results in major problems of interpretation and therefore of comparability between studies. Such problems must be confronted by any researcher who wishes to make use of the official data on occupation and class, and in order to elucidate this major problem of interpretation and to try to suggest a viable strategy of classification for future research, I shall review some of the main alternatives to the Registrar-General's Classification.

The official five-class schema was especially influential in sociological work of the inter-war years, with writers such as Beveridge and Carr-Saunders helping to popularise its use, while undoubtedly the most influential of the alternative classifications, the Hall–Jones schema originating in a study of Merseyside, was used in the London School of Economics social mobility study of the 1950s.[48] The Hall–Jones classification comprises seven classes (see figure 6.1), which can be collapsed into the five social classes of the official classification. It was constructed without the benefit of a formal coding scheme, occupations being allocated to the various classes at the coding stage by comparing the recorded occupational title with a list of exemplars for each class.[49] The Hall–Jones classification was constructed through *ad hoc* adjustments to the official classification, but the researchers subsequently sought to test its validity through empirical research. They argued that it was necessary to derive a scale of stratification from which valid class boundaries could be identified.

Figure 6.1   *The Hall–Jones classification*

1 Professional and higher administrative
2 Managerial and executive
3 Inspectional, supervisory and other non-manual: high grade
4 Inspectional, supervisory and other non-manual: low grade
5 Skilled manual and routine grades of non-manual
6 Semi-skilled manual
7 Unskilled manual

The researchers held that the fundamental element in social stratification was the popular assessment of relative social standing, this assessment being based on occupational evidence. For this reason, class was to be measured from perceived occupational status in a national opinion survey. Despite their intention to see if their intuitive schema corresponded with that derived from a national survey, only a few of the example occupations were subsequently re-allocated in the light of the survey result.[50] The Hall–Jones schema was not strictly derived from the national survey.

The Hall–Jones class schema and its coding procedures took the same intuitive form as those that produced the Registrar-General's Classification. Despite their view that occupation must be seen as the determinant of class position, the schema is equally compatible with the argument that occupation is an indicator of social class. The absence of a systematic coding scheme, however, seriously undermines its reliability as an alternative to the official scheme. Any attempt to use the Hall–Jones classification in documentary research – or any other type of social research – must bear in mind this fundamental problem. Without an adequate code book, comparable to the official *Classification of Occupations*, there can be no guarantee that different researchers will classify the same evidence in the same way. This problem of reliability was not seriously confronted for many years, with even the most influential of studies using *ad hoc* variants of the Hall–Jones schema.[51] Only when a new study of social mobility was planned, aimed at replicating that of Glass, were the main problems of the Hall–Jones schema identified and confronted.

In this study, directed by John Goldthorpe and Keith Hope, the initial solution was to base a coding scheme around the official *Classification of Occupations*. The OPCS unit groups in the 1970 edition of this booklet were cross-classified with the six official 'employment statuses' to produce what were termed 'occupational grading units' (OGUs). The occupations of individuals, whether derived from interviews, from civil registration or from other sources, could therefore be allocated to one of these OGUs through the same reliable procedures that are followed by OPCS. Goldthorpe and Hope devised a classification of the OGUs on the basis of the 'expert judgements' of economists and industrial sociologists, the aim being to produce categories which were homo- geneous in terms of 'the net extrinsic and intrinsic, material and non-material rewards and deprivations typically associated with the occupations which they comprised'.[52] As a result, the OGUs were grouped into 124 categories which reflected the major sources of variation in market and work situation that Goldthorpe and Hope assumed to comprise the main determinants of class.[53] The researchers were, therefore, following analogous – though more rigorous – procedures to those used by Stevenson in his estimation of the 'environmental' determinants of class.

Goldthorpe and Hope next wished to reduce the 124 categories to a limited schema of social classes. They did this not directly but through the intermediate step of constructing a scale of stratification from a national survey of opinion. Respondents were asked to rank a sample of occupations drawn from the 124 categories, and the scores for the various occupations were used to scale the categories themselves. The resulting 'Hope–Goldthorpe' scale was the basis on which 'adjacent' categories – those close to one another in score – were merged to form 36 large occupational categories, which were then further reduced to the final social classes. Goldthorpe recognised seven such classes, though he sometimes reduces these further into three core classes (see figure 6.2).

The idea of using popular gradings in the construction of a class schema is rooted in the assumption that social classes are to be seen as convenient and conventional categories derived from the continuous distribution of life chances along a single scale. I showed in the previous chapter that this is one possible view of the nature of the Registrar- General's Classification. In the Hall–Jones study this assumption was made explicit, but the scale derived from popular gradings was used only to validate the already existing class schema. In Goldthorpe's work, however, popular evaluations entered into the construction of the

Figure 6.2   *The Goldthorpe classification: version 1*

I Higher professional and admin.; large manufacturers and proprietors II Lower professional and admin.; small manufacturers and proprietors	SERVICE CLASS
III Routine non-manual workers IV Small employers, proprietors and self-employed	INTERMEDIATE CLASS
V Lower technical and manual supervisory workers VI Skilled manual workers VII Semi- and un-skilled manual workers	WORKING CLASS

class schema itself, and occupation came to be regarded as a determinant of class rather than simply as an indicator. It was a growing recognition of the need to separate class analysis from occupational status which led Goldthorpe to construct a second version of his class schema, based firmly on the idea that social classes are real social groups divided by fundamental differences in their life chances.[54]

The construction of this second version of the schema (shown in figure 6.3) was associated with a revision of the underlying occupational coding procedures that separated them completely from popular gradings. Occupations are reliably classified into categories derived from a cross-classification of employment status with the 1980 OPCS occupational unit groups. These atoms are then combined into an eightfold class schema, which can be 'collapsed' in various ways. The degree of collapsing is limited only by Goldthorpe's assumption of a fundamental class opposition between 'service class' and 'working class'. With the addition of the loose 'intermediate class', this is similar to Stevenson's original model.[55]

There is one major problem inherent in any use of occupation as an indicator of class position. The service class and its constituent groups encompass both bureaucratic employees and capitalist employers, the latter having a market and work situation based on a personal and impersonal structure of property ownership which cannot be grasped through occupational categories.[56] Despite Goldthorpe's recognition of an 'elite', distinct from the service class – but too small to be visible in a sample survey – there are crucial technical difficulties in identifying such a class from the census or civil registration records, where no information on income or wealth is available. And an occupationally

Figure 6.3 *The Goldthorpe classification: version 2*

I Higher professional and admin.; large manufacturers and proprietors II Lower professional and admin.; small manufacturers and proprietors	SERVICE CLASS
IIIa Routine non-manual workers IIIb Personal service workers	INTERMEDIATE CLASS
IV Small proprietors; farmers and small-holders	PETTY BOURGEOIS
V Lower technicians and supervisors VI Skilled manual workers VII Semi- and un-skilled manual workers; agricultural workers	WORKING CLASS

based class schema cannot, in any case, easily allow for the existence of a property-based upper class.

With that major qualification in mind, it might still be concluded that an occupationally based schema provides a useful general purpose measure of class structure. The OPCS/GRO occupational coding schemas and the modifications and extensions proposed by Armstrong (for the nineteenth century)[57] and Goldthorpe (for the latter part of the twentieth century) might then be seen as comprising a set of valid and reliable procedures for handling occupational data. On the basis of these procedures, the Registrar-General and Goldthorpe class schemas could be used to produce satisfactory mappings of the British class structure below the level of the upper classes.

But a major problem has been shelved throughout this discussion. Stevenson's original intention was that the occupation of the head of household should be used to classify the whole of the household. Goldthorpe's study took this one step further by concentrating its attention on men and male occupations, on the assumption that men are typically the heads of their households. This assumption has been questioned in a number of recent commentaries, and the central question has become: 'Do women's jobs matter for purposes of class analysis?'

Goldthorpe has in fact put forward a powerful defence of what he terms the 'conventional view'. The family, he argues, is the unit of stratification. It is the unit of 'reward' and 'fate', and this unity offsets any internal divisions of gender and age. The position of a family in the stratification system is therefore determined by the 'family head', defined as the chief breadwinner of the family.[58] Wives are both dependent and subordinate within the family, and their life chances, as individuals, are determined by the class position of the family. Goldthorpe argues that

> married women are required by conventional norms to take major responsibility for the performance of the work that is involved in maintaining a household and rearing children. This requirement then in various ways restricts their opportunities and prospects in regard to paid employment and, moreover, forces them to a greater or lesser extent into a situation of economic dependence on their husbands, so that the possibility of any effective challenge to the prevailing norms is in turn greatly reduced.[59]

Even where wives engage in paid employment, this tends to be part of a family work strategy within which the husband's employment is the dominant factor.[60] The 'timing, duration, and character' of the wife's work is conditioned by 'conventionally imposed domestic and family responsibilities' and by the market or work situation of her husband.[61]

Goldthorpe recognizes that such an approach may face difficulties in handling families without male heads and families in which the man and woman are dual earners. The first case can be dealt with quite easily by classifying the family on the basis of who actually *is* the head: i.e., by discovering the family member who has the greatest commitment to, and continuity in, labour market participation. A residual, but not unimportant problem is that Goldthorpe's original class schema was based on occupational coding procedures which were explicitly geared towards those occupations typically held by men. Any attempt to use it to classify women by their own occupations would be difficult or perhaps misleading. This problem has been partly resolved in Goldthorpe's second schema, where the occupational grading units are based on a recognition of variations in male and female employment.[62] The problem of 'dual earning' families is less easily resolved. The correct procedure, argues Goldthorpe, is to take account of the 'work time' involvement of the partners (i.e., whether it is full time or part time) in order to discover the 'dominant' partner in terms of labour market participation. The family as a whole may then be classified on the basis of the occupation of this person, male or female.[63]

This approach to class analysis has, however, been criticised by a number of feminist writers: indeed, Goldthorpe's re-formulation of the conventional view was itself shaped as a response to such criticisms.[64] The common element in these contrary positions is a rejection of the idea that the class position of the members of a family can be derived from the occupation of one of its members. While some take the view that a social class schema must allow the 'joint' classification of families by the occupations of both partners, more radical writers have argued that classes have individuals and not families as their basic units. Advocates of the latter position therefore hold that individuals, whether male or female, must be classified by their own occupations, and that a useful class schema must recognise the important differences in the advantages attached to male and female occupations. What seems to lie behind such positions is a correct appreciation of the limitations inherent in the assumption that the conventional nuclear family is the typical form of household in nineteenth-century and twentieth-century Britain. The many 'single parent', single person and other 'unconventional' households cannot adequately be grasped by a schema which centres on the family.

But the alternatives proposed are not, in general, preferable solutions. They are unable to recognise that the life chances of an individual are a consequence not only of her or his own market and work situation but also of the position of the *household as a whole*. Indeed, Goldthorpe has demonstrated quite clearly that the life chances of those married women who are not the dominant breadwinners in their families are more completely explained by the market and work situation of the economically 'dominant' partner than they are by the woman's own employment. Goldthorpe's 'conventional view' can adequately handle the theoretical and empirical problems raised by his feminist critics if a relatively minor shift is made from the family to the household as the fundamental unit.[65]

Though all the problems for class analysis raised by feminist writers have not been resolved, the 'conventional view' has survived remarkably well. It would seem that the modifications suggested by Goldthorpe mean that the Registrar-General and Goldthorpe schemas can, indeed, be used to produce adequate mappings of the class structure. Their use in studies drawing on census and vital registration data, and in other types of study, is a valid procedure for maximising comparability in social research.

Measuring the class structure

There is a long-standing tradition of research aimed at converting census and vital registration data into a moving picture of the 'changing social structure' of British society. The aim of this research is to document 'social trends' from this unique source of data and so provide a backdrop for more detailed research using other sources. Studies by Carr-Saunders and his associates,[66] for example, were influential in the development of the Hall–Jones classification and the Glass study of social mobility,[67] thereby influencing a whole generation of social researchers. I propose to discuss this work and to show how, despite the reservations of some social statisticians about the concept of class, their work demonstrates the indisputable reality of class relations in Britain.[68]

In 1927 Carr-Saunders and Jones, of Liverpool University, argued for the need to treat official social data from a 'morphological point of view' to present a statistical 'picture' of British social life. The morphological approach, they argued, involves relating various measures together so as to disclose the 'structure' of the society. They were, however, somewhat sceptical of terms such as 'class structure'. Their book was originally titled *The Structure of English Society* but was changed to *A Survey of the Social Structure of England and Wales* during publication,[69] and by 1958 the title referred more blandly to *Social Conditions*. Their justification for this change in title was that 'the term social structure has come to be used by sociologists in a special sense' and that the scope of the book had been extended – in fact, the scope was virtually identical. It seems clear that Carr-Saunders and his colleagues were reluctant to use any terminology that smacked of Marxism.

Their implicit model of the 'morphology' of society is very close to the environmentalism of the early census statisticians: the division of the population by housing, industry and occupation is seen as the basis upon which to analyse variations in education, crime, religion, patterns of unionisation, and political activity.[70] Within this model there is an acceptance of the idea that the household is the fundamental unit of analysis, a unit in which members are dependent on their communal income and resources: 'society is not composed of units thrown together by chance like so many grains of sand. It consists of groups of persons who . . . have come together consciously and of set purpose. These groups are typically family groups – father, mother, and children, with whom may be living other relatives. The best term is perhaps "household".'[71]

Their survey of British society begins with a standard age and sex breakdown of the population over the period 1881–1921, with later volumes extending this forward to 1951 and back to 1801.[72] The number of family households is calculated from the recorded figures for the number of 'private families', though the researchers recognize that there is a discrepancy between 'the official conception of "private family" and our conception of a "household"'.[73] This discrepancy between official and sociological conceptual instruments centres on the assumption of Carr-Saunders and Jones that a household consists of two or more people: they exclude single persons living alone from their concept of 'household'. For this reason they make a number of 'corrections' to the official figures in order to bring them closer to their own concerns, taking account of such figures as the numbers of married, widowed and divorced persons. On this basis they conclude that Britain had, in 1921, 8 million households, with an average household size of just over four people.

The next step in their analysis is to examine the housing statistics. Households live in houses: 'A household without its own front door cannot regard its home as its castle'.[74] They discovered, in fact, that many houses and flats were occupied by two or more households and concluded that Britain exhibited high levels of overcrowding, as measured by the number of persons per room. Britain's overcrowded houses were a reflection of its high level of urbanisation. The majority of the population lived in areas of relatively high housing density – about 40 per cent of the 1921 population lived in towns with 100,000 or more inhabitants. The British people, they conclude, 'are for the most part shut off from any continuous contact with country conditions. They pass their lives in man-made surroundings – the fields are no longer visible at either end of the main street'.[75] The bulk of the population was found to be living in Greater London or in the large industrial areas north of the Severn–Humber line.

The early environmentalists, it will be recalled, saw housing and industry as the basis of class differences. True to this tradition, Carr-Saunders and Jones complemented their measures of housing with assessments of the industrial distribution of households. Their initial industrial and occupational classifications followed closely the evolving SIC and SEGs of the Registrar-General's office. In place of the Registrar-General's social class schema, however, they introduced an *ad hoc* schema of their own, distinguishing four groups: 'owners, agents, and managers', 'foremen and subordinate superintending staff', 'skilled workers', and 'other workers'.[76] Having looked also at employment status and source of income, they conclude: 'We have employed various methods of classifying the population and no methods as yet have brought to light the existence of social classes.' The Registrar-General's Classification, in particular, they claim, 'is not based on any clear principle of fundamental importance to us'.[77]

What they seem to mean by this is that class differences had declined in salience since the nineteenth century and no longer occupied a central place in the description of social structure. Class is seen as the resultant of many factors working together to produce divided and opposed groups. Conditions in 1921 were such that the old upper and middle classes have been dissolved as distinct and cohesive groups. Only the wage-earners retained some degree of class cohesion, but since they formed the only true class it was felt to be inappropriate to speak of class *divisions* in Britain.[78] Carr-Saunders and Jones conclude: 'The belief in the existence of social classes . . . the interests of the members of which are identical, or nearly so, and opposed to the interests of the rest of the community, is the result of studying social theory of doubtful value and of neglecting social facts.'[79]

Here the positivist credentials of Carr-Saunders and Jones are to the fore: class divisions have indubitably declined and it is only sociologists committed to Marxist-inspired theories who fail to see this. Their rejection of the relevance of class analysis – though not of environmental factors *per se* – leads them to reject the Registrar-General's Classification. Social research, they argue, must focus on the detailed environmental circumstances of households.

This was in 1927, and was repeated in their volume for 1937, but by 1958 Claus Moser had become the leading figure in the research group and a more qualified and sensitive view of class was adopted. The Registrar-General's schema was used early in this volume to present standard mortality ratios, and when the topic of class was discussed more fully, in a chapter largely written by Moser, they argue: 'The difficulty of the concept lies, not in deciding whether social classes have reality, in the sense that social class attitudes have a share in everyday behaviour and thought, but rather in defining appropriate class boundaries for statistical purposes.'[80] For Moser, class boundaries may still be important predictors of attitudes and behaviour, even when strong assumptions about cohesion, consciousness, and interests are rejected.

The multi-factored nature of class means that it cannot be defined in terms of any single variable, but Moser and his fellow researchers now accepted that occupation served as the most useful indicator of class position. Indeed, they explicitly refer to the findings of Hall, Jones, and the Glass group on occupational gradings. Although the Registrar-General's Classification 'leaves much to be desired',[81] it should be used by investigators of social structure because it is easier to operationalise than the more accurate classification of the British population into 'upper middle', 'lower middle', and 'working' class. This ambivalence about the Registrar-General's schema is apparent also in Marsh's similar 1958 book on social structure. Marsh argues: 'If there are five social classes in the population then they probably correspond to the divisions shown . . . and as occupational differences play a fundamental part in a society like ours in attracting or repelling people towards or from each other it may well be that the Registrar General's classification is as good a guide as any to our social class structure.'[82]

The continuing salience of social class in Britain is demonstrated by Moser in a study of the social differentiation of towns which he carried out with Scott.[83] The researchers studied all towns in England and Wales with a population of 50,000 or more in 1951.[84] Their initial problem was to try to define 'town' in a way that would allow them to use census statistics. In fact, they felt constrained to use administrative categories rather than a strictly sociological concept, as there appeared no obvious way of adapting census categories to theoretical concepts. Only at the conclusion of their research did they argue that travel-to-work areas might be used to identify the boundaries of local labour markets and, hence, of towns in the sociological sense.

The units they employed comprised 80 county boroughs, 64 municipal boroughs, 12 urban districts, and the London County Council – 157 'towns'. For each of these areas they collected census statistics for 1951, information on retail sales from the 1950 census of distribution, local authority housing statistics, and electoral statistics. A total of 57 variables were recorded for each of the 157 towns, and principal components analysis was used on the 57×57 correlation matrix.[85] The details of this procedure are not relevant to my present concerns, but it involves a search for 'underlying' variables which measure the overlap between closely associated variables. The 'components' or 'dimensions' identified by the method are the 'common factors' underlying the 57 variables and can be regarded as indicators of important sources of structural variation between towns. If 2 or 3 components are identified, then the towns can be plotted on a scatter diagram to show clusters of similar towns, but if more than 3 components are identified a three-dimensional picture will not suffice. In such a situation, the analyst must simply identify the main clusters and can only produce a mapping of them through a series of two-dimensional cross-sections.[86]

In fact, Moser and Scott discovered four components which structured their data: *social class* (underlies such variables as percentage in post-school education, percentage in private housing, birth-rate, Conservative voting);[87] *pre-war population change* (underlies such variables as percentage in one-person households, illegitimate births, percentage of elderly); *post-war population change* (underlies such variables as rates of house-building); and *overcrowding.*[88] These components reflect clearly the concerns of the environmentalists among early census statisticians, and show both the extent to which these concerns shaped the statistical categories used and the accuracy of their assumptions. The most important component in explaining the data was the social class composition of the population of the towns, as measured by the Registrar-General's schema. The two 'population change' components relate to the findings of Carr-Saunders and Jones on urbanisation, reflecting the expansion or contraction of an area and its general 'age'.

The components defined 14 clusters, groups of towns with a similar position on each of the variables. London appeared distinct from all other towns, reflecting the fact that a vast metropolis is not a single unit in terms of social composition.[89] These clusters included such groups as seaside resorts (e.g., Worthing, Blackpool, Brighton), commercial centres (e.g., Southampton, Plymouth, Bristol), textile towns (Halifax, Burnley, Oldham), old residential suburbs (Ilford, Twickenham, Crosby), working-class industrial suburbs (Willesden, Walthamstow, Leyton), and metal-manufacturing towns (Scunthorpe, Dudley, Smethwick).

Moser and Scott saw their study as providing a firm basis for the classification of towns from census statistics and as a way of allowing subsequent researchers to draw representative national samples. Equally important, however, was the possibility that locality studies could be seen as part of an overall national picture. Locality studies which have begun from a morphological position have generally sought to relate such variables to wider social processes. For example, working in the tradition of Charles Booth, Dyos has traced the expansion of Camberwell in the nineteenth century as part of the suburban expansion of Greater London, and he goes on to look at social segregation and its consequences.[90] Anderson's study of Preston used both published and unpublished census data to analyse family structure. A 10 per cent sample was drawn from census enumerators' books and a more detailed family reconstitution was undertaken for one district.[91] Foster's work in Oldham used a sample drawn from the 1851 census to study the local 'bourgeoisie' and its relation to Oldham's working class. Supplementing census material with other sources allowed him to examine the social cohesion and internal structure of the class and to explore some of the cultural correlates of these features.[92]

These studies are merely pointers to the ways in which census data have been used, but it is striking that none have made reference to gender divisions and women's work as salient aspects of the structure of class relations. In this they are typical of social research. It is only recently that the matter of gender has been taken seriously.[93]

The records of health, welfare and education

In this chapter I have used census and vital data to show how the questions of authenticity, credibility, representativeness and meaning can be handled in an area where previous research has provided effective solutions to many problems. By making explicit what is generally implicit, I have tried to highlight these solutions. In many other areas, there are fewer tried and tested solutions, and the quality appraisal criteria must be raised explicitly by all researchers. It may be, one day, that research in such areas will be able to draw on accepted resolutions to these questions of data quality, but that day has not yet come.

Records of the health, welfare and education of the population have frequently been used by analysts of 'social structure' in order to show how, for example, medical treatment or educational attainment are related to social class. For instance, the OPCS reports on mortality and life expectancy have been complemented by DHSS statistics on the careers of hospitalised persons.[94] Such data have not, however, been given the sustained critical attention that has been accorded to those derived from the census and vital registration. Even so, American writers in the ethnomethodological tradition have discussed the ways in which such data are produced and have suggested limits on the uses to which they may be put in social research. Consideration of their views will demonstrate the crucial problems of authenticity, credibility, representativeness and, above all, meaning which such data involve. But it will also implicitly, highlight further difficulties in the handling of census data.

Whereas the collection of census data involves some degree of research interest among its administrators, Garfinkel has shown that the problems of using medical records for social research reflect the fact that the records are organisationally produced for purely clinical purposes. The information collected embodies the way in which the clinical concerns of the participants have been administratively organised, and researchers invariably require information which departs from these organisationally relevant purposes and routines. The clinic has particular administrative routines which constitute taken-for-granted ways of doing things. Even where researchers are given some official sanction to modify the system of record-keeping so as to produce the additional information they require, the taken-for-granted routines of the clinic will tend to undermine this aim.[95]

Medical records are produced by clinical practitioners – doctors, nurses, technicians, etc. – and by non-clinical administrators. The actual information recorded in case files reflects 'the wary truce that exists among the several occupational camps as far as mutual demands for proper record-keeping are concerned'.[96] For medical staff the case file is regarded as a *therapeutic* record which documents the 'contractual' relationship between the patient and the practitioner. Although files appear to be straightforward 'medical' records, there is a structure of obligation and trust surrounding the relationship, and the record is one way in which clinics demonstrate that they have honoured a patient's claims for adequate medical care. The record is an account of the doctor–patient relationship which documents the fact that medical obligations have been met. The therapeutic purpose of the record means that 'the contents of clinic folders are assembled with regard for the possibility that the relationship may have to be portrayed as having been in accord with expectations of sanctionable performances by clinicians and patients'.[97]

For administrators, on the other hand, the record is regarded as an *actuarial* record; it is part of a system of supervision in which the operations of the organisation are monitored. Administrators are concerned that resources are being used efficiently and that they are able to make the required statistical and financial returns to their superiors. the actual case file represents a compromise between the therapeutic and actuarial purposes of the records, though the former is invariably accorded 'enforced structural priority'.[98] The priority accorded to the therapeutic interests of medical staff means that administrators are unable to ensure that the actuarial information they require is systematically recorded.

But, further than this, administrators – and therefore social researchers – face insuperable difficulties in interpreting the meaning of medical records. The clinical folder is elliptical and vague, resting on a vast body of taken-for-granted assumptions, and its therapeutic meaning can only be grasped by participants who understand the situation in which it was produced. The record is constructed so as to allow medical staff to reconstruct the therapy and so legitimate their actions. These difficulties of understanding mean that administrators will tend to regard the medical records as 'bad' records producing erratic and unreliable results. Garfinkel documents the same feeling among researchers:

> When any case folder was read as an actuarial record its contents fell so short of adequacy as to leave us puzzled as to why 'poor records' as poor as these should nevertheless be so assiduously kept. On the other hand, when folder documents were regarded as unformulated terms of a potential therapeutic contract, i.e., as documents assembled in the folder in open anticipation of some occasion when the terms of the therapeutic contract might have to be formulated from them, the assiduousness with which folders were kept, even though their contents were extremely uneven in quantity and quality, began to 'make sense'.[99]

The social researcher who wishes to use such records must try to uncover what medical staff take for granted. For Garfinkel and some other ethnomethodologists, this is all that sociology can achieve.[100] For others, it is merely a prelude to using records as resources rather than as topics. Cicourel and Kitsuse, for example, have tried to use Garfinkel's methods as a way of studying educational opportunities.[101] They are concerned with how people come to be defined, classified and recorded in case records and official statistics, and with the consequences that this has for individual careers and for educational policy. The research involved interviews with students, parents and counsellors from an upper-income suburb in the Midwest. The high school that the students attended had a high national reputation for the quality of its students and was in the forefront of educational innovation. In particular, the school had a highly developed counselling system, and Cicourel and Kitsuse aimed to show that educational achievement was much more a consequence of this administrative system than it was of student behaviour and attributes.

The school's administrative structure was formed into a 'grid' in which teaching divisions, based around four year-grades and college entry, were cross-cut by subject departments. Counsellors and social workers, each subordinate to a specialist head, were allocated to each of the teaching divisions. There was therefore a complex intersection of 'line' and 'staff' authority, with crucial implications for administrative routines. Teaching was organised into 'college' and 'non-college' curriculums, the allocation of particular students depending on parental choice at entry and on selection by ability. The school's selection procedures, however, depended not only on the officially recorded academic record produced by their junior high schools, but also on what Cicourel and Kitsuse term 'organisational contingencies'.[102] The flow of students through the opportunity structure of the school – and therefore their chances of college entry – depended upon the organisation of the counselling system.

Each student was allocated to a counsellor who had access to their cumulative school records, containing medical, social and psychological information as well as academic attainments. The counsellor monitored the student's academic performance and allocated them to one of five categories: excellent, average, underachiever, overachiever, and 'opportunity student' (lacking in both ability and performance). Cicourel and Kitsuse argue that the criteria used in defining these categories involved a mixture of academic and social factors, including appearance, manner, family background, attitudes towards school and peers, and participation in clubs and leisure activities, as well as academic grades.[103] Students were differentiated in terms of their personal characteristics, and the organisation of the counselling system did not allow for any recognition that students' qualities might also be a consequence of the system of teaching. Student case files reflected the psychologistic and 'social problem' concerns of counsellors. Conceptual instruments used by counsellors reflected their professional interests within a bureaucratic system: 'the bureaucratisation of the counselling system in large, comprehensive schools leads to an emphasis upon and concern for professional status among counsellors, and . . . this professionalisation will produce a greater range and frequency of student problems'.[104] The organisational structure of the school generated professional competition and status anxiety, resulting in educational records geared towards the occupational interests of the counsellors.

Cicourel and Kitsuse go on to show how professional interests determined the contents of the surviving records. The social workers were more established than the counsellors and had a higher professional status in the organisation. As a result, they were able to enforce the confidentiality of their files – they could include a great deal of confidential personal information because they knew that only fellow social workers would have access to the files. The counsellors, on the other hand, had to permit teachers access to their files. In order to maintain confidentiality, the counsellors complied a set of 'official' files containing academic and general information and a completely separate set of 'secret' files to which only they had access. Only the official files were recognised as part of the bureaucratic system, and so only they were retained in the central registry when the students had left the school. Social workers' files stored in this registry, therefore, were markedly different in style and content from counsellors' files relating to the same students.[105]

These conclusions were arrived at after interviews with those responsible for producing the records. Cicourel and Kitsuse did not themselves observe any counsellor–student interactions and so were not present at the time that situated decisions were made. A study by Macintyre pushes the analysis of administrative records to this final step.[106] Macintyre observed the interactions between patients and medical staff in an Aberdeen antenatal clinic, aiming to discover how case sheets were compiled. This compilation involved data collection at five separate points during the patient's visit to the clinic: a nurse initially recorded the medical and social history, a health visitor took down background data and information on welfare benefits, a nurse recorded the results of certain physical investigations, the obstetrician made a physical examination and used the case-sheet data to decide on the management of the pregnancy, and finally a clerk collected the specific information required for the procedures chosen by the doctor. The routinised operation of the clinic was such that patients passed through each stage in turn: the medical encounter was completed and the case sheet was compiled.

At each point in the administrative routine, however, specific questions had to be asked or observations made by the medical staff. While the questions were specified on a standard form, they were qualified, extended or adapted according to staff perceptions of patients – staff evolved a categorisation of patients and varied their approach according to the 'type' of person that they felt they were dealing with. Responses to questions were taken as confirming or refuting the initial typification and, therefore, as ways of illuminating the meaning of responses to later questions. According to Macintyre the key element in a typification was the husband's occupation.[107] Thus a woman factory worker married to a schoolteacher would be typified as a 'teacher's wife'. Although both husband's and wife's occupation had to be recorded, the former had priority in informal clinical typifications.

This is especially interesting in relation to the earlier discussion of census and vital registration. The assessment of occupation – central to official 'class' analyses and to the social class schemas of secondary users – can be seen in the light of Macintyre's commentary on the occupational classification of patients in the clinic. She discovered that the recording of such information varied with the kind of staff worker who was collecting it. Nurses assumed women with young children to be housewives, and entered this on the case sheet without asking, reflecting the fact that 'occupation' was not regarded by nurses as being a particularly relevant piece of information. Health visitors, on the other hand, saw occupation as relevant to a woman's ability to claim maternity benefit and so invariably asked a specific question about employment outside the home. The clerk saw occupation as relevant for hospital activity analysis (HAA) and administrative statistics which were to be processed using the Registrar-General's Classification. Clerks therefore asked specific questions and probed for full details.

The informal typifications made by staff in the clinic determined both the perceived competence to answer specific questions and the reliance which it was felt could be placed upon answers. Questions concerning the date of the last menstrual period, for example, were adapted according to the patient's perceived ability to answer accurately, and answers to questions about genetic disorders were assessed on the basis of the perceived medical competence of the patient. Of particular importance was the use of what survey researchers call 'leading questions'. If, for example, a nurse judged that a woman was unlikely to have experienced any psychiatric disturbance the patient was simply asked, 'And you've never had any trouble with your nerves, have you?' – a question which virtually required a 'No' answer.[108] Common sense and implicit theories of social behaviour ensured that the records showed the very answers that the theories would predict.

Of particular importance for researchers interested in the relationship between social class and health, Macintyre reports that medical staff themselves used implicit theories of class characteristics to shape their decisions. They regarded middle-class women, as gauged by husband's occupation, as being more competent in giving accurate answers to technical questions and more likely to respond well if given explanations about the purpose of the questions. Working-class women were regarded as less competent and less in need of explanation. Questions on the availability of a relative or friend as a contact for the health visitor depended on implicit theories about the isolated nuclear family of the middle class and the supportive extended family of the working class: women perceived as middle class were asked for the name and address of a neighbour or friend; working-class women were asked 'And does your mum live in the city?'[109]

Typification shaped the production of the record in such a way that the profile of responses confirmed the initial typification. Answers which were regarded as ambiguous or uncertain were clarified with reference to answers to later questions, and this tended to produce a consistent and coherent profile of responses on the case sheets. In this way, each member of staff took over the typification that had been compiled for the patient by those who had already seen her. The patient's identity, for clinical purposes, could be read from the case sheet by all members of the medical staff. Health visitors, for example, questioned patients in the light of the information already collected by nurses and so used direct questions and prompts rather than open-ended questions: they already 'knew' what kind of response was likely. Clerical staff involved with the patients also shared in these typifications. By the time that the booking clerk saw the patients a great deal of information had been collected, and the clerk could build up a clear picture before seeing the patient: 'this means that she can "sum up" the patient in advance in ways that the nurse cannot, thus allowing for more definitive typifications and less room for negotiation. The patient already, to some extent, *is what the records say she is*.'[110] Macintyre remarks that patients themselves, by this stage, had learnt to respond in the 'right' way, in accordance with the typifications that had been placed upon them in the earlier stages of the recording process.

Macintyre concludes that researchers who use the completed medical records and discover confirmation for their theories may do so because medical staff have drawn on these very theories to make the typifications that have shaped the records. She argues, however, that a knowledge of how the records are constructed can help the researcher to discount these effects and so begin to move from treating the records as topics to treating them as resources. Records can be assessed for their credibility within the conventions of the administrative structure for which they were produced, but only so long as the researcher is able to achieve some degree of understanding of these conventions.

Business and industrial records

I have shown that the problem of interpretative understanding is of cardinal significance in the assessment of all other aspects of data quality, and I have argued that an appreciation of this can allow researchers to treat documents as resources rather than simply as topics. But if documents are to be used as resources, researchers must have some procedures for handling the problem of interpretative understanding. How, in practical terms, can this be achieved and demonstrated? In chapter 2 I discussed the background to textual analysis as the means for handling this problem. In the remainder of this chapter I shall use studies of industrial records to explore this further. In particular, I shall look at the claims of content analysis to have provided a definitive solution to this problem.

While content analysis, which originated in the study of mass communications and propaganda, has evolved clearer and more rigorous techniques of reading than have other approaches to textual analysis, its philosophical basis is less well developed. Its advocates have argued that its systematic methods of analysis make it more objective, and hence scientific, than literary approaches, though the two approaches have tended to share a concern for the 'objective' internal meaning of the text rather than the intended meaning of the author or the effects of the text on its readers.[111]

The claims of content analysis are grounded in the application of clear and easily followed procedures. The content of a text is analysed by the frequency with which certain categories of meaning appear. These categories are constructed by the researcher, as in any piece of textual analysis, but the aim of content analysis is to minimise the discretion of the individual researcher once these categories have been chosen. The objectivity of content analysis is said to be guaranteed by the use of rigorous and replicable procedures. Objectivity lies in the techniques, not in the initial theoretical perspective that orientates the research.

The core of content analysis therefore lies in its technical measurement procedures. Holsti has argued that the categories that are used – for example, positive, neutral and negative references to democracy – must meet a number of formal criteria, which can be summarised as comprehensiveness, exhaustiveness, mutual exclusiveness, and independence. Comprehensiveness means that it is necessary to examine all relevant sources, and not just those that support the researcher's hypothesis. It is necessary for a researcher interested in newspaper bias, for example, to collect information from papers which are pro-government as well as those which are anti-government. Categories must be exhaustive and mutually exclusive in that it must be possible to classify all relevant items to one, and no more than one, of the categories: there must be no residual, unclassified items, and no item may be capable of classification into two or more categories. Thus the researcher must ensure that an adequate typology or system of categories is constructed before carrying out the analysis. Independence requires that the classification of one item must not affect the classification of any other; each individual item must be treated in its own right.

If a system of classification is to meet these criteria, and especially exhaustiveness, mutual exclusiveness, and independence, it is important that clear definitions be given of each category, together with rules for determining the allocation of particular items to the appropriate category. This has led content analysts to argue that content analysis can be carried out as a purely technical process. Once the initial categories are chosen, it is possible for techniques to be applied by assistants who have not been involved in the development of the theory and to be checked for technical objectivity by adherents of rival theoretical frameworks. The origin of the categories is assumed to be irrelevant to the formal validity of the method. It has even been argued that content analysis could be undertaken by an appropriately programmed computer, using index and data-base systems as alternatives to human researchers.

The units of analysis may be words, sentences, articles or any other appropriate unit, so long as the same unit is employed in each document studied. Holsti has tried to formalise this by distinguishing between the recording unit and the context unit.[112] The recording unit is, as the name implies, the basic survey unit for which information is recorded, for example the word; but it is obvious that a particular word makes sense only 'in context', and thus the context unit may be the sentence in which the word is embedded. Holsti gives an example drawn from medical records in which a mental patient is recorded as saying 'I am in Switzerland'. In this sentence, the word 'Switzerland' may designate simply the country Switzerland – and may, therefore, reflect an American patient's derangement in time and space – or it may be used by the patient as a symbol of freedom from hospitalisation. The only way of choosing between these two possibilities, Holsti argues, is by reference to the whole sentence or speech in which the statement is found, and it may even be necessary to draw on wider background information.[113]

This contextual determination of meaning is one of the crucial obstacles to the computerisation of content analysis, and also a major limitation on the reliability and replicability of the technique, as comprehension of the meaning of an item in context is a matter of interpretation and, therefore, of individual discretion. Although some of these problems can be minimised through pilot and pre-test surveys aimed at gauging the reliability with which different researchers come to the same decisions, the contextual determination of meaning involves an irreducible element of subjective interpretation on the part of the researcher.[114]

Like other approaches to textual analysis, content analysis faces difficult problems of validation, in that its success depends upon the interpretative abilities of the researcher and on his or her ability to convince readers of the validity of the interpretation offered. As I argued in chapter 2, this problem can be resolved only if the separation of the text from its author and audience is rejected. I will illustrate this point through two examples of textual analysis.

Both Strinati[115] and Vogler[116] have explored class consciousness and industrial organisation with the use of business and trade union documents, yet their strategies have differed. In each case, the documents were regarded as topics, to be examined for what they disclosed about their producers, but Strinati employed literary techniques of textual analysis and Vogler employed content analysis. Their sophisticated use of these methods, however, show the ways in which analysts can overcome some of the problems that have been discussed.

Strinati studied the published and unpublished volumes of oral and written evidence submitted to the Donovan Commission on industrial relations,[117] supplementing this with the annual reports and other publications of the Confederation of British Industry, Trades Union Congress, and various other bodies. The authorship of these documents was not regarded as problematic for Strinati's purposes, his main concerns being their credibility and meaning, but a difficulty of the project was its failure to confront the issue of representativeness. No details are given as to whether an exhaustive coverage of Donovan documents was made, nor is there any indication of the criteria used to select additional documents for study. A possible conclusion therefore is that, however valid Strinati's interpretation of the documents may be, he is generalising from an unrepresentative collection of papers.

The problem from which Strinati began was to study the programmes and objectives of organised labour and 'fractions' of capital which shaped the role of the State in industrial relations during the 1960s and 1970s. The theoretical framework that he employed was used to define the social groupings of interest, and the relevant sections of the available documents were allocated to these groupings according to their authorship. Thus, CBI and Engineering Employers' Federation documents were allocated to 'industrial monopoly capital' on the basis of membership and financial evidence. The other groupings identified in this way were 'petit-bourgeois capital', 'foreign, multinational capital', 'money capital', and the TUC. Each of these groupings was characterised by a particular programme and objectives on the basis of a reading of their documents, illustrative extracts from which were included in Strinati's book. Thus industrial monopoly capital is argued to have espoused a programme of 'corporatist control' which existed in tension with rather weaker 'liberal' views. On the other hand, the TUC held a combination of 'social democratic' and corporatist views.[118]

The central problem that Strinati had to resolve was that of how to validate these readings of the documents. In common with similar studies, Strinati attempts to demonstrate its validity through illustrative quotation: supplying extracts from the documents and, in effect, inviting the reader to share his interpretation. The reader must, of course, take it on trust that the illustrations are representative of the documents studied, and textual analysts should perhaps be more concerned with establishing criteria of sampling and selection for their illustrative material. Strinati's main response to the question of validity is to demonstrate the adequacy of the interpretations as explanations of the subsequent behaviour of the social groupings in question. That is to say, he strives to show that the internal meanings disclosed through his analysis correspond with the received meanings constructed by the relevant audiences, and this is demonstrated by using the disclosed meanings to predict the actions of audience members.

Vogler studied working-class consciousness as reflected in trade union documents, her aim being to explore 'corporatist' and 'class' forms of consciousness and, in particular, variations in national and international class orientation. Her research design followed from theoretical debates which generated the typifications of consciousness that she employed and suggested the crucial periods to study. The 1930s and 1970s were chosen to reflect theoretically important features in the development of capitalism, and her concern was to examine variations in solidarity and cohesion between these two periods. Her assumption was that the use of the word 'we' by unions is an indication of who is included and who is excluded from the desired solidaristic grouping. The frequency and context of the word 'we' is an indicator of the type of class consciousness:

> Whom are the unions referring to when they use the word 'we'? and who are 'they'? Are 'we' a class against capitalism regardless of national boundaries? Or are 'we' a nation in an international struggle with other nations? What is the extent of 'class' or 'corporate' identity – is it purely sectional, or is it national or does it extend beyond the nation state to the international level?[119]

Vogler studies union and TUC documents, taking a representative sample of unions in different economic sectors. Lack of availability of documents for some unions meant that the sampling reflected the existence or non-existence of sources, and it is necessary to know whether the unions analysed (those whose documents were published had survived and were available) differed in any significant way from those that were not analysed. Vogler's sample was further constrained by the needs of comparison, as she sought unions which existed in both the 1930s and 1970s – so losing those that had merged or been substantially reorganized over the intervening period. Vogler is aware of these problems of representativeness but, like Strinati, believes that an awareness of the limitations of the data enables the researcher to generalize from unrepresentative material.

The documents studied were union journals, supplemented by presidential addresses when journals were not available, and Vogler categorised these as 'ideological' documents, in the sense that they were written mainly for the unions themselves and were intended to reinforce a sense of collective identity. Vogler's categorisation, there-fore, does not concern itself exclusively with the contents of the documents. Instead, she relates them back to their process of production, though no direct evidence is presented to substantiate the claim that their authors had such an 'ideological intent'.

This approach is extended to other documents, which are classified as 'ideological/practical' and 'practical' – the former being publications substantially geared to policy concerns, and the latter being evidence to committees which were almost exclusively practical in orientation but which were written for an outside audience and structured by the requirements of official discourse. Vogler's conclusions are that, in the 1930s, the frequency counts show that 'we' were a class against capital at the national level. There was a strong sense of national working-class identity. The TUC documents in the 1970s show a national corporatist orientation, while individual union documents show a combination of sectional and national corporatism. 'Class' con-sciousness, she argues, was supplanted by national and sectional forms of consciousness.

The validity of this interpretation is demonstrated by Vogler through a literary textual analysis of a wider range of documents for the whole period 1930–79 and, most crucially, by results from studies of union action. The latter were used to assess the practical adequacy of the interpretations, as had been the case with Strinati, and this assessment led Vogler to reconstruct some of her own data. Her examination of the 1930s had thrown up an anomalous observation: the 'practical' documents evidenced 'syndicalism' (a sectional form of national class consciousness), which did not accord with the general pattern and was discrepant with her theoretical expectations. Vogler concludes that this should be regarded as an invalid result, as it was not supported by behavioural evidence. The finding was an artefact of the structuring of the documents as 'interest group' evidence in official discourse.[120] This is not, however, a failure of content analysis, as the analysis generated the anomaly in the first place, and examination of the intended audience suggested an explanation. Despite what Vogler says, the result *was* valid as a report on the internal content of the documents, and its appearance shows the power of content analysis. Vogler unfortunately re-classifies the result as evidence of national class consciousness, producing a coherent frame of reference at the expense of distorting the meaning. It may be, in fact, that national class consciousness mediated through the genre of official discourse *appears* as sectionalism, but the fact remains that it does so appear and is available in this form to its readers.[121]

In both Strinati and Vogler, therefore, interpretations of meaning are validated in terms of empirical adequacy, relating the meaning of the texts to the intentions of their authors and their effects on their audiences. It should be clear, however, that certain important problems of reading remain. It was argued in chapter 3 that all accounts in social research are inherently contestable in the light of their 'value relevance', and it is important to see the extent to which the work of Strinati and Vogler has been shaped by their initial frame of reference.

Both authors adopt a 'class' frame of reference, drawn from the works of Marx and Weber, and this undoubtedly determined the concepts and categories employed. Their work is not 'relevant' to the values of those who adopt markedly different theoretical frameworks. A feminist, for example, might claim that their readings of the documents ignore the single most important feature of the discourse: their silence about women. Vogler, for example, does not try to measure the extent to which 'we' refers to 'we men' or 'we men and women'. It is possible to argue that the most significant element in male working-class consciousness in both the 1930s and the 1970s was its lack of concern for women. Such a claim would of course have to satisfy the criteria of empirical adequacy, but it is clear that any truth claims that Strinati and Vogler may wish to make for their analyses can at least be questioned in terms of their relevance to values. And if the work of, say, Vogler and the hypothetical feminist were equivalent with respect to their practical adequacy, there would be no impartial way of choosing between them. They would be equally valid descriptions of male working-class consciousness, constructed from differing theoretical and value standpoints.

7 The Public Sphere and Mass Communication

The private though official documents discussed in the previous three chapters are those whose publication is, largely, independent of their production. They are produced within the private sphere for administrative purposes, and, unlike many State documents, publication is a secondary matter. Many such documents remain unpublished and are available to the public only through archival access, if at all. Their impact on the public sphere and public opinion is therefore limited and indirect. The State, on the other hand, undertakes a massive publishing operation, geared to the administrative needs of public and private agencies and to expanding the information available to public opinion. The intention to publish – to make a document available in the public sphere – is an important element in determining the form and therefore the quality of the document. In this chapter, I shall turn from State and unpublished private documents to those privately produced documents which are explicitly intended for publication, and whose character therefore differs significantly from those previously discussed.

The documents in question are those whose production and publication is central to the commercial or organisational activities of their producers. Newspapers, for example, are produced for sale in a competitive market, as are reference books and television programmes. There is also of course a large number of private documents which are not produced as commodities, but which still fall under type 8 in figure 1.2. Membership lists of professional bodies, for instance, may be published as a service to members, with any sales to outsiders regarded as of secondary importance.

Clearly, in considering a document for which publication is the major factor, the 'public' for whom it is intended must be a fundamental point of reference. Documents of this kind were virtually unknown before the development of a reading public, such as did exist being produced either for specific patrons or for a highly restricted audience. Only from the late seventeenth and early eighteenth century did a large reading public exist in England and other European countries, the formation of a reading public being an integral part of the formation of a public sphere of informed opinion. This laid the basis for the mass circulation of books and periodicals, which was made possible by innovations in the technology of printing. This in turn opened up the prospect of the 'broadcast' publication of sounds and images by means of the electric and electronic technologies of cinema, wireless and television. It is the aim of publication for a broad 'public' that differentiates these types of document from those aimed at more restricted audiences.

In illustrating the nature and use of these published documents, I shall consider them in two broad categories: those regarded as media for mass communication and those with more limited circulation, such as directories, almanacs, and yearbooks.

Public opinion, the media and the audience

The earliest form of written 'publication', dating from about the eighth century, involved the manual copying of books at medieval scrip-toriums. Such volumes were often produced in fairly large numbers and for commercial purposes, the main purchasers being monasteries, universities, and similar institutions. But it was not until the fourteenth century that retail sales through dealers to the clergy, lawyers, doctors and other 'professionals' became at all widespread. The invention of printing in a commercially viable form encouraged this market to expand, enabling book producers to reach a wider audience. This in turn allowed an extension in the range of published documents. Whereas small-scale circulation had concerned mainly 'books' (rela-tively large, bound volumes), the larger audience were purchasers of shorter, and cheaper, chap books, broadsheets, and ballads.[1] The growth of the market for such items was limited by the opposition of both Church and State to the production of non-Christian, and, especially, fiction, books. In England there were even limitations on the reading of the Bible by those who were not 'gentlemen'.

Despite such restrictions there was a more-or-less continuous growth in the publishing market from the end of the seventeenth century, when the numbers of merchants, tradesmen, shopkeepers and clerks increased to such levels that it was possible to speak of a true 'middle class' reading public. This public was a receptive audience for newspapers, periodicals, magazines and novels,[2] as well as for the other kinds of publication such as almanacs, chapbooks, technical books, and bibles. The growth of the reading public was especially marked in Britain during the late eighteenth century, when the Methodist Sunday schools and reading classes began to broaden the social base of the reading public. This was furthered by the introduction of steam printing in the 1830s and the later abolition of newspaper taxes, but it was not until the First World War that there was a true 'mass' reading public for newspapers.

Other publications remained more restricted in their circulation. The publication of cheaply produced books began with Tauchnitz, Penguin, and similar 'paperback' publishers, but these only achieved mass circulation levels in the period after the Second World War. The mass production of paperbacks became possible only when publication became a market- rather than an author-led process: publishers aimed to identify what kinds of books would sell and then to discover authors who could produce those kinds of book. The stage of mass production in publication depended upon the conversion of the reading public into a mass of consumers whose demand for books could be met in the same way as the market-generated demand for any other commodity. The development of the mass culture that has ensued is often criticised on the grounds that it leads to a mediocrity which undermines the traditional 'high' culture of the literary and artistic middle classes. The mass market, mass communications and mass culture are seen as inextricably linked to the rise of 'the masses' in economic and political power; they are also seen as facets of the development of a 'mass society'.[3]

The Press in Britain during the seventeenth and eighteenth centuries was a restricted and tightly controlled enterprise.[4] Although government licensing, aimed at the prevention of sedition and treason, ended in 1695, a stamp tax and advertisement tax imposed severe financial restrictions, and large-scale circulation was further inhibited by the expense of postal distribution. Newspapers therefore concentrated on the provision of the information that the middle classes needed for the conduct of their businesses – foreign and financial information and commercial advertisements, but not political commentary – and they appeared weekly or even less frequently. The first daily newspapers were local or provincial in scope: the *Worcester Post* began in 1690, the *Stamford Mercury* in 1695, and the *Norwich Post* in 1701.[5] The first London daily newspaper was the *Daily Courant*, published from 1702, and this was followed by the *Post* (1719), the *Journal* (1720), and the *Advertiser* (1730).

Political comment, ideas and opinions were handled by periodicals and magazines, which had wider cultural aspirations than the fiercely practical newspapers. The first was Daniel Defoe's *Weekly Review* (published from 1704), but it was William Cobbett and others who spearheaded the establishment of an independent press by devoting their periodicals purely to opinion – thereby avoiding taxation as newspapers. Cobbett's *Political Register* (published from 1802) built up a massive sales volume of 44,000, and the *Black Dwarf* (1817) had sales of 12,000. At this period, *The Times* newspaper, a daily, had a circulation of only 10,000.

The success of the political periodicals encouraged the daily press to seek greater independence from government controls. The reduction of taxes on newspapers in the 1830s and their final abolition in 1855 meant that newspapers could broaden the scope of their news coverage to include political commentary and could begin to build up their circulations by means of retail sales rather than subscriptions. By the late nineteenth century a cheap daily press for the middle classes was in existence, its popularity culminating with Northcliffe's *Daily Mail* in 1896. Working-class readership on the other hand was largely restricted to the Sunday press which, from the 1820s, had expanded through the publication of sensational crime stories and sports reporting: the *Dispatch* and the *Chronicle* were each selling around 50,000 copies by the 1830s, and by the 1840s *Lloyds Weekly* and the *News of the World* had reached circulation figures of 100,000.[6] This success of the Sunday papers had an influence on the daily press, which included more and more sensational and 'trivial' items, rather than the foreign, financial and political news on which it had previously concentrated. The *Daily Express* (1900) and the *Daily Mirror* (1903) forwarded a new type of popular daily paper with a mixture of news, magazine, and sensational reporting, together with pictures and a variety of typographical styles.

The success of the *Mail*, the *Express* and the *Mirror* transformed the Press into big business and made newspaper publishers a political force. Whereas the early papers had been predominantly by-products of the printing industry, the twentieth-century papers were parts of large, national publishing operations which rapidly took over the businesses of their predecessors. Press ownership became concentrated in the hands of large combines with many newspaper and magazine titles, both national and local, and their mass circulations were built up by means of low cover prices and heavy dependence on revenue from advertising. The market for newspapers was inextricably intertwined with the growth of a mass market for other consumer commodities. Newnes, Northcliffe and Pearson, and later Hulton, Beaverbrook and the Berry brothers, engaged in aggressive and unprincipled circulation wars with one another; they saw their newspapers as vehicles for their political views and as routes to power and influence. The moulding of public opinion through the columns of mass-circulation newspapers was an effective means of influencing government policy, and the 'press barons' became powerful figures behind the political scene.

In the United States, James Bennett spearheaded the introduction of the popular press with his *New York Herald* in 1835.[7] A crucial factor in the press's development was the introduction of automatic typesetting machinery in the 1870s; this allowed an expansion of advertising space and therefore a lower cover price. The New York *Morning Journal* was bought by William Randolph Hearst in 1895, and his influence led to the 'yellow press' tradition of low-level, popular journalism. Hearst's major achievement was to provide a model for the formation of national newspaper chains and their mass production and distribution methods. By the 1920s, the Hearst group comprised 31 papers, 6 magazines, and various other communications interests. In the USA, more than one-third of newspaper circulation was in the hands of 70 chains by 1929, and by the late 1970s the 12 largest chains controlled 38 per cent of daily circulation.[8]

The circulation of newspapers has been declining since the end of the 1950s, due partly to increased labour and material costs though mainly to competition by other media: television as a source of information, comment and entertainment has diminished the market for newspapers, and the transfer of much advertising to television has forced newspapers to increase cover prices and so become less competitive. These new media of communication evolved from earlier forms, adopting the mass orientation of the press. Thus television is perhaps the logical outcome of developments in the theatre: changing technology allowed live theatre to be transformed into cinema and subsequently into radio and television.

Popular drama first became a commercial genre in England in the 1570s, with the establishment of a number of theatres and the emergence of professional actors and dramatists.[9] After closure and set-back during the Puritan period, the theatre expanded rapidly in the eighteenth century, with a polarisation emerging between officially sponsored and licensed 'legitimate' theatre and the popular theatre of pantomime and spectacle. Variety theatre was the basis of the massively popular music-halls which sprang up in large numbers from the 1840s. By 1900 there were 63 London theatres, more than 300 provincial theatres, and innumerable music-halls, this great sphere of entertainment coinciding with the related establishment of football and racing as spectator events.[10] The turn of the century saw the beginning of a period of concentration in ownership, as with the Press, impresarios such as Stoll and Moss presiding over large, national theatre chains.

This was short-lived, however, because of the competition offered by cinemas. The first cinema show in England was in 1896; the big period of growth was between the two world wars, when the huge Odeon and ABC groups came to dominate British cinema. The home of cinema of course was the United States, where the movies rapidly became a major popular entertainment. Run initially by the owners of small arcades, the industry soon moved into 'electric theaters'. The making of films was also a small-scale business for a long time, but it also became highly concentrated. Between 1908 and 1914 – the period of dominance in American industry of the so-called 'Money Trust' of bankers and financiers – there was a competitive drive towards concentration and the establishment of Hollywood as the production centre of the industry.[11]

Theatre productions are by their very nature transient and leave no direct documentary record. But a large amount of documentary material grew around the requirements of theatre production: plays were published, programmes produced, and song books printed. With the coming of cinema, the film itself became an additional documentary record of the studio production. Despite differences in material form, a cinema film is every bit as much a document as is a newspaper. Disc, tape and film recording of sound further expanded this range of documentary sources, and were important elements in the development of radio and television.

In Britain the establishment in 1927 of broadcasting by the BBC – a public service that depended upon the creation of a large audience but not upon advertising revenue – was followed by limited television broadcasting from 1936 to 1939 and a regular television service from 1946. Commercial television was allowed by the government in 1955, with the formation of a publicly regulated licensing system for a limited number of stations operating under strict guidelines. These commercial stations were, unlike the BBC, operated as privately owned businesses and soon became as concentrated in their ownership as were cinemas and newspapers. Radio broadcasting developments in the United States were somewhat earlier: Westinghouse set up domestic services in 1920 and RCA, funded by General Electric, began a year later. The system remained a private oligopoly as other firms entered the field, and all the initial companies were local operators until RCA set up the NBC in 1926. CBS and other network systems followed, and they became the focus of further concentration in the industry. General Electric began experimental television broadcasts in 1928, and the radio giant RCA and its NBC associate soon followed suit. Although NBC began a regular service in 1939 and a network broadcast in 1940, development was slowed down by the Second World War. By 1948, there were 36 stations on air, and by the mid-1950s the television system was dominated by NBC, CBS and ABC.[12]

Concentration of ownership thus became a feature of all areas of mass communication, with a higher level of concentration in these industries than in industry generally. In Britain, two firms dominated the production of gramophone records by the 1930s, two firms dominated cinema by the 1940s, five firms accounted for about 70 per cent of newspaper circulation in the 1950s, and commercial television in the 1960s was dominated by five network companies with monopoly powers in particular broadcasting regions.[13]

At the same time, there were increasing links *between* sectors, as multi-media conglomerates were formed. The driving force behind these large conglomerates was declining profitability in particular sectors, which had resulted from the competition of others. Rank, the one-time British market leader in cinema and film production, for example, responded to a decline in these areas by diversifying into the manufacture of television and hi-fi equipment, into other leisure-related industries, and into commercial television. In some cases, firms facing a declining market were bought out by expanding firms from other sectors. EMI, for example, was a market leader in records and in radio and television production, and it bought out a leading cinema chain and acquired interests in broadcasting.[14] In the United States, CBS controls a major television network and is also involved in gramophone records, films and books. RCA owns a television network and is involved in the publication of books and gramophone records as well as in the electrical and service industries.

The proprietors of such conglomerates differ from the press barons of the first half of the century, adopting a more entrepreneurial role towards what is seen almost exclusively as a 'business'. As a result, newspaper editors, for example, are allowed greater political autonomy by the proprietors. They are able to carve out a particular political identity for the paper and thereby to build up a large enough readership in a particular sector of the market. Instead of newspaper content being proprietor-led, as under the press barons, it is market-led, and proprietors are more willing to countenance profitable papers which do not closely follow their own political preferences.[15]

Many of the large conglomerates are owned not by entrepreneurial proprietors but by institutional shareholders. These enterprises become locked in to the extensive system of intercorporate shareholdings and interlocking directorships which comprises the system of impersonal possession in both Britain and the United States.[16] A study of the 200 largest British business enterprises of 1904, 1938 and 1976 found that none of the media enterprises were interlocked in 1904, just over a half were interlocked in 1938, and all but one were interlocked in 1976.[17] These interlocks were with financial enterprises and with enterprises operating in the aerospace and electrical industries, a trend seen by Mattelart as indicative of the close links between the mass media and military provision that lay behind the internationalisation of mass communications through computer and satellite technology.[18]

Images, content and meaning

The documentary products of the mass media are a major source of evidence for social research and, like all documents, can be assessed through the quality control criteria of authenticity, credibility, representativeness and meaning. Therefore any attempt to explore the contents of these documents must examine the way in which the structure and organisation of the mass media have shaped them.

The discerning reader of a daily newspaper will recognise the problems of authenticity that arise from errors and misprints. Many of these will be both obvious and easily corrected: few readers would fail to recognise that '*Grauniad*' is a typographical misprint for '*Guardian*' on a page header of that paper. But misprints of many names and statistics may be far from obvious and pose considerable problems for researchers using newspapers to study unfamiliar subjects or periods. On occasion, misprints may be obvious but difficult to correct: there may, for example, be numerous jumbled lines with whole or part sentences missing. In such circumstances, it may be impossible to reconstruct a sound copy.

Such errors can be multiplied when microfilm copies of newspapers are used instead of the originals, as mistakes and omissions can be made in the filming process. The published quarterly index of *The Times*, for example, records that the issue of Friday, 5 March 1920 contains a report of the funeral of James Rowlands MP on page 19. A researcher consulting the official microfilm copies of *The Times* – available at most large libraries and normally supplied by the National Newspaper Library in preference to the originals – will not find this report. Only a close examination of the film shows that page 19 has not been filmed and that page 19 of the issue of the 4 March has been inserted in its place. A mistake in the master microfilm has been reproduced in all library copies of that microfilm, and the article in question can only be found in an original paper copy of the correct issue of *The Times*. This error is only apparent from a check in the index for a specific item. A researcher analysing the film itself, without reference to the index, would discover such an error only if the whole film had been systematically checked for completeness before any analysis was undertaken.

Whereas the name of the author of a book is generally shown prominently on its cover and title-page, authorship in newspapers and television programmes is often indicated in smaller bylines or credits, while many newspaper and television items are not attributed to particular authors at all, reflecting the fact that they are collective products in a stronger sense than is the case for most books. Even where a particular journalist is credited with authorship, an article will have been subjected to sub-editing and transformation in line with the house style, and the journalist will have little or no control over this. Similarly, a television or radio news-reader – invariably credited by name – may have played only a very small part in the writing of the news reports he or she is reading. This can make it difficult for a researcher to impute intent, as it may not be known who is responsible for particular aspects of the text: who writes the unsigned leading articles in national newspapers, and do they always intend to represent some supposed editorial position of 'the paper' rather than their personal views?

Even where a non-fiction book is attributed to a particular author, this may be more of a mask than a revelation. In 1981 a book by Jennifer Aldridge and John Tregorran was published under the title *Ambridge: An English Village Through the Ages*.[19] The authors did not in fact exist, but were characters in the popular BBC radio soap opera, 'The Archers'. A running story-line in the series concerned the undertaking of a local history survey of the village of 'Ambridge' in which the Archer family was supposed to live. The survey in the story was written up and published in book form by 'The Borchester Press', owned by local businessman 'Jack Woolley'. The book actually published is presented as if it were this fictional book. The title-page indicates that it is published by The Borchester Press 'In association with Eyre Methuen', and adds 'By arrangement with the British Broadcasting Corporation'.

Nothing in the book indicates that it is a spoof produced as a novelty spin-off from the radio series. The 'authors' and their co-researchers are credited in author biographies, and the text reports the 'history' of the village, describes archaeological 'discoveries', and includes numerous photographs ostensibly showing residents of 'Ambridge'. It is, to all intents and purposes, identical to the numerous genuine works of local history produced by enthusiastic amateurs. Only the rather lavish style might cause an unknowing reader to question its authenticity. Even close examination of the book fails to discover any internal, textual evidence which would suggest that it is not authentic. A reader knowing of the existence of the radio programme might be expected to guess at the book's status, but other readers would be dependent on external evidence: 'Ambridge', 'Felpersham', and 'Borsetshire', for example, cannot be found on any genuine maps of the British Isles. In this case, a cursory knowledge of the geography of Britain should be enough to suggest that there is something 'wrong' with the book; but more determined forgeries and frauds will give less obvious signs of inauthenticity.

Related to this question of authorship is a problem of credibility centring on the deliberate inclusion of spoof items in newspapers. Sometimes the spoof may take the form of simple exaggeration or the use of in-jokes presumed to be understood by regular readers, but every year on 1 April (All Fools' Day) many newspapers and television programmes include one or more items designed to fool readers and viewers. The fact that many *are* fooled each year suggests that researchers may be misled if they happen to consult an issue for 1 April in the course of their research. Even if they believe themselves to have discovered such an item, they must search for external evidence to establish that, implausible as it might seem to them, the story is *not* genuine.

There is a common presumption that newspapers are not subject to a high level of distortion or falsification, though a number of important cases of falsification have been documented. In fact, it is important to ask how sincere newspaper reports can be expected to be, as their sincerity will affect their accuracy. Undoubtedly the major source of insincerity in newspaper and television reporting is the influence of owners and controllers acting on the basis of the perceived political or financial interests of themselves or of external bodies. Such influence can result in considerable distortion of the reports that journalists file, though the extent of this is largely unknown and it certainly varies over time and from one media organisation to another. To identify the commercial and political interests that may underlie a text is rarely a straightforward task, though direct political commentary may often be obvious enough to the researcher for him or her to be able to assess the extent of any distortion in factual reporting. Less obvious forms of distortion are far from uncommon, especially where editors and journalists depend upon politicians for their information. Politicians may pass on false information to journalists, intending to promote their own careers, to defend their interests, or simply to dramatise the events in which they are involved and so give them greater public significance.

If journalists and editors are unable to discern this lack of sincerity, newspaper and television accounts, no matter how sincere their producers, cannot be regarded as credible accounts. The strongest form of distortion introduced by the insincerity of politicians is undoubtedly direct censorship, particularly in time of war.[20] At such times the proximity of reporters to the events they describe is generally restricted by the military authorities, and so it may be impossible for reporters to arrive at an independent assessment of what has happened. Their reports are inevitably dependent upon the information with which they are supplied by the military authorities and by politicians. Even if they are aware that the information is subject to censorship, as any good journalist should be, they may be unable to discern the particular areas in which censorship is strongest and so may be unable to sift 'reliable' from 'unreliable' information.

The most common problem of credibility in newspaper and television reports, however, derives not from a lack of personal sincerity on the part of the journalist or of those with whom he or she deals, but from the administrative routines of news-making that affect its accuracy. Apparently factual reports are frequently compiled from press releases, with journalists checking the basic story and following up one or two points. Such reports invariably include quotes from persons involved in the story – 'Mr X said . . .' – and a researcher may wish to use these quotes as evidence about the person concerned. But it should not be assumed that those quotes are direct transcriptions of the named person's speech. The conventions governing the press release as a genre require the inclusion of quotes in the text of the release.[21] This makes it more likely that a busy journalist will use the story and will use more or less the words intended by the author of the press release. But the author of the release, who will not normally be the person to whom it refers, is most likely to have manufactured the quote with little or no reference to the person who ostensibly 'said' it. These conventions are understood by journalists and those with whom they deal, though they are less often understood by readers of newspapers and viewers of television. Researchers using such sources must apply an understanding of the conventions of the press release as a way of inferring the meaning of the text.

Public libraries, especially copyright libraries, have done a great deal to ease the problem of representativeness of documents in this area. By stocking books and protecting them against physical deterioration, libraries ensure both their survival and their availability. But this is not true for all publications. Many minor publications do not get into libraries, and many publications from earlier centuries have not survived to the point at which they can be collected and indexed. Moreover, books get lost or stolen from even the best-organised libraries, and researchers must take fairly obvious precautions to ensure that they have a satisfactory collection of source material available to them. The National Newspaper Library in Britain similarly takes great care of the national and local newspapers in its custody, though its stock is far from comprehensive; but there are few archives for television and film productions. Even when old film has been stored, there is no guarantee that it will survive. Like paper, it is subject to the attack of insects and decay, and celluloid film deteriorates to the point at which it can self-ignite and explode. Material retained in the archives of film and television organisations may be subject to restricted access provisions for researchers, but it is difficult for a researcher to know whether the archived films and tapes are retained in the form in which they were broadcast, include unbroadcast material, or have been edited prior to storage. Editing is a continuous feature of television and film production, and the 'final' released or broadcast version is, in fact, merely one stage in this process.[22]

I argued in chapters 2 and 3 that assessing the quality and significance of documentary sources is a theoretically informed and value-relevant process. The achievement of an interpretative understanding is a hermeneutic process which employs the methods of semiotic or content analysis. These methods have been particularly widely used, and their relative merits discussed, in studies of the mass media. When researchers approach these documents as topics for analysis, attempting to understand the social conditions of production of the documents themselves and to grasp their internal meaning, these questions of interpretative understanding are raised in an especially acute form.

The traditional methods of content analysis when applied to the mass media assume that the frequency of items can be taken as a valid expression of the objective, or internal, meaning of the text that contains them. The meaning of the text is seen as inhering in its manifest content. The approach therefore tends to be atomistic, decomposing the text into its individual elements, rather than concerning itself with the structure of the text as a whole. Hermeneutic and semiotic approaches to textual analysis aim to overcome this limitation by their holistic focus on the meaning of the whole text. Advocates of these approaches argue that 'significance' is a qualitative rather than a quantitative matter and that the researcher must attempt to grasp the underlying, latent content of the text. This is to be achieved by exploring the connections between the individual elements and by discerning any 'codes' (conventions of stylisation and genre, etc.) which are used to process the raw material of cultural assumptions and images and transform them into texts. Yet beyond this general guidance there is little positive indication of the criteria which should be used in assessing the validity of a particular researcher's interpretation. While rejecting the content analysts' criterion of 'frequency', no other criterion, or set of criteria, is put in its place.

The direction in which mass media researchers have moved in an attempt to resolve this problem is to consider more closely the audience, or audiences, who read the texts. A semiotic analysis may, like content analysis, result in a particular description of the internal meaning of the text, but this has no privileged methodological status. As I argued in chapter 2, the text escapes the intended meanings of its authors once it is inscribed and available to others, but the 'objective' or internal meaning which it acquires in the process of its production is only one element in the complex of factors which determines how it is read by an audience. Indeed, the researchers who are studying a text in order to discern its internal meaning are simply one of its many audiences, employing particularly lengthy and formalised techniques to read it. Other audiences may well read the text differently from the researchers, and so will construct a different interpretation. The received meaning of a text varies with its audience. It cannot be assumed, for example, that the political bias or gender stereotyping which seems apparent to a researcher who has spent many months undertaking an analysis of newspapers will be equally apparent to an ordinary reader who skims the daily paper in fifteen minutes. Audiences for texts are diverse, and there is always a *choice* of readings. The interpretative understanding of a text depends upon a knowledge of its audiences.

Mass media studies have tended to view the audience variously as a 'mass', a 'public', or a 'market' of readers, viewers and spectators.[23] Each way of conceptualising the audience involves a different set of assumptions about its role in the interpretation of textual messages, and only recently has research begun to explore the plurality and diversity of the audiences for mass media productions and to examine their active role in the construction of media messages. The received content of a text, as opposed to its intended or internal content, has only recently been seen as something in which audiences themselves are active participants.

Audience members have frames of interpretation, shared to varying degrees, which are derived from their experience and socialisation and which are the basis on which they ascribe meaning to that which they view or read. Morley has shown that audience interpretation is, furthermore, context specific: a person can make different readings of the same source material when in different situations.[24] Audience members make implicit situational decisions about how their interpretative frameworks and implicit theories are to be applied in constructing a reading of a text. A shop steward, Morley argues, is likely to interpret a newspaper report differently according to whether he or she is reading it at home or among colleagues at work. Morley concludes that researchers must obtain the fullest possible information about the audiences for the texts with which they are concerned. For contemporary and recent documents this can be achieved through interviews, but for earlier periods scant documentary evidence on audiences will have to be used, with all the problems of circularity which this involves.

The aim of such research is to discover *how* people watch television, read newspapers, or listen to the radio. What criteria do people use in choosing what and how to view, and how are their responses shaped by such choices? Class, gender and ethnicity, among other factors, are important determinants of variations in these criteria, and their varying intersection in different contexts (home, work, school, cinema, etc.) are responsible for differing situational decisions and responses. Although the internal meaning of a document, as disclosed by careful and objective techniques of analysis, may constrain the possible readings which audiences can place upon its text, it does not uniquely require one particular reading. The intended, internal, and received meanings of texts must be regarded as separate but interdependent elements in the process of mass communication.

The interplay of the various processes I have described in attempting to use published documents as topics of research can best be illustrated through work in the area of newspapers. The earliest and, until recently, the most widespread approach to the analysis of newspapers was content analysis, where researchers have measured, for example, the number of column inches given to particular topics. Typical of such procedures is the research carried out for two reports on the British press, the Political and Economic Planning (PEP) report of 1938 and the Ross Commission of 1949.[25] The PEP report gives four of its pages to an analysis of what it terms the 'distribution of space' in the eight main daily newspapers of the time. The results of this content analysis are presented in diagrams and there is very little commentary or interpretation, it being assumed that the figures speak for themselves. What seems to be shown in these figures is that, behind their surface similarity, *The Times* and the *Daily Telegraph*, for example, differ in certain ways.[26]

There was, in 1938, rather more news in *The Times* and more advertising in the *Telegraph*; nearly a half of the latter comprised advertising material. The two papers are shown as similar in the proportion of space given to pictures, sport, financial news, and general news, but rather different in their use of feature space: both papers gave about one third of the feature space to the arts (books, radio, theatres, music, etc.), but the bulk of *The Times* feature space was taken up by articles and letters, whereas feature space in the *Telegraph* included far more gossip, stories and 'women's' features. The overall similarity between the papers is brought out when they are compared with the smaller *Daily Mirror* and *Daily Sketch*. These two papers gave more space to display advertisements (and hardly any to classified ads), and included a higher proportion of pictures and feature articles than did the other two papers. Their news coverage included very little financial news, and their features material consisted almost entirely of stories, women's and children's features, and strip cartoons.[27]

It is far from clear that the research reported by PEP, of which I have given only a short extract, conveys any more information than would be apparent through a more superficial scrutiny. The main advantage of their quantitative approach is its *reliability*: the results are 'objective' in the sense that they can be checked by other researchers. The definitions, measures and procedures followed are in general clear and systematic. The objectivity of the report is limited only when it fails to establish clear definitions. This is the case, for example, with its inclusion of the category 'women's features', which reflects conventional cultural understandings rather than scientific categorisation. A completely impressionistic analysis, on the other hand, cannot be replicated and checked in the same way, and this has always been one of the strongest arguments put forward by advocates of quantitative content analysis.

It is for this reason that similar methods were used in the Report of the Ross Commission of 1949, which used research specially commissioned from Silverman on newspaper content and bias.[28] The study was a cross-sectional comparison of 1927, 1937 and 1947, taking nine papers which were published throughout the period, and the most detailed analyses were those of *The Times*, the *Daily Mail* and the *Daily Mirror*, which were seen as 'representing the three main types of national daily'.[29] Silverman's techniques were more rigorous than those of PEP, though certainly not themselves unproblematic. He took a selection of papers in each of the years studied, aiming to produce a sample that was representative of the seasons and the days of the week. Articles were classified by their predominant theme, and the numbers of column inches for each theme were calculated. These were then converted into percentages of the 'total print', the area of newsprint less margins and titles, so as to standardise for the varying sizes of the papers.

Further measures, such as 'news space', were calculated on a similar basis.

Silverman's results show a number of clear differences among the three papers.[30] He found that the size of *The Times* declined from 30 to 24 pages between 1927 and 1937, and that in the same period the proportion of advertising declined from 42 per cent to 33 per cent. Most of the increase in editorial space went to news, though features and news on political, social and economic matters fell slightly from 22 per cent to 18 per cent. *The Times* was found to have a level of foreign news coverage as low as that of the other papers, but more than one third of its news space was given to financial news. Only 3 per cent of the feature space was given to 'women's features' by 1937, about a quarter of the feature space going to the arts.

The *Mail* remained constant in size between 1927 and 1937 at 20 pages. Its advertising content declined from 51 per cent to 41 per cent, the extra editorial space going to news and features. Coverage of social, political and economic news fell slightly from 13 per cent to 10 per cent of news space, while pictures and cartoons increased their presence from 21 per cent to 25 per cent. News on law and the police fell from 12 per cent to 9 per cent, but sports coverage increased from 27 per cent to 36 per cent. Over the inter-war period, 'women's features' in the *Mail* declined from 23 per cent to 15 per cent of the feature space, part of the freed space going over to children's features.

The *Mirror* increased in size from 24 to 28 pages. The advertising content declined from 33 per cent to 26 per cent, with the main editorial increase being in the area of news coverage. Social, political and economic news made up only 4 per cent or 5 per cent of news coverage, and while the picture and cartoon content fell from its extremely high level of 48 per cent in 1927, it remained at a high level of 37 per cent in 1937. Law and police news increased from 15 per cent to 20 per cent, and sport remained constant at 36–7 per cent. About 17–18 per cent of the *Mirror*'s feature space comprised women's material, and a further 10 per cent was for children. Of the feature space, 20 per cent was given to 'light' features, compared with no coverage of this type in *The Times*.

The Ross Commission made no attempt to use content analysis to disclose bias, regarding it as a method simply for establishing the distribution of space among various topics. This reflects the level of development of content analysis, which only came to be used to measure the positive and negative references to particular items in the big growth of content analytic research in the United States during the 1940s and 1950s. Bias was investigated only through very simple techniques of literary textual analysis. Newspaper reports were compared with the independently derived knowledge of the same events which was available to the Commissioners – for example, knowledge from parliamentary reports in Hansard, official statistics, and so on – in order to see whether there was a correspondence between the two. The limitations of this approach of checking one set of documents against another should be obvious, as no document may be regarded as giving an unproblematic and perfectly credible account. Such a strategy has, however, been frequently used by others also.[31]

Silverman analysed coverage of a by-election and concluded that news and comment were not generally separated and that, with the possible exception of *The Times*, the political standpoint of a paper was apparent from its 'factual' news coverage. There was little sign, he argued, of any attempt to give a balanced coverage of different party viewpoints.[32] The Commission Report itself elaborated on this, claiming that, while the topics covered in the newspapers reflected their political standpoint, the 'quality' papers did report accurately and impartially on the subjects they chose to cover. 'Popular' papers, on the other hand, were seen as subject to 'extensive partisanship' and 'distortion for the sake of news value'.[33] These biases were argued to follow from the ownership and control of the papers and from their operation as capitalist undertakings. Ownership pressure towards commercial viability led editors to provide what they thought their section of the reading public was looking for in a newspaper. Where two or more 'popular' papers pursue a similar segment of the market, there is a tendency for convergence in style and political outlook.

A study by Raymond Williams sought to use similar methods of content analysis to up-date the results of the Ross Commission to 1961, and Williams extended the same approach to women's magazines and children's comics.[34] Important for my purposes is that he attempted to extend content analysis into the area of style and presentation. Analysing the coverage of a Transport and General Workers' Union conference, he showed that the *Mirror*, the *Mail*, and *The Times* each gave 23 column inches on their inside pages. The *Telegraph*, the *Daily Herald*, and the *Daily Worker* covered it on the front page. Over and above the quantity of material, Williams argued, its positioning was an important determinant of its meaning.

He attempted to push this analysis further by looking at the type of language and imagery employed. All newspapers except the *Worker* personalised the conference around Frank Cousins, the union's General Secretary, and Williams argues that this personalisation was reinforced by the imagery of fighting and battle: union members were variously described as 'rebels' engaged in 'bomb battles', and Cousins was depicted in a cartoon as a boxer. Such issues are difficult to handle in the same kind of objective way as the distribution of space, but a number of studies have successfully applied content analysis to the measurement of political imagery.[35] What Williams raises, however, are issues which have since been taken further by hermeneutic and semiotic writers who have emphasised that the very categories used in content analysis depend upon an interpretative judgement on the part of the researcher.

Some of the problems involved in moving in this direction can be seen in attempts to analyse still and moving pictures in the mass media. Marjorie Ferguson carried out a study of the cover photographs used by three women's magazines over the period 1949–74, aiming to show how the intentions of the editors and cover designers were transformed into the finished product.[36] She interviewed editors and concluded that the intended meaning of a cover design was to identify the magazine to its audience by signalling its content and readership and by differentiating it from its competitors. The final cover resulted from the ways in which designers used photographers and models to attempt to express this intended meaning. Ferguson identified four distinct types of cover, each involving different conventions of stylisation for representing femininity: 'Chocolate box', the smiling, sweet image of femininity; 'Invitational', the 'mysterious' image of femininity; 'Super-smiler', full-face, windswept, 'aggressive' image; 'Romantic or sexual', overtly sensual or sexual imagery.[37]

Figure 7.1   *Women's magazine covers, 1949–74*

	Woman (%)	Woman's Own (%)	Woman's Weekly (%)
Chocolate box	50	21	86.0
Invitational	22	54	3.5
Super-smiler	14	8	3.5
Romantic or sexual	7	4	3.5
Other	7	13	3.5
	(N = 28)	(N = 24)	(N = 28)

Source: M. Ferguson, *Imagery and Ideology*, p. 108 (see note 36).

Figure 7.1 shows Ferguson's results. In both *Woman* and *Woman's Own* the first two types predominated: half of the *Woman* covers were of the 'chocolate box' type and half of the *Woman's Own* covers were 'invitational'; one-quarter of the *Woman* covers were 'invitational' and one-quarter of the *Woman's Own* covers were 'chocolate box'. The remaining covers of these two magazines were more mixed but tended to be 'super-smiler' rather than 'romantic or sexual'. These magazines, she concluded, competed for the same market and were seeking to emphasise only slight differences in identity. *Women's Weekly*, on the other hand, had over four-fifths of its covers of the 'chocolate box' type, and Ferguson claims that this showed its pursuit of a different audience and a relatively greater emphasis in its content on knitting and other aspects of the female role of domesticity.

This approach has been extended into the realms of moving pictures by Tuchman, who has demonstrated what she calls the 'symbolic annihilation' of women in television presentations.[38] Drawing on the work of other researchers, she uses conventional content analysis techniques to show that over the period 1952–74 between 60 per cent and 80 per cent of the people appearing in American television programmes were male, this figure varying from 60 per cent in comedy shows to 80 per cent in plays. In addition to this, it was very rare for women to be shown in an occupational role or described in an occupationally relevant way – though this was very common for men. Even in soap operas, where women appeared more often, this remained the case. These two features – the absence of women and the trivialisation of their work – were reinforced by a third failure, which Tuchman terms 'condemnation'. Women, she argues, were invariably depicted as incompetent or inferior to men. Strengthening the conventional gender stereotyping, single women were less likely to be presented in an approving light than were married women. Typical of such condemnation of women workers, she argues, was the fact that in medical series men appeared as doctors performing operations while women doctors appeared only to be pulling files from cabinets.[39]

The work of Ferguson, Tuchman, and others concerned with pictorial images is based upon numerical 'head counts' of the presence and absence of women in the mass media and also on a full content analysis of the representations conveyed in such diverse areas as news, entertainment and advertisements. The method therefore goes beyond the mere frequency count to an assessment of the significance of particular items and approaches. 'Trivialisation' and 'condemnation', for example, are measured by judging the extent to which women are portrayed as 'submissive', 'dependent', 'unintelligent', 'sex objects', and so on. But such judgements should not involve simply the exercise of personal judgement; they require the construction and use of coding categories similar to those employed in the analysis of words. It is only when personal judgements are combined with a reliable set of coding categories that any degree of objectivity can be achieved.

Judith Lemon, for example, analysed crime dramas and situation comedies on American television.[40] Using codes for 'dominance', 'occupation', 'sex', 'race', and 'family role', pre-tested for reliability between different researchers, she tried to ensure that her findings could be checked by other researchers. Even those who reject her particular assumptions about what is or is not significant in a media image can at least check that, from the standpoint of her own assumptions, the results are valid and reliable. Lemon found that men were more likely than women to be shown in high-status occupations in each type of programme, and she argued that this was generally responsible for men appearing in dominant roles in interaction. But male dominance was found to be a general feature of the programmes even where occupational status was not relevant. Male dominance was, furthermore, unaffected by the presence of a female star.[41]

In a different area of the media, the Glasgow Media Group examined all British television news broadcasts over a period of six months to assess the reporting of industrial and economic affairs.[42] Using a categorisation grid covering the length, subject and style of the reports, and cross-checking for inter-researcher reliability, they concluded that reporting was biased in favour of an 'establishment' point of view and effectively excluded or trivialised alternative accounts of events. This bias is seen as inherent in the news genre itself; it is not a direct reflection of the personal opinions of programme-makers. Editors and journalists have certain taken-for-granted criteria of 'news interest' and 'news worthyness' which are part and parcel of the organisational requirements of their jobs. News broadcasts are constrained by organisational imperatives of space and duration which govern the length and order of presentation of items. Events for reporting are chosen to fit these predetermined formats.

In existing semiotic textual analyses,[43] the interpretative categories and codings are rarely made explicit, and the reader must take it on trust that the researcher is not simply displaying his or her arbitrary preferences. A reading of a text which is unconstrained by reliability-tested coding categories and uses the conventional techniques of literary analysis cannot easily demonstrate its validity as a reading of the text. Nor, as already argued, is it the case that the internal meaning – however disclosed – will correspond with the received meanings constructed by audiences. The bias that is apparent to researchers may not be experienced by audiences, or may be constructed differently by them.

Directories, almanacs and yearbooks

I have looked at the use of published documents of private origin in so far as they can be used as *topics* of research, but it is also necessary to look at the ways in which they can be used as *resources* for telling us about the world beyond the documents. Indeed, as I have previously emphasised, these two concerns are interdependent. A knowledge of, for example, how newspapers process events to construct a particular image of reality is an essential element in any research which aims to use newspapers as sources of evidence about the events themselves. In the discussion that follows I shall be taking for granted the numerous points raised in the previous sections and shall concentrate on the additional problems involved in using such documents as resources. In order to broaden the discussion, however, I shall consider these problems in relation to a different set of documents: those published reference books conventionally designated by such terms as 'directories' and 'yearbooks'.

Published reference books have long had an important place in social research, though they have rarely been compiled for such purposes. Such books have been produced by private organisations as part of their own internal operations and by publishing companies aiming at a wider public, and they appear under a bewildering range of designations: 'Directory', 'Manual', 'Almanac', 'Guide', 'Register', 'Yearbook', 'Calendar' and even 'Diary' have been used, and rarely in a consistent or self-explanatory way. There are in fact three major genres, commonly identified as directories, almanacs and yearbooks.

A directory is, strictly, a listing, typically of the inhabitants of an area or of the members of an organisation or association, but the term has often been applied more generally to large and heavy reference books.[44] The best contemporary exemplar is perhaps a standard telephone directory, listing all the telephone subscribers in a given area,[45] together with their telephone numbers, and organised alphabetically by surname, first name, and address.[46]

'Almanac' is the earliest term for an annual calendar of dates which also contains information related to these dates. Originally, religious and astronomical data were included, such as the dates of festivals and the phases of the moon, and this was subsequently extended to such things as records of the weather and political events, and anniversaries for the coming year.[47] A contemporary exemplar of the almanac is *Whitaker's Almanack*, published annually since 1868, which begins with a fifty-page calendar showing astronomical data, the times of sunrise and sunset in various cities, religious festivals, and the births and deaths of prominent persons. The *Almanack* continues through a further thousand pages containing notes on astronomical observations and the measurement of time in different calendar systems, a day-to-day account of political, artistic, scientific and sporting events of the previous year, notes on the legal system and tax regulations, historical weather records, a large digest of international information, and substantial directory sections covering the peerage, the government and civil service, the judiciary, the military, the Church hierarchy, and other organisations.[48]

Whitaker's Almanack attempts to extend the principle of the almanac to cover the regular up-dating of general information, and it also contains material that more particularly characterises yearbooks. A yearbook is, naturally, an annual publication, its defining characteristic being that it aims to bring a particular subject area up-to-date: the same basic material is presented year after year, with the names and figures altered to reflect changes during the course of the year. *The Statesman's Year-Book* is a contemporary example: it gives, for instance, population figures for every country every year, which change as each country carries out a census or devises new estimates of population; it also lists such things as the personnel of each country's government and state apparatus, the names changing with each retirement, election or revolution.[49]

The distinctions I have drawn between directories, almanacs and yearbooks are far from clear-cut. They are analytical distinctions aimed at identifying ideal types with which actual publications can be compared. Because of this overlap in actual content, reference books are diverse in both title and content, especially those that are termed 'manuals', 'guides', or 'handbooks'. These and similar terms originally designated short and handy source-books of practical relevance to particular occupations or activities, often gleaned from more complex unpublished sources: typical are the investment and shareholders' manuals of Bradshaw (for British private railway companies), Garcke (for the electrical industry), and Moody (for American companies),[50] the numerous technical manuals of the steel, coal, oil, publishing and other industries, and the consumer manuals of Baedeker (for tourists) and Bradshaw (for railway travellers).[51]

Virtually no area is without its specialist reference books – whatever titles are used to describe them – and very few of these have no relevance to social research. The highly technical summaries of horse-racing form, as published in Cope's *Racegoer's Encyclopaedia* or in the *Guide to the Turf*, can give useful insights into patterns of ownership and competitiveness in the horse-racing industry, the movement of prices, the organisation of stables and training, and the activities of gamblers. A comprehensive reference book for an uncommon or unusual industry, activity or locality can often provide the single most useful means of orientation for a researcher fresh to that area; and as the research proceeds, many such books will constitute a systematic source of research data. The whole range of published reference books cannot be reviewed here.[52] I propose to focus on those which have been particularly widely used in social research and which highlight the advantages and limitations of all such sources, concentrating my examination on commercial and biographical directories.

Commercial directories emerged in Britain at the end of the seventeenth century in response to growth in the scale and extent of the national market and increase in the distances over which trade transactions took place.[53] In such circumstances, a merchant would often have no knowledge of the names and addresses of other merchants with whom he might trade. To meet this gap in knowledge, lists of traders and merchants were produced *ad hoc* by printers and, increasingly, by registry offices. The latter were advertising and employment agencies which maintained registers of businesses for their own use and began to sell copies of these registers to other firms. Making their earliest appearance in London,[54] the publication of commercial directories spread to the provincial cities of Birmingham, Manchester and Liverpool in the eighteenth century. Only towards the end of that century, as the canal system opened up trade even further, was there anything like adequate coverage of the areas outside London, and even then only the major cities were at all well served. Commercial publishers of the eighteenth century treated the production of directories as an adjunct to other activities: printers, land agents, post officials, and even the police produced local directories. For this reason, they were diverse in style and content. But major changes occurred as a result of two interdependent phenomena: the growth of the postal system, and the nineteenth-century establishment of a national railway system. The railway not only stimulated trade and travel but also aided the establishment of an efficient national post.

The Postmaster-General in Britain set up a provincial penny post in 1764, and there was a big expansion in the mail.[55] Postal officials sought information on names and addresses so that they could accurately deliver letters, and began to use existing directories and to become more closely involved in the production of new ones. Users of the system also sought a way of discovering the addresses of those with whom they wished to correspond. This established the principle of the 'Post Office

Directory', a directory produced by Royal Mail officials themselves.[56] In 1835 Frederick Kelly, chief inspector of inland letter carriers, became responsible for the London directory. He stressed its official character and was able to use postal messengers and agents to collect and check the information he published. There were, however, criticisms of this as an abuse of the position of a public servant, and Kelly established the fiction of a separation between his public and his private activities by forming the directory-publishing operation into a separate firm headed by his brother. Through various changes of ownership, *Kelly's Post Office London Directory* is published to this day.

Similar Post Office directories began in other towns during the nineteenth century, and a number expanded into county, regional, and national directories. Most important of these were the directories of James Pigot, who began his directory publishing in Manchester and set up a national series of directories, and William White, who was especially active in Yorkshire and the Midlands. By the 1850s, however, Kelly was dominant in the field, having taken over Pigot's and a number of other firms, and it was under Kelly that the classic form of the commercial directory was created. A series of county directories covered almost the whole country,[57] and these were published also in regional compendiums as well as having their city sections published separately. The form of the directory was the same, regardless of the county covered. Each contained a parish-by-parish listing of upper- and middle-class residents, farmers, merchants and manufacturers, together with a general county index. Large towns and cities were covered street by street, and the commercial premises were often listed also in a 'classified' section. These various listings were preceded and interleaved with political, administrative and commercial information, and the directories also contained a topographical account of the history and geology of the area. The classic commercial directory, therefore, combined the basic principle of the directory with some features of the yearbook and the travel guide.

These general commercial directories became the basis of a differentiation into numerous more specialised directories, each linked to specific markets or industries. The earliest to emerge were the various 'Court' directories, which listed only the nobility and gentry and those who wished to trade with them in the consumer markets for luxury goods. They were produced for London, above all, although a number of county volumes were issued later. The most important of the Court directories were those of Boyle, which began in 1792 and ceased publication in the 1930s. In its final form, under the title *Webster's Royal Red Book*, the directory contained a short almanac and a yearbook of public officials as well as an alphabetical and street listing of London upper-class society. Like their general and biographical counterparts, which are discussed below, the Court directories played a particularly important role as registers of social acceptability when the traditional upper classes were challenged by *nouveau riche* industrialists. Closely related to them were various short-lived resort directories, produced for seaside and spa resorts, which listed local 'society' people and were linked with guidebooks to provide information on leisure and accommodation for fashionable visitors. Such directories were rapidly superseded by the more useful guides to British and foreign resorts produced by Murray from 1836, Baedeker and Black from 1839, Nelson from 1859, and Ward Lock from 1896.[58]

Specialist trade directories evolved in the late nineteenth century as the various trades became more extensive and distinct from one another, and directories of merchants and manufacturers made their appearance. By concentrating on industrial and commercial information these directories began to meet the requirements of large-scale enterprises operating in national and international markets. The changing nature of industry and the establishment of an effective system of postal addresses meant that the original rationale for the general commercial directory began to be undermined.

Many of the general directories began to disappear, and the Kelly county series ended in the 1930s. Perhaps the biggest force for change was the spread of the telephone, which reduced reliance on the postal system.[59] With the development of the telephone network came the telephone directory, which supplanted the Post Office and County directories as popular sources of local information. The growth in the number of subscribers since the Second World War has meant that the telephone directory has come to approximate a full list of house owners in an area; though it is not yet a full list of *households*, as many remain without a telephone.

In the United States, the telegraph monopoly Western Union turned down Alexander Graham Bell's offer of the patent and rights to the telephone, just as the British Post Office had turned down the British rights. Bell therefore formed his own company, which developed a web of international subsidiaries and associates. The telephone was seen predominantly as a business instrument at first, and its use expanded with the growing need to monitor the large national and multinational production units that were developing in the United States at the turn of the century. The telephone's early development, therefore, was an aspect of the central surveillance of a business over its operations.

The form of the modern telephone directory in Britain is a result of the establishment of a legal monopoly of telephone provision throughout the whole country.[60] Initially, telephone provision was in the hands of a number of competing enterprises, each producing its own directory, listing only their own subscribers. As most subscribers were commercial, the directories were often subdivided by industry.[61] Through a series of mergers a large private undertaking emerged by 1889, and this entered into a partnership with the Post Office telephone system in 1901. Eventually, in 1911, the Post Office acquired and operated the whole system.[62] Similar State-owned systems developed in West Germany and in France. The Société Générale de Telephone was set up in France in 1881 as a State-backed monopoly, with the State subsequently setting up its own rival system; in 1889 the State bought up the private system. In the United States, by contrast, the Bell telephone interests came under the control of the A. T. & T. conglomerate, and the system remains a privately owned network.[63]

The early Court directories were paralleled by the establishment of genealogical directories of the nobility and gentry. The predecessor of the *Debrett* peerage volume appeared in 1769, taking the *Debrett* title in 1802. This provided an alphabetical directory of living peers with notes on their lives and ancestors and listings of their living relatives. The *Burke* series, beginning in 1826, also adopted the alphabetical format but included full genealogies, of varying accuracy, from the earliest recorded members of the family lines. Both *Burke* and *Debrett* extended their coverage from the peerage to the baronetage, but only *Burke* attempted a comprehensive coverage of the landed gentry – this was published in 1833–5.[64] Each of the main *Debrett* and *Burke* works was published in a continuous series up to the end of the 1970s, the peerages being published almost annually in their early years but less frequently as time went on.

It is uncertain whether *Debrett* and *Burke* will continue at all regularly, as the market for them is far smaller than formerly and they have been largely superseded by simpler biographical reference books covering a wider range of peope. *Burke* from 1907 included a biographical directory of knights who were not also peers or baronets.[65] The main sources for such information are *Who's Who* and *Kelly's Handbook to the Titled, Landed and Official Classes*. The Kelly volume tried, from 1874, to cover all members of the established upper classes and those who held public or other prominent offices.[66] *Who's Who*, similar in its coverage, was launched in 1849. It has remained an annual publication ever since, and has been complemented since 1915 by *Who was Who*, which brings together the biographies of all those people listed in *Who's Who* that have died during each period covered.[67]

Similar in style, though concerned only with those active in Parliament, are *Debrett's House of Commons* and *Dod's Parliamentary Companion*; the latter has been published in a continuous annual series since 1832. Similarly, Whitaker and Dod published biographical peerage directories, and Walford published a biographical directory of the landed gentry. The success of the *Who's Who* format has led to the appearance of numerous, but often short-lived biographical directories in specialised areas. These books generally include people prominent in a particular trade or profession who may not qualify for inclusion in *Who's Who* itself, and they often form sections of trade and professional yearbooks: examples include 'Who's Who' volumes for insurance, finance, education, the theatre, sport, and yachting, perhaps the most specialised of all being *Who's Who in Corrugated Paper*.

Outside Britain, genealogical directories are uncommon, though biographical directories on the model of *Who's Who* have proliferated. Burke has published volumes on Irish families and the 'colonial gentry', as well as a volume on *Prominent Families of the USA* (1980),[68] but these were all essentially British in focus: the American volume, for example, was a directory only of certain families of British origin. The European nobility was covered comprehensively in the annual *Almanach de Gotha*, which followed the style of *Debrett* but gave briefer notes for each entry. Ruvigny's *Titled Nobility of Europe* appeared in 1914, adopting the *Debrett* format for the upper levels of the European peerage. The date of its appearance, however, was inauspicious, and the First World War meant that it disappeared along with many of the families listed. The lower levels of the German nobility were comprehensively listed in the *Handbuch des Adels* and related volumes, but no European country has produced a genealogical directory comparable in scope to *Burke's Landed Gentry*. The *Almanach de Gotha* ceased publication with the Second World War, and it was only recently that a less comprehensive, though geographically more extensive, publication appeared under the title *Royalty, Peerage and Nobility of the World*.[69] Virtually every country, however, has its own version of *Who's Who*, together with specialised counterparts. *Who's Who in America* has been published since 1897.

Most distinctive of these is the American *Social Register*, which is similar in intention to the British Court directories and arose with the nineteenth-century expansion of the American economy and its upper class.[70] The Social Register Association was founded in 1887, and the first volume, for New York City, appeared the following year. The book was explicitly intended as an arbiter of the dividing line between established and newly rich families, and its compilers aimed to list all the members of acceptable 'Society' – described by the original editor as the 'Best People'. The volume listed names and addresses together with the maiden names of married women, so that kinship links through marriage could be seen, and it added the education, clubs and similar connections of the people listed. Through the 1890s volumes were published for other cities as a national series was established. First to be covered was the East Coast, then the Midwest, until, in 1906, San Francisco was reached. By 1910 a *Social Register* had been published for twelve cities, and these have all appeared in annual volumes to the present.[71] The editors aimed to be selective on the basis of established social groups. Provided that those who apply can afford the subscription, the decision on inclusion depends upon their acceptability to existing members; applications must therefore be supported by written references from people already listed.[72]

The annals of the rich and powerful

I propose to discuss the use of these documents from the standpoint of the appraisal criteria for documentary sources. While many of the problems raised in earlier discussions of the appraisal of documents are relevant here also, I shall concentrate on certain questions which are particularly germane to the use of published reference books in social research, illustrating these points through studies of elites.

First, then, the question of authenticity. The author of a published reference book is not always known, and such volumes often appear under the collective authorship of the publisher's office. Occasionally an 'editor' or 'compiler' may be named, but his or her role in the collective process of production will be far from clear. Most clear-cut, perhaps, are the *Burke* volumes: they were edited successively by members of the Burke family, who determined their overall shape and coverage. But even these pose problems of authorship. The rights to publish the peerage were sold in the late 1970s to a syndicate which aimed to sell advertising space in future volumes. Their first act, in 1980, was to reissue the 1970 edition with an expanded advertising section and a 13-page supplement of changes over the decade. Many libraries bought this book under the impression that it was a new edition. Journalists investigating those responsible for producing the book and who would be responsible for any future editions, found that their business documents had not been filed at Companies House. When the chairman of the company was asked if the relevant documents could be examined at the company's office, he is reported to have said: 'If you try to inspect them, I will personally break your legs.'[73]

Where books are published in relatively large numbers, the forgery of whole volumes is hardly viable, but plagiarism and pirate publication is another matter. A number of cases of plagiarism in nineteenth-century directory publication are known: a directory might be given a name similar to that of an established directory and the whole contents of the directory simply reprinted under a different name. Satire, on the other hand, is more difficult to achieve in this area than in many others, though comic writers and performers have successfully satirised school registers and other listings.[74] *John Bull* magazine published a parody of *Whitaker's Almanack* in 1907 under the title *Witty-Cur's Almanack*.

The question of soundness is perhaps a far more important issue. Alphabetical listings or volumes with numbered pages can be checked very easily for their physical completeness, but misprints and missing entries may be almost impossible to discern. Listings in a directory generally adopt a particular style which is far removed from that of conventional texts. Abbreviations and incomplete sentences are normal, and so it is difficult to discern missing words or even misprints by reading an entry. Where the whole entry for a particular name has been excluded, there is virtually no way that this can be known.

Assessing the credibility of a published reference book can be undertaken only if the researcher takes account of the processes through which it was produced. The collective authorship of most reference books is often associated with a lack of public information on the ways in which those responsible for the book collected and collated information and how they processed it for publication. There are at least three groups of people whose role in production may affect the credibility of a book: the individuals who are listed, those who collect the information about them, and those who edit it into its final form. Collectors and collators are members of commercial publishing enterprises or of sectional trade or professional associations, and the requirements of these organisations will set the constraints within which they work. The sincerity of most of those involved may rarely need to be questioned, though there is little evidence on which this can be assessed, but the commercial motivation behind most such books must be expected to shape their contents and coverage in significant ways.

The individuals who are listed have a particularly strong influence on the contents of the book whenever they are asked to provide information to the compilers. *Who's Who* and *Burke*, for example, both depend upon information supplied by those whom they list. Compilers may send regular questionnaires, extract information from subscription forms, or write letters seeking clarification on particular points, and they rarely have any opportunity to check all the information supplied. This information must generally be taken on trust, and any gaps in the information supplied can only rarely be filled by the compilers themselves. Indeed, some biographical reference books adopt a policy of retaining information as it is supplied, making only minor editorial and stylistic changes. Some of the earlier editors of *Burke*, for example, have been criticised for their willingness to accept fantastic and unsubstantiated genealogies from some of the families listed in their volumes. For whatever reasons, the entries in a particular book may vary slightly from one to another in terms of what is and what is not included. When this is combined with the necessary changes from one edition to another that must be made as a person advances in his or her career, there can be serious problems of comparability.

Who's Who for 1952, for example, includes, for the first time, an entry for the Honourable Anthony Neil Wedgwood Benn, Labour MP and heir to the first Viscount Stansgate, and mentions his education at Westminster School. As Wedgewood Benn wished to pursue his career in the House of Commons and was politically opposed to the House of Lords, he did not use the title of Lord Stansgate that he inherited in 1960, and in 1963 he eventually managed to renounce the peerage. These facts are duly recorded in the relevant issues of *Who's Who*, though the volumes since 1970 have not included the fact that he attended a public school. His politics followed an even more populist strain, and from 1976 to 1982 he had no listing in *Who's Who* at all, having decided that inclusion in such a directory was incompatible with his political position. In 1983, however, his entry reappeared under the name Tony Benn. The more aristocratic *Debrett's Handbook* for 1982, however, places greater emphasis on independent research and less reliance on information supplied by individuals than does *Who's Who*: it includes an entry under 'Right Hon., Tony (Anthony) Neil Wedgwood Benn', and records his attendance at Westminster School.

The sincerity of those who provide information to compilers may also be questioned. It was reported in the national newspapers in 1987 that all editions of *Burke's Peerage* since 1963 had contained an error, because particular information had not been supplied by a listed family.[75] Two female members of the Bowes-Lyon family who had been in mental hospitals since 1941 were, from 1963, listed in *Burke* as having died, though both were still alive. Though the fact was not reported in the newspapers, the two women were also not listed in *Debrett* at this date. A spokesman for the family ascribed this to the 'vagueness' of a particular family member when filling in forms, but some suggested that the information had been deliberately suppressed as the women in question were cousins of the Queen Mother. This suspicion was strengthened by the existence of a legend that a nineteenth-century heir to the family earldom had become insane and been incarcerated in a secret chamber in Glamis Castle, his death being reported in both *Burke* and *Debrett*.

Even when the researcher believes entries to have been sincerely and accurately supplied, it is necessary to take account of the inherent element of selectivity which arises from the editing requirements of a reference book. Over the course of their careers, for example, individuals will update and add new elements to their biographies and, because of pressures of space, will have to delete items previously included. Any particular biographical entry, therefore, is a cross-sectional 'slice' through a person's life and may be an unreliable indicator of that person's attributes and characteristics at other stages of his or her life. This is especially problematic when using a volume such as *Who Was Who*, which includes only the final entry for the person in question, an entry compiled shortly before death and perhaps after numerous alterations have been made to the annual entries in *Who's Who*.

Where a reference book is compiled from existing sources, a particularly important role is played by the data collectors. Many of the larger publishers have employed agents and full-time staff to undertake this work, though the methods and technical instruments they use to collect the information are rarely known. The Kelly organisation, for example, used a mixture of full-time agents and local correspondents such as postmen, tax-collectors, clergymen, and Poor Law overseers. The local correspondents in rural areas were required to act almost like census enumnerators, travelling around an area collecting information on a house-to-house basis – indeed, many of them combined census work with their work for directory publishers. This procedure was too expensive to follow in large urban areas, but local correspondents still provided the full-time agents with detailed local information. This information had similar reliability problems to those discussed in relation to the census, the problems perhaps being greater because directory publishers had no legal sanctions behind their work.

To an extent, the coverage of commercial directories can be assessed by comparison with parish registers and census data. Shaw has shown that a Manchester directory of 1811 covered just 11 per cent of the population, and an 1861 directory for Ashby de la Zouch covered 17 per cent.[76] In a more systematic investigation of Lancashire in 1821, Shaw concluded that coverage was fairly high for urban areas but low for small villages – the more important markets and customers were more likely to be covered than others. The 'private residents' who were included, for example, were those wealthy people who were accorded social recognition of their status in the community by those who collected the information. Only the more important trades and crafts people were included, and those who rented their accommodation on a weekly basis – the majority of the population – were not included at all.[77]

Representativeness is easier to assess for some directories than it is for others. Good catalogues exist for the earlier commercial directories, showing where known copies are available,[78] the *Burke* series is well documented and fairly easily available, and *Who's Who* was fully indexed in 1982; but many handbooks and yearbooks are unrecorded in catalogues. Many such reference books are short-lived and are not always covered by the copyright laws, and so no library or archive has maintained a complete record of their publication. Even when catalogues exist, copies may not have survived or may be inaccessible. All except the very earliest directories, almanacs and yearbooks were published in large numbers and so stood a good chance of survival; yet they are generally regarded as ephemeral items, going rapidly out of date, and so their survival depends, in practice, upon the deliberate efforts made by libraries and archives. For this reason, not even the national copyright libraries have complete runs of even some of the most common reference books. Some trade and professional associations will have followed a deliberate policy of retaining copies of their own yearbooks, though this practice is far from widespread. The Kelly publishing organisation, now part of a large international publishing group, maintains a large though not complete archive of its own publications, but public rights of access and search are limited. For many other reference books, especially those of the nineteenth century, access to surviving copies can be difficult, as their location is frequently unknown.

The problem of survival may become progressively more important in the future. While surviving copies from the past can, in general, be repaired and maintained, despite the damage caused by acid to wood-pulp paper, there can be no surviving documentary records unless the document is in a non-transient form. Where data are stored electronically on computers and transferred over telephone lines to other computers, there may be no need to print copies of the document on paper or microfilm. Information about telephone subscribers, for example, is now stored on computer and can be made available on-line, making the printed directory increasingly redundant. The data are continually updated and so no running archive of past information is maintained. If printed directories are eventually superseded by on-line directories, the researcher of the future may have greater difficulty in locating sources for the late twentieth century than he or she would in locating seventeenth-century directories.

Problems of literal understanding are unusual in directories, almanacs and yearbooks, though idiosyncratic or archaic punctuation and typefaces may pose some minor problems. Interpretative understanding, however, is a great problem, as these documents rarely indicate their criteria for inclusion or their methods of data collection, and many fail to include even a rudimentary introduction to the abbreviations and definitions used. Where occupational titles and trades are listed, for example, problems comparable to those involved in the handling of census data will arise, but directories include such additional problems as the meaning of the terms 'private residents', 'principal seats', or 'landed gentry'.

Similarly, the date to which the data relate may be uncertain. Time is taken to collect the data and to process it, and there will be additional delays as it is printed and distributed. There will be varying margins of error in books, depending on the time-lags introduced at each of these stages. The date shown on the spine of a reference book is often one year ahead of the actual date of publication, and the latter 'may be anything up to a year ahead of the year to which the data relate.[79]

When the criteria for inclusion in a reference book are unknown or unclear, the significance of its text may be hidden. In some cases this will be unproblematic, if given a little thought. A telephone directory, for example, does not show its criteria for inclusion, but it should be obvious that it includes only telephone subscribers. Despite the growth in the number of subscribers since the Second World War, the directory should not be taken as a list of householders or of house owners, for many households remain without a telephone.[80] This is a particular problem if it is intended to use directories as sampling frames in research.

Other sorts of directory pose less obvious demands on interpretative understanding, and this problem can best be illustrated by considering the use of directories in research on 'social elites'. *Who's Who*, *Burke* and the like have frequently been used in studies of upper-class groups, as it has generally been assumed that they are adequate indicators of social status, wealth and political power. Those who study 'elites' in terms of their social background have regarded such reference books as essential sources of information. A directory has often been seen as a more or less complete enumeration of the elite in question, obviating the need to draw up a questionnaire and undertake a systematic inquiry.

Such assumptions have frequently been questioned, however, and many researchers into elites have been sophisticated in their use of bio-graphical reference books;[81] even so, numerous methodological problems remain.

Typical of the best in American research of this kind is the work of Baltzell, who carried out a study of 'an American business aristocracy, of colonial stock and Protestant affiliations, and centered in the older metropolitan areas along the Eastern Seaboard'.[82] He saw this group as a hereditary upper class, a social elite which could be defined independently of its appearance in reference books. Nevertheless, he regarded those books which had been published in order to document the boundaries of this group, and to serve as records of membership, as essential sources of factual information on upper-class members. He used *Who's Who in America* and the *Social Register* for 1940, supplemented by the *Directory of American Biography* for earlier periods, identifying Philadelphians in the national elite from *Who's Who* and then examining their family backgrounds in the *Social Register*. The intermarried, local families comprised the established 'old family core' of Philadelphia. Those who were unlisted, Baltzell argued, tended to be incomers who might eventually move on to full elite status. Baltzell showed great sophistication in the use of his sources, examining, for example, family size and household composition.

A typical British study of elite social background is that of Boyd, who used *Who's Who* and other directories to study the recruitment of civil servants, the judiciary, the armed services, the Church of England bishops, and clearing-bank directors.[83] As well as using directories as sources of information on elite members, however, Boyd also used them to define the boundaries of his various elites. His argument was that *Who's Who* aimed to reflect the recognition of achievement and the status accorded by the established social orders themselves. For this reason, anyone listed in *Who's Who* could be regarded as a member of those same established social orders. Boyd recognised, however, that many people who qualified for inclusion would not in fact be listed – they might have been uncontactable by the compilers or might have refused to give the information requested. He therefore approached the compilers to discover the criteria used for each occupational group and then applied them himself in defining the boundaries of the elites; in each case, formal career attainments were given by the compilers as their criterion of selection. *Whitaker's Almanack* was used by Boyd as a full listing of the relevant levels of the occupational groups, and biographical directories were used to compile information on as many of the people as were listed.

Boyd took serious account of many problems of authenticity, credibility and representativeness – looking particularly at the problems posed by the varying compilation dates of the directories, which led to difficulties in the cases of individuals who were promoted in the course of the years studied. But the fundamental problems of interpretative understanding were not tackled. The most useful – indeed, almost the only – discussion of this issue is to be found in an important article by Bell.[84] Bell looked at the social processes of production of directories, aiming to show that they could not be taken as unproblematic indicators of an elite social group.

The elite to be studied must, Bell argued, be defined independently of the documents used to provide evidence on their social background. Although he illustrated this contention with reference to the *Dictionary of National Biography*, his general points are applicable to all biographical directories and to all research which uses directories as sampling frames, rather than simply as sources on particular individuals. Though nomination for inclusion in the *DNB* is a posthumous recognition of status, it reflects the status concepts of its editors and not those embodied in the State machinery or held by the general public. Bell felt, however, that the criteria may sometimes be close to those followed by the established social groups themselves: the nineteenth-century volumes of the *DNB* were based on editorial nominations circulated to members of the Athenaeum Club for comment.

Today, however, the procedures are less clear-cut and the whole process is more diffuse. There tends to be a higher proportion of people included on the grounds of their official positions in the hierarchy of the State or because of public titles. Coverage of private business is far less comprehensive, formal criteria of achievement in that case being less clear-cut and more contentious. On the other hand, many people prominent in literature and science, where formal criteria of achievement are almost non-existent, are listed in the *DNB*.

A number of the points raised by Bell are relevant even where the directories are used simply as sources of information on social background. If a researcher searches only in directories for the biographies of members of an independently defined elite – as was the case with Baltzell – the results will be based only on those who are listed in the directories. These people may not be typical or representative of the elite group as a whole, and the study will be biased to an unknown degree by the inclusion criteria employed by the directory compilers. For this reason, Useem's study of the 'inner circle' of business leaders in Britain took two estimates of social background. One measure was the proportion of people in the elite group who were shown, for example, as having attended public schools, and the other measure was the proportion of people listed in the directories who attended public schools. The former measure gives a lower estimate, while the latter measure gives a higher estimate. Use of the two measures indicates the range in which the actual level is to be found.[85]

It is possible to gain some idea of the diversity in biographical reference books from the typology in figure 7.2.[86] The typology is defined by two dimensions: the editorial intention and the subjects' rights of control over information. Editors may aim to give a complete coverage of all those with a particular attribute or those falling into a particular category, regardless of their own personal views of merit. This inclusive intention is aimed at producing a document of record which has relatively unambiguous and publicly recognised criteria of listing. On the other hand, editors may wish to exercise their own judgement on the merits of those who might be listed, in which case they select from among the pool of potential entrants. This selective intent may be aimed at identifying real rather than merely nominal achievements.

Figure 7.2   *A typology of directories*

	Subjects' rights	
	To opt out	*Not to opt out*
Editorial intent:		
inclusive	1	2
selective	3	4

Whatever criteria is used by editors, directories may differ in the role accorded to the subjects themselves in the provision of information. At one extreme, the subject may have no right to opt out, the editors compiling an entry from whatever sources are available. At the other extreme, subjects will have not only the right to opt out completely, but will determine the data which are included in the entry by supplying this themselves. While *Who's Who* and telephone directories exemplify category 1, the inclusive directory with the right of opting out, *Debrett*, *Burke*, and other peerage directories come closer to category 2. In the latter cases, subjects provide much of the information, but the editors strive to insure that there is an entry for all who qualify for inclusion. The *DNB* and occasional publications such as *Who's Really Who*[87] fall into category 4, as the editors adopt a selective stance and exercise control over the content of the entry. Category 3 would seem to be a null category, as the intent to be selective would seem to preclude any absolute right for the subject to opt out. Certain directories may, however, approach this as an extreme.

This chapter concludes the main discussion of public and private documents, but the various types of personal document remain to be discussed. Although official certificates and forms, receipts and so on, may enter the personal realm of the household, their conditions of production and the form they take are fundamentally different from those produced within the personal sphere itself. In the following chapter I will review this type of document and touch on some of the ways in which they too may enter the public sphere or be used alongside official documents.

8   Personal Documents

Personal documents have been defined as those produced outside of the official sphere of State and private action, though they may enter the public sphere through subsequent publication (see figure 1.2). Typical personal documents are letters, diaries and other household paperwork, and these documents shade over imperceptibly into the realm of domestic ephemera. Certificates and similar ephemeral items have been discussed in earlier chapters in terms of their status as certified copies of official documents, and they were related to such official records as receipts, bank account ledgers, land registration records, and so on. Many such items appear in family archives and domestic sources alongside other, more strictly personal documents. Documents actually generated within the personal sphere itself, or produced commercially as a direct service for the personal sphere, include letters, diaries, household accounts, personal memoirs, family photographs and portraits, and address books.

Personal documents and ephemera together comprise the archaeological record of a household and, if available to a researcher, can provide a unique insight into family life.[1] Subject to selective survival from the past, such evidence will normally be unrepresentative of the whole range of documentation that passed through the household, but can be assessed and utilised in exactly the same way as any other source material. Unfortunately, household documents rarely survive intact and *in situ*, though fragments of whole records survive in surprisingly large quantities. In most cases it is the records of the wealthiest and most prominent families which have been best preserved, especially when family life has been inextricably tied in with the fate of a business undertaking or a landed estate. In such cases the family and official records have often been maintained in a personal archive or have been deposited at a local or national record office.

In this chapter I shall consider two major classes of personal documents as illustrations of the whole range: first, diaries, letters and autobiographies; the more strictly 'written' sources; and second, photographs and paintings. The latter, like the visual media considered in the previous chapter, should be regarded as true documents, although they are produced by brush and camera rather than by pen or typewriter. The diaries and life histories considered in this chapter should be distinguished from those solicited by researchers from their respondents. When researchers ask people to keep a diary as part of an investigation, for example, the resulting document is not a strictly 'personal' document in the sense that I use that category. Such source material is more akin to the interview and oral history transcripts with which it is usually associated.[2] Along with questionnaires and interview schedules, therefore, such source material has been excluded from the remit of this book – though the historical records of past research are, of course, useful private documents in their own right for subsequent researchers.

Diaries, letters and autobiographies

Personal documents appear in substantial numbers only as literacy and the means for writing spread outside the official sphere of the State. When writing skills remained the monopoly of clergy and servants of official power, private individuals were unable to record their thoughts and experiences in permanent form. Even when the production of documents became more common, people remained dependent upon official action – for example, as a means of distributing letters. Some of the earliest letters to survive in Britain are those of the Paston family in Norfolk, carried by hand as an adjunct to the family's business undertakings.[3] Letter-writing only really became widespread with the introduction of an official postal service, and letters survive in large numbers only from the era of the penny post. Changing technologies – especially the introduction and spread of the telephone – have reduced the volume of personal mail relative to the size of the population, and it remains to be seen what implications this will have for the survival of personal letters as documentary sources.

Whereas letters are generally written for others, diaries are generally written for oneself. The qualification 'generally' is important, as diaries are often written with publication or the judgement of posterity in mind, and many letters are written in the hope that they will survive as a personal record. There was a rapid growth in diary-keeping after the

Reformation, and especially in the second half of the seventeenth century, largely due to the rise of a literary culture. By the seventeenth century, diary-keeping had become a gentlemanly hobby for many members of the English upper classes, and few survive from before this time.[4] The best known of the seventeenth-century diarists are Samuel Pepys and John Evelyn, whose diaries were published a hundred or more years after their deaths.[5] Evelyn's diary covers the period from the 1630s to 1706, and his friend Pepys, a civil servant at the Admiralty, wrote between 1660 and 1669. Both moved in the upper social circles, but while Evelyn wrote mainly about political matters of national importance, Pepys gave more attention to everyday activities. From the seventeenth and eighteenth centuries the diaries of clergymen have survived in especially large numbers, reflecting their generally higher level of education and literacy than many of their contemporaries. Josselin of Essex, Woodforde of Norfolk, and the travelling preachers George Fox and John Wesley all produced diaries which survived and were published.[6]

Diaries shade over into autobiographies, many of which were produced by members of the working classes of the nineteenth century as acts of religious self-justification. Autobiographies may, in general, have been written with the firm intention that they should survive and be published, especially those of the upper and middle classes, and are firmly linked to the cultural changes associated with the rise of a reading public. For this reason the genres of autobiography and novel, for example, are sometimes difficult to distinguish. It should also be noted that personal diaries and records may be closely linked with official records when the person held official position, and in some cases records of official actions are to be found in private papers.[7]

In this section I shall examine how one particular diary – that of Ralph Josselin – has been used in historical research, and I will show how the quality appraisal criteria can be used to assess its value as evidence. In order to do this, I shall first review these criteria as they apply generally to personal documents.

The first criterion – authenticity – is of fundamental importance in the consideration of personal documents, perhaps more so than in any other type of document. It is of course of fundamental importance to know who is supposed to have written a diary or letter, and so the question of authorship needs always to be given particular attention. This is especially true in the case of the writings of the famous. In the early 1980s German and British newspapers announced the discovery of extensive wartime diaries ascribed to Adolf Hitler which would, if genuine, have been invaluable to historians. Despite concerns about their authenticity, as their provenance was unclear, a prominent British historian examined them and announced them to be genuine. Subsequently, following chemical testing on the paper and ink, it was realised that they were modern forgeries and that those who had bought the diaries had been duped.[8]

The question of the authorship of diaries also occurs when, as is often the case, they are incomplete or unsigned. In these cases, the identity of the supposed author must be inferred from other sources before the question of forgery can even be considered – and assuming the document to be correctly ascribed to a particular author, the question of soundness needs also to be considered. Sir Lewis Namier's study of eighteenth-century politics involved the use of 500 volumes of papers belonging to the Duke of Newcastle, which had been deposited at the British Museum. The Duke had kept accounts in his personal papers of how the Treasury secret service fund had been spent, including the quarterly payments to himself. Namier's problem was to discern the authorship of the papers, which were written in a number of different hands and some of which were rough notes or copies of final accounts. Newcastle employed a number of secretaries to keep and write his accounts and to provide copies to the King, and Namier had to assess the identity of each hand and the role of the Duke in their compilation before he could reconstruct a coherent and meaningful set of accounts. Through careful consideration of handwriting, Namier infers the role of John Roberts, H. V. Jones and the Duke himself, and goes on to make further inferences about the nature of the lost final accounts.[9]

The authenicity of a diary may also be questioned when there is the possibility that someone other than the author has edited or suppressed the document. Members of the family of the author, for example, may destroy sections that they find embarrassing to themselves or which place the author in a poor light, and this may be especially likely if there is an intention to publish. The wife of the Reverend Kilvert, for example, is reputed to have destroyed two large sections of her husband's diary, much of which referred to their courtship.[10]

The issue of credibility involves not only the assessment of the factual accuracy of diaries and letters as descriptions of the world, but also the question of the extent to which, accurate or not, they sincerely report the author's perceptions and feelings. Indeed, the latter question is often the more important. As Burnett has argued in his discussion of working-class authobigraphies, 'The autobiographer's version of what happened to himself possesses a personal validity which is different in kind from any second-hand account, however skilled the reporter may be in techniques of observation and analysis. . . . The very partiality of the account is, therefore, part of its value.'[11] The value of personal documents, that is to say, lies often in their status as recollected experience rather than recorded fact.

Assessment of sincerity rests upon a knowledge of the motivation behind the personal document. Was a diary, for example, produced purely to record an individual's innermost thoughts, or did the author have at least one eye on publication? Diaries which enter the public sphere through publication result in a public reassessment of the author's character and life; for this reason those diarists who intend their diaries to be published may seek to present a particular definition of themselves in the pages of the diary in an attempt to pre-empt this reassessment. Even purely personal diaries are motivated for a variety of reasons and will involve various attempts at self-presentation. Some diaries, for example, are little more than account books, in which details of purchases and payments are recorded, while others are aids to memory which record notes on people and events which are, for whatever reason, important to the diarist. Numerous diaries of the seventeenth and eighteenth centuries, however, reflected the religious introspection of the diarist and an attempt to reflect on his or her behaviour in the light of religious precepts in order to try to improve conduct in the future.[12] Diarists rarely seem to record the reason why they keep a diary, and so this has to be inferred from the contents of their writings or from whatever else is known of their lives.

It is possible that only certain types of people are likely to keep a diary: the methodical and introspective routines of diary-keeping may appeal mainly to those with a methodical and introspective character. Bagley has argued that to keep a diary 'the diary has to become a major, if not the most important, interest in the diarist's life'.[13] The diarist, therefore, will tend to have some strong practical or literary interest for maintaining a personal record for any period of time; and self-justification or the impulse to record what are regarded as important personal or family events might be expected to dominate the motivation of many diarists and autobiographers. People reflect on whole periods of their life and then construct, or reconstruct, diary entries in the light of the self-image that they have built for themselves. As people periodically reconsider themselves, so their perception of what to record and how to record it will change. As the project of keeping a diary becomes incorporated in a person's self-perception, so the diary may become more of a self-justificatory autobiography rather than a daily record of events: the construction of the diary becomes a central element in his or her moral career and self-definition.[14]

If the credibility of personal documents may be questioned on the basis of the typicality of those who produce them, then it may be seen how important it is to raise the issue of the representativeness of the surviving diaries themselves. By their very nature, such personal documents as diaries and letters are dispersed among numerous hands, and few private or public archives have large collections of surviving documents. Indexes to collections are few in number and rarely comprehensive, though some attempts have been made to produce printed bibliographies. Matthews's *British Diaries* and *British Autobiographies*, supplementing Ponsonby's works, have attempted to survey surviving documents, but coverage is partial – concentrating on published volumes and public archives – and both Matthews and Ponsonby are now outdated.[15] Typically the researcher who wishes to make use of diaries must attempt to construct a list of potential sources from which to sample. In his study of trench warfare in the First World War, Ashworth, for example, had to rely on the patchy survival of published diaries and reminiscences of private soldiers. In order to compensate for some of the more obvious problems of representativeness, he aimed to get source material that represented the range and number of divisions operating as part of the British Expeditionary Force.[16]

In recent years, existing bibliographical sources have been considerably supplemented by the work of Burnett and his colleagues in discovering and listing working-class autobiographies, which are not well covered in published sources and often remain in private hands.[17] Building from existing sources and undertaking a systematic search of major archives as well as advertising for information on privately held documents, they sought to identify books, articles, pamphlets and manuscripts of autobiographical material. Burnett recognises the atypicality of those who wrote – predominantly skilled manual workers and upper domestic servants – but feels that, overall, autobiographies survive in large enough numbers to make the construction of a representative sample possible. Vincent's commentary on the same source material tellingly adds that 'The one major silence is that of women'.[18] Very few of the surviving diaries were by women and Vincent concludes: 'The answer must lie . . . in the absence among women of the self-confidence required to undertake the unusual act of writing an autobiography, and in particular from the increasing exclusion of women from most forms of working class organisations . . . which provided the training and stimulus for self-expression for so many of the male autobiographers.'[19]

In the case of letters, it is even more difficult to ensure that a sample is representative, as indexed or calendared letters are even more heavily biased towards the upper classes than are diaries. In research on letters, there is often little alternative but to construct a selection of source material from scratch. In their classic study of migration and settlement amongst Polish arrivals in the United States,[20] Thomas and Znaniecki used, among other sources, letters exchanged between migrants and those still in Poland. There is little information in the original book on how the letters were obtained, but it was subsequently disclosed that many were purchased through a journal published 'for the benefit and enlightenment of the peasants'.[21] Further letters were obtained by an assistant in Poland, but about a third of this extra material was lost when the assistant was forced to flee the country when the First World War broke out. Thomas said: 'I have speculated on how much difference in our final results this loss meant, but on the whole I do not think it was very much.'[22] No reasons are given for his coming to this judgement, though equally there are no reasons to assume that the loss in itself introduced a bias. More problematic for this kind of research is that the inherent bias in letters made available to researchers, especially when payment is involved, is unknown.

More fortunate in research using letters was Towler, who explored popular religious atteitudes from the whole archived collection of letters sent to the Bishop of Woolwich after the publication, in 1963, of his book *Honest to God*.[23] These letters were unsolicited by either their recipient or the researcher, and all 4,000 letters received had been retained by the bishop. Nevertheless, while having a representative – indeed, complete – collection of all the letters written, Towler did not have a representative sample of the British population; and those who wrote letters must be expected to differ in certain respects from those who did not. The researcher who wishes to make use of such material must ensure, as Towler did, that they are adequate for their particular purpose and that the degree of unrepresentativeness can at least be estimated.

The issue of literal meaning poses serious problems in those personal documents which are handwritten or which have been at all damaged. This is further exacerbated in many diaries whose contents were intended to remain secret from contemporaries by the use of codes or personal shorthand. Samuel Pepys, for example, entered many sections of his daily diary in code form. Even where there is no deliberate intent to conceal, the use of a shorthand script may make a reading difficult, especially when personal names are abbreviated. Ralph Josselin, in his diary, used 'K' to refer to the King and 'OC' to refer to Oliver Cromwell, as well as using numerous initials for local and less well-known people. He also used abbreviations such as 'agst' for 'against' and 'go' for 'glory', and archaic written forms such as 'i' for 'j' and 'ye' for 'the'.[24]

Shorthand and abbreviations are used by diarists because the meaning of the contractions is obvious to them and there is no need to write them in full. For the same reason, many words and phrases which appear ambiguous or obscure to a later reader may have been perfectly clear to the author. Similarly with letters, the writer assumes a background of taken-for-granted assumptions, shared by the intended reader, which make it unnecessary to spell everything out in detail. Writer and recipient share a particular cultural world in which elaboration is frequently unnecessary, not only in relation to particular people and events, but also in relation to certain social conventions and institutions. A writer who says, in a letter to a close friend, 'Don't forget to send me your club' will not need to make explicit the fact that he or she is the collector for a hospital savings association or a Christmas savings club – this will be obvious and apparent to the recipient. For the researcher, however, considerable investigation may be required before the meaning of the text can be discerned.

The assumptions drawn on by the writer of a personal document will reflect the genre and sub-genre of the document. Thomas and Znaniecki, for example, recognised five different types of family letters among those they studied.[25] In the 'ceremonial' letter, the language and style was especially formal and elaborate, as the letter had been sent to mark a special family occasion such as a wedding or a funeral and served as a substitute for a speech in a face-to-face meeting. 'Sentimental' letters, on the other hand, were intended to revive the feelings of the individual, independently of any special occasion. Such letters were simply ways of keeping in touch and maintaining family solidarity. Closely related were 'informing' letters, which had the distinctly practical aim of passing on information about what had happened to other family members. Family 'business' letters were also practical, though discussing details of jobs, family property, and so on. Finally, they identified the 'literary' letter, where the writer seemed more likely to be practising literary techniques and to engage in deliberate aesthetic stylisation.

Autobiographies, also, fall into a number of sub-genres. In considering working-class autobiographies Vincent identifies two major types: the spiritual and the 'oral tradition' autobiography.[26] The spiritual autobiography originated in the religious conflicts of the seventeenth century and continued well into the nineteenth. In such a document the author aims to discuss his or her discovery of God and how the truth of the Bible illuminates the author's own experiences and salvation. Such autobiographies often tell of redemption from poverty and drunkenness, and the whole tone is didactic with a strong stress on moral values. Autobiographies in the oral tradition, on the other hand, are essentially written versions of the old ballad and story-telling tradition in which people pass on stories of their life much as they might have told them orally among family and friends. Such autobiographies, argues Vincent, were generally attempts to record events and reminiscences for grandchildren – something not possible for most people before widespread literacy.

In a related book, Burnett adds a third type, the political or radical autobiographies of those involved in the labour movement. By contrast with the spiritual autobiographies, the radical autobiographies have as their main theme the idea that 'power lies in the hands of the people, and that through organisation, self-help and education the new Jerusalem can be built in this world.'[27] Such writings were very much a minority phenomenon but nevertheless constitute a distinct sub-genre of working-class autobiography.

Although the motivation of the author is a particularly important factor in explaining the choice of genre, it is also necessary to consider the intended audience and the form of publication. Working-class autobiographers who wrote for their local community and were dependent on its support were perhaps more likely to adopt assumptions and conventions which would differ from those writing for a middle-class audience and, perhaps, religious sponsors.

The interpretative understanding of a particular text goes beyond the identification of genre, though this is a central part of the process. An adequate interpretation of the meaning of a document draws on all the issues of authenticity, credibility, representativeness and literal interpretation to achieve a reconstruction of the intended meaning of the text and its reception by particular audiences. The difficulties involved in this task can best be illustrated through a particular study, and I shall use Alan Macfarlane's discussion of Ralph Josselin to this end.

Macfarlane is critical of the prevailing view among sociologists and historians writing on the development of English society. This view holds, he argues, that the sixteenth century was crucial in the transition from feudalism to capitalism, as it saw the emergence of a capitalist peasantry. Macfarlane's argument is that the concept of a peasantry has no application to England and that many of the features of capitalist modernity can be traced back many centuries further.[28] This argument is developed through the use of parish registers and other parish level data, and it is exemplified through extracts from the diary of Ralph Josselin.[29]

Josselin was an Essex vicar who owned land and farmed in his parish of Earls Colne through much of the second half of the seventeenth century. Macfarlane's book *The Family Life of Ralph Josselin* was based on a copy of the original diary kept by Josselin, Macfarlane having rejected a published copy of 1908 which concentrated only on political opinions and involvement. The copy that Macfarlane used was made in the 1930s and was in private hands until deposited in the Essex Record Office. Macfarlane made various checks on the diary and believed the copy to be both authentic and sound. Only later, when preparing the copy for publication, did he discover it to be inauthentic – about one-half of the original diary was not included in the copy. This discovery posed problems not only for the analysis presented in Macfarlane's book, but also meant that he had to reject the copy and seek to publish an authentic transcript of the original.

The copy had been produced by the owner of the original, Colonel Probert, who had reduced it in length by cutting out almost all the repeated religious utterances and anything which he regarded as offensive or bizarre. For example, details of the worm infestation of the Josselin family and of Josselin's suppurating navel were suppressed. Examples of religious sentiments excised are 'A drunkard came into my house, lord thy name be blessed in keeping mee from that sin' and 'the lord make his word effectual upon me and my people, and grant that wee may worke with god and prevaile with him for the naciun and mercyes for familyes for soule and body'.[30]

Macfarlane claims that 'The editor's method was to snip and re-stick passages, but sometimes they were stuck in the wrong order and dates were muddled'.[31] While being labelled 'A full transcript' on the front cover, the Probert copy was highly misleading.

The task facing Macfarlane therefore was to obtain and publish the original diary in full. It had been acquired, it was believed, by the lord of the manor of Earls Colne in the eighteenth century and had stayed in that family until it had been lent or stolen in 1850. Later in the century the family subsequently received the diary back from a London dealer in second-hand books, into whose hands it had fallen. Nothing of its history is known during the time it was missing.

Having obtained permission to use the original, Macfarlane had to try to convert it into a publishable text which was an authentic copy. The original was of course handwritten, and so certain conventions were followed which would show the original line- and page-breaks on the different-sized printed page. To aid the task of literal understanding three hundred years after the diary had been written, it was necessary to alter some of Joselin's abbreviations, while indicating that the alteration had been made. Macfarlane was concerned that, having himself been caught out by an inauthentic copy, he would publish a copy of the highest authenticity. Particular problems arose where parts of the diary were torn or frayed and words were missing, and Macfarlane notes that the diary seemed to have deteriorated since being 'copied' in the 1930s, although he could not be sure that the words in that copy were an accurate reflection of the contents of the diary at that time.

How, then, did Macfarlane use the diary in his own work? The diary concentrates on religious matters and refers to additional material in notebooks and almanacs which have not survived. Josselin interweaves these religious concerns with an account of his family life and local and national events of the Civil War and Restoration periods. Macfarlane's original book, based on the inauthentic copy of the diary, showed that Josselin was a rentier with a home farm and that he was a rationalistic, individualist capitalist in his outlook. To the extent that Josselin's views were typical of small landowners, Macfarlane argues, the idea of a peasantry is singularly inappropriate to describe the English situation. The question of representativeness is, of course, crucial. Josselin was untypical of other small farmers because of the very fact that he kept a diary, because of his university education, and because he was a Puritan vicar. But Macfarlane claims that these facts do not detract from the credibility of his account of the life of a small-scale owner-occupier farmer.[32]

A primary concern of Macfarlane was to outline Josselin's family life, and he uses the diary to reconstruct not only the household and farm accounts, but also the life-cycle demography of the family and the social meanings of kinship. His concern with demographic matters was intended to supplement parish register family reconstitution methods, and can be illustrated through his analysis of Josselin's family size. Josselin married in 1640 at 23 years of age,[33] and he and his wife had ten children in twenty-one years, before they stopped increasing the size of their family in 1663. A problem that Macfarlane begins with, therefore, is the extent to which the couple used contraceptive or family-planning methods, and whether the end of what Josselin terms 'breeding' was due to a deliberate decision or to his wife's arrival at the menopause. Macfarlane concluded that breast feeding may have been used in a deliberate way to prevent conception, and that abortions may have been induced towards the end of the child-rearing period. However, Josselin's silence about sexual matters and his wife's menstruation made it difficult to be precise.

In looking at the quality of kinship relationships, the diary should be especially informative. Macfarlane notes that Josselin writes more about the family when he is away from home than when at home. Whole years pass at home without any mention of the children: are these 'meaningful silences' evidence of a lack of concern or of a deep and taken-for-granted affection? He infers that Josselin and his wife had a close relationship without any sharp domestic division of labour: important decisions were taken jointly, there were shared friends and leisure interests, and both were involved in child-rearing, the major differences being Josselin's greater involvement than his wife in land and property management. Macfarlane also notes that a wealthy household with servants was unlikely to have many 'housework' tasks divided between husband and wife. The rather limited concern for wider kin which is apparent in Josselin's diary, argues Macfarlane, shows that the nuclear family was of more importance than the extended kinship network. The only extended kin with whom close relations were sustained were those who were also defined as 'friends'. That is to say, Josselin's diary shows that the seventeenth century was not dominated by the extended family. Members of the nuclear family households were selective about those of their kin with whom they sustained close links.

When Macfarlane discovered the full version of the diary, he recognised that certain changes in his account of Josselin's life were necessary, especially in relation to his millenarian beliefs and to his state of health. The broad picture of family and kinship, however, remained intact: 'On the whole . . . it would seem that the full diary adds further documentation to support many of the arguments sketched in the analytic work, rather than contradicting its conclusions'.[34]

However, major attention had to be given to the whole question of Josselin's credibility as a witness, regardless of which version of the diary is used: can we rely on what he tells us as an accurate and sincere account of the world as he saw it? Macfarlane is able to check the diary's credibility in many factual areas by comparing Josselin's observations against other local sources. Josselin did fail to mention some local events which appear in other records, but Macfarlane claims that the errors were generally slight copying mistakes rather than serious mistakes of substance. Some problems arise, however, from Josselin's selective attention to aspects of village life. Examples are Josselin's underestimation of the level of convicted theft in the area, as compared with the quarter sessions records, and the fact that he mentions by name only about one in twenty members of the parish. It is, equally, the case that there is no way of discovering whether Josselin failed to mention important matters which are also missing from other records. On the other hand, Josselin records a number of local events which are unrecorded elsewhere. He mentions, for example, a number of baptisms, marriages and burials which do not appear in the parish registers, though it is difficult to know which source is to be believed, as Josselin was ultimately responsible for the registers as well.

Macfarlane's study of Josselin and his discussion of the diary as a source illustrate exceptionally well the advantages and limitations of this type of documentary material. Of particular importance is his examination of the ways in which the question of authenticity impinges on the interpretation that can be placed upon the diary. Such questions arise in relation to all of the personal documents discussed in this section, and becomes especially pressing when the document enters the public sphere through publication. Whether or not publication is by the author personally, the very act of publication blurs the line between personal and private documents. A diary has already 'escaped' its author's intent by being committed to paper, but a published diary enters a further series of escapes in the publishing houses and distributors. The personal document becomes an element in mass communication.

Photographs and visual sources

I have argued at a number of places in this book that visual documents are to be considered in the same light as handwritten or printed and typeset documents. They are texts whose meaning must be disclosed like any other. It is, perhaps, in the area of personal documents that they acquire their greatest significance – certainly in terms of numbers – as personal portraits and photographic records have survived in such large numbers.

Medieval forms of professional art involved tempera, where pigment mixed with egg yolk or size is applied to a plaster or chalk surface, and fresco, where a water-colour is applied to a plaster surface before it dries. Such techniques were particularly appropriate to the grand scale of architectural painting under State or Church patronage, and it was not until the development of oil painting that the wealthy families produced by capitalist expansion incorporated painting into the personal sphere of the household.[35] Although the technique of mixing pigments with oil was known in the ancient world, it was not until the sixteenth century in Europe that it became a major art form. Oil painting on canvas rapidly created new ways of seeing and recording the world, establishing the modern ideas of perspective and pictorial likeness. Oil, unlike other mediums, could convey 'reality' and substance in the people and objects portrayed. The European aristocracy and merchants – especially those of Florence – used their huge wealth to sponsor artists and stocked their houses with paintings. 'Artistic images, through the techniques of oil painting, became commodities and possessions.'[36] The artists' patrons sought, above all, images of themselves and their property – images appropriate to an age of 'possessive individualism'[37] – and the idea of the true likeness became established as the principal criterion for assessing a painting.[38]

Family portraiture remained essentially the prerogative of the wealthy, until photography made personal portraits more widely available. The principles of the camera obscura, like those of oil painting, had been well known for many years, but it was not until the nineteenth century that a technique was devised for allowing the camera image to be recorded in a permanent form.[39] Professional portraits and other artists had used the camera obscura as an aid to accurate drawing, and during the eighteenth and nineteenth centuries projected images were a popular form of entertainment. Chemical research had discovered ways of producing images of objects on light-sensitive materials, but not until the 1820s was this combined with the technology of the camera obscura. Camera images were initially too faint to produce a permanent image in the available exposure times, and the earliest experiments of Niépce involved eight-hour exposures. In 1827 Niépce met Louis Daguerre, who owned a Parisian theatrical diorama of paintings produced with the help of a camera obscura, and it was the co-operation between these two that produced the first major leap in photographic technology.

Daguerre invented a technique which involved more sensitive recording equipment and hence much shorter exposure times. In 1839 he patented the daguerreotype technique for recording architecture and landscape in black and white, and modern photography was born. Exposure times were still around five or six minutes, and portraiture was not possible until improvements in lenses made a much brighter image available. From the early 1830s, however, William Fox-Talbot was working on a technique which produced a negative image from which numerous positive copies could be made, and it was Fox-Talbot's technique which became the basis of modern photographic technology.

Although amateurs began to make use of photography in the 1850s, it remained almost exclusively a technique for the professional and the serious amateur. Francis Frith, one of the more important commercial photographers, travelled widely and produced large numbers of landscape and townscape photographs. In the same period, Roger Fenton and Mathew Brady undertook photographic coverage of the Crimean War and the American Civil War. Though becoming progressively cheaper, portraiture required more complex technology than landscape, and it remained an exclusively professional, studio skill until the 1880s. From the mid-1850s, studio photographers began to produce small portraits, 4 by 2 inches – the so-called 'carte-de-visite' – and, later, the larger 'cabinet' cards, 6 by 4 inches. These forms of professional portraiture, produced fairly cheaply, rapidly became popular among the middle and working classes. They were highly stylised in both pose and background, as were portraits in oil, and the rigid poses reflected not simply the preferences of the photographers and the character of the sitters, but also the long exposure times and the mechanical supporting devices employed to prevent sitters from moving.

Technical advances in lens and shutter design from the 1870s allowed a closer approximation to 'instantaneous' photography, in which very short exposure times allowed moving subjects to be photographed. Professional photographers such as Peter Emerson began to experiment with naturalistic rather than posed photographs, and it became possible to produce a documentary record of ordinary human situations. Such applications, however, produced private, commercial documents rather than the personal documents under consideration in this chapter.

Not until George Eastman simplified and cheapened basic photographic technology did photography spread beyond the professionals and the wealthier classes. It was the introduction in 1888 of Eastman's 'box' camera and cheap roll film, under the trade name 'Kodak', that introduced the era of amateur 'snapshot' photography.[40] A whole new mode of photography, one which tied it to the routines and practices of everyday family life, existed alongside the commercial, studio mode of photography. Amateurs could 'point and shoot', producing documents of family life which differed in almost all respects from the documentary record created by the studio photographer.

Snapshot photography rapidly spread from the United States to Britain and to the rest of Europe. Major events in the life of the family, holidays, and weekends were all recorded on film by family members themselves. But snapshot photography, as will be shown below, was more than simply picture-taking. It was part and parcel of a particular style of family life. The heyday of the black-and-white snapshot was the period from 1910 to the 1950s, 'the period when cheap cameras were in universal use for the simple purpose of recording private lives'.[41] After this time, advances in film and camera technology – above all, improved lenses and colour film – became available to family photographers and initiated a new era of family photography. Many amateurs could produce photographs of a high quality, and even those who persisted with the 'point and shoot' style were able to produce a technically superior product. 35 mm cameras and multi-exposure 110 cameras have allowed people to produce larger numbers of acceptable photographs and so have made it less likely that each photograph will be lovingly retained in a family album or collection. In an age of relative affluence the colour photograph, unlike the black-and-white snapshot, is disposable.

For a time, the moving ciné film became popular among enthusiastic amateurs, though it remained very much the professional medium discussed in the previous chapter. Video recording, widely used in the mass media from the 1980s, has begun to achieve the position once held by amateur ciné, but it has not yet achieved the popularity of snapshot photography. While amateurs seem happy to put up with the jerky and erratic movement produced by a poorly handled camera, much as they tolerated the poor quality of most black-and-white snapshots, the disadvantage of moving film for amateurs is the special equipment necessary to view it. Printed photographs are self-contained documents, texts which are immediately visible and can be easily handled, stored and displayed within the personal sphere of the household. Moving photographs are none of these.

It is impossible to illustrate the use of personal pictorial source material in social research through case studies, as few good studies which rely predominantly on such material exist. I shall therefore discuss those few useful studies that exist only in terms of their relevance to specific appraisal criteria. For this reason the appraisal criteria will be considered in a slightly different order from that followed in other parts of this book. First, the problems of authenticity and credibility will be looked at together; this will lead to the raising of certain aspects of the question of meaning, and especially that of literal meaning. I will then go on the the wider issue of interpretative understanding, and finally I shall consider the question of representativeness.

The question of authenticity is frequently seen as a particularly acute problem when assessing oil paintings, especially when considering 'old masters'. When large amounts of money can be made from forgery – or by copying in the style of an artist – the question of authenticity is bound to be raised.[42] But the authenticity problems also arise out of the purely technical issues of copying. Is a reproduction of an oil painting, for example, an authentic copy of the original? And does the mere fact of reproduction alter the authenticity of the original itself?

Berger among others has argued that, before reproduction by camera became possible, the painting was a unique aesthetic item. Once reproduction became possible, the painting became simply 'the original' of its numerous copies – it acquires a distinct market value as an original, and this price is bolstered by studying its provenance so as to establish its authenticity as an original. By virtue of the possibility of technical reproduction, therefore, the oil painting becomes an authentic, and thereby valuable, 'work of art' rather than simply an authentic expression of the artist's subjectivity.[43] As we have seen in all other examples of documents considered, the document 'escapes' its author's intent and hold once it enters the public sphere, and its meaning comes to be increasingly defined by its various audiences. In the case of the oil painting, argues Berger, the crucial question is no longer the authenticity of the image in the picture as an expression of the artist's perception; rather it is that of the authenticity of the physical fabric of the picture.

The reproduced painting also emerges as a new form of art within the household. The 'same' image can enter into many homes through printed reproductions, and the image becomes part of each person's home – its meaning is interpreted by a different, and highly differentiated, audience. 'The painting enters each viewer's house. There it is surrounded by his [sic] wallpaper, his furniture, his mementoes. It enters the atmosphere of his family. It becomes their talking point. It lends its meaning to their meaning. At the same time it enters a million other houses and, in each of them, is seen in a different context.'[44]

The photograph is, by its very nature, a reproducible medium, and the whole idea of an 'original' photograph is something of a contradiction. The authenticity and meaning of a photograph, even one developed and printed by the photographer, simply cannot be assimilated to the case of the painting. Even if the negative produced from the photographer's own film is regarded, for present purposes, as being the 'original', it is necessary to consider the fact that the printed version must necessarily be a 'copy'. Not only can technical faults arise in copying, but the very technology of dark-room reproduction requires that the printer exercise some discretion over exposure and development time. For this reason, many photographers prefer to undertake their own printing, so that the finished product conforms to their vision of the original subject-matter. But then the question of credibility is put forcibly in front of us. How credible is a photographic record of an event, even one which can be regarded as 'authentic'?

Any use of camera and dark-room equipment involves some technical control over lighting and exposure, and a degree of control over the subject. In combination, these factors mean that the photographer is an active agent in constructing the event that is recorded. 'The camera never lies', we are told, but the photographer can. The photographer's active role in constructing the meaning of the situation leads to the conclusion that, whether intentionally or not, the photograph is a selective account of reality – as selective as any other account. Within the technical constraints of the medium, the photographer is able to emphasise or minimise particular aspects of the scene or to alter its whole appearance, even without dark-room 'trickery'. Props and poses are central to the photographer's art, as are alterations of light and shade and variations in focus. Once an occasion is past, all that may survive is the photographer's contrived version of the happening.

Similar issues of selectivity arise with the production of oil paintings, where the artist also has control over what is recorded on the canvas. This involves not simply a control over specific representations in the picture – distorting or inaccurately depicting a person's face, for instance – but an ability to shape whole ways of seeing. The conventions of perspective drawing, for example, were unique to European art, being first established in the Renaissance. This technique centres everything in the picture upon the eye of the observer and so corresponds to our modern subjective perception of reality. The introduction of perspective drawing, in place of conventions which tried to depict a scene from numerous different angles or from some transcendental position, was part of a reconstruction of prevailing cultural patterns in a more 'rational' direction. The camera works on precisely this principle, recording the basic shape of the world as it would appear to any one else standing in the photographer's place. Perspective drawing and photography have, therefore, in European cultures, a high prima facie credibility. For this reason, modern artists can question prevailing ways of seeing only by departing from these conventions, just as photographers can do so only by resorting to photomontage or other ways of altering the camera image.

Western culture places great emphasis on the photograph as a credible record of the world, particularly in such matters as a person's physical appearance. The police, for example, will issue a photograph, a photofit or even a sketch of a wanted person in preference to a verbal description, as the visual image is regarded as more accurate and more memorable. Studies of other cultures, however, have shown how much of an acquired cultural trait this is. In his fieldwork on Dowayo linguistic categories, Barley tried to use pictures of lions and leopards. He discovered that the Dowayo could not tell the animals apart in pictures, despite being able to do so in reality and even despite being able to identify them from preserved parts of their bodies. They could not even recognise the difference between men and women in a drawing. The only forms of visual art in Dowayo society were the photographs that they were required to include on their identity cards, issued by the Cameroon government. Barley shows that, partly because of the absence of photographers in the area and partly because of their inability to discriminate visual images, many people would share the same photograph. This practice was possible because the Dowayo officials responsible for checking identity cards were unable to tell whether a particular photograph bore any resemblance to the bearer of the card.[45]

Such considerations might inevitably shape the researcher's interpretation of a particular visual image. At the level of literal understanding, for example, a photograph of a Victorian family may appear to give us evidence about dress styles, affluence, and demeanour, and also about attitudes, intimacy and formality in family relations. Similarly, the background may provide evidence on street activity and forms of transport, and also on occupational and residential segregation. But can these perceptions be relied upon? Were the family dressed in 'Sunday best' and adopting a pose, and what part did the photographer play in constructing the scene?

These questions will be considered more fully below in relation to the issue of interpretative meaning, but it should be clear that further aspects of literal interpretation are involved. It is important to gain some idea of who or what is depicted in a photograph. This may be extremely difficult, as studio photographs and snapshots are often labelled inadequately if at all. It may even be difficult to discern the sex of young children in Victorian and Edwardian photographs, as in many families both boys and girls were clothed in dresses for the first years of their lives. Moreover the dating of photographs may be difficult if they are not labelled. And if the date is estimated from the dress styles of the subjects an inevitable circularity occurs: in order to date the photograph, we must assume that the dress styles accurately reflect the fashions current at the time the photograph was taken, but this may be precisely what we want to question by dating the photograph accurately. The basic problem is that the more internal information which is used to date or identify a photograph, the less information there is left to serve as evidence in our research. In such circumstances, recourse to external evidence is necessary – for example by checking the address of the photographer shown on a studio portrait against lists of photographers in trade directories or surviving business records.[46]

The central problem of interpretative meaning in handling personal photographs is that of photographic genres. It is around this that all other considerations revolve. In relation to the argument of this chapter, only two genres need be considered: professional photography and 'home mode' photography. Professional photography encompasses a wide range of activities from commercial studio photography, through postcards and news reportage, to art photography. In the context of the personal documents considered here, it is only studio photography that is relevant. The 'studio' in question may be high street premises or a booth at the end of a seaside pier, but the defining characteristic of studio photography, as I use that term, is that the photographer takes pictures of private individuals as a commercial service to them. Common extensions to the studio mode are when the photographer sets up a temporary studio in a school, for example, or visits a private house to take photographs. This is to say, the central characteristics of studio photography are to be found in the social context in which it occurs and the social conventions by which it is shaped.

'Home mode' photography comprises photographs 'produced and accumulated by and for family members within the context of family life'.[47] The photographs are produced for personal rather than for public or artistic use, and it is no coincidence that the golden age of the snapshot, from 1910 to the 1950s, is the same as the high point of the conventional family household and the ideal of domesticity and home-making.[48] The social context for home mode photography, therefore, is the family itself. Snapshots are taken by and for family members and are retained within the domestic sphere, typically within a family album.

In addition to the normal studio photograph, there is a further sub-type of professional photograph which frequently finds its place in the family album. King calls this the commercial snapshot.[49] These are photographs produced by commercial photographers at seaside resorts, the photographer taking unsolicited photographs on the arrival of families at the railway or coach station, sitting on the beach, or strolling along the promenade. Such part-time photographers often produced pictures which were technically no better than those taken by families themselves, but they were frequently bought as mementoes by families with no camera of their own. The typical collection of family photographs will consist of a mixture of studio pictures, home mode snapshots, and commercial snapshots.

The studio photographer aims to achieve a considerable degree of control over the subjects of the photograph and the context in which they are photographed. Professionals generally strive for a degree of technical and aesthetic competence which most amateur 'snapshotters' would not seek; for this reason, great attention is given to the film and lighting quality, and much greater ruthlessness is exercised in discarding technically imperfect pictures. The photographer's level of control is especially apparent in the choice of background and pose – central elements in the aesthetics of studio photography. It has often been pointed out that the poses, props and backdrops used by photographers vary over time, as fashions and preferences among them change; and the subjects of studio photographs have in general acquiesced in the aesthetic contexts chosen for the pictures. For example, as Steel argues, Victorian photographers of the 1850s invariably posed their subjects sitting in a chair and holding a book,[50] whereas by the 1860s the preferred pose was standing with one hand resting on the back of a chair, and much greater attention was given to the use of columns and curtains as backdrops. In the 1870s, studio photographers aimed to create an 'outdoor' impression through the use of a rustic bridge and stile, to which were later added artificial rocks, swings, and even railway carriages to create the impression of travel. By the 1890s, backdrops became even more extravagant, with the use of cockatoos and bicycles.

Clothing was the one element in a studio photograph over which the subject had some control, though people's choice of clothing reflected their own acceptance of the criteria of the studio genre and the aura of formality which was attached to a visit to the photographers. Studio styles differed for adult and child photography. Adults were invariably dressed in 'Sunday best' formal attire, and rarely had their photographs taken in ordinary, everyday clothes. Where adults were depicted in everyday rather than formal clothes, it was usually in a military or some other uniform. By contrast, conventions of baby photography surrounded the extent of undressing, and the completely naked baby on a white fur rug became a studio fashion in the 1890s. With older children the conventions of adult photography were followed, and children appear in formal dress or in school or scouting uniforms.

The conventions of the studio express the attempt to convey a particular image of the subject and, in doing so, draw heavily on the taken-for-granted assumptions of family and gender roles. Photographer and subject connived to present a stylised presentation: who is seated and who standing symbolise authority relations, and whether the subjects are smiling or serious can convey an image of respectability or convivality. Such conventions and usages reflect the attempt to construct and define a particular image for public presentation within an accepted framework of norms and values. Nevertheless, a close examination of studio photographs can often disclose discrepancies between the image and the reality: a middle-class drawing-room setting for people in ill-fitting and shabby clothes can signal social aspirations rather than established social standing.

Home mode photography is far less governed by conventions of technical perfection, but it has its own distinct, aesthetic conventions. Snapshots produced by family members themselves are produced almost exclusively within the personal sphere and reflect, even more closely, the assumptions and norms of the family itself. Yet the lesser degree of technical control which home mode photographers have over their photographs can make them important pointers to other aspects of family life. The snapshot, like any document, escapes its author the moment the shutter is released, and its meaning for others can often lie in what it unintentionally conveys about the family.

Family photographs are intended by their authors to buttress family pride and to sustain a particular sense of identity and definition of reality.[51] Family photography is often geared to presenting the image of 'the family' as a corporate entity, over and above its individual members. The solidity and substance of the family is indicated through the use of house fronts and porches as backdrops to symbolise the family's standing and territory. Wedding photos emphasise the unity of the two sides of the family, brought together in one place on this particular occasion and forming an image of the extended family that many members would like it to have in reality. The photograph is used by family members to stand for, and so create, a sense of group identity.

Home mode photography tends to be organised around specific events of importance to the family. Frequently these are formal rites of passage for family members, ceremonial occasions such as weddings, christenings, anniversaries and other family gatherings, but recurrent events such as holidays and Christmas celebrations are also important. Such events can be used to present a particular image of the family: children happily opening presents in front of the Christmas tree, or sitting on the beach during a sunny family holiday at the sea.[52]

It is also important to recognise the part played in family interaction by the very act of taking a snapshot. The end result, the photograph itself, may be almost incidental to the sense of cohesion and occasion that is created by taking the photograph. The act of getting out the camera and the ritual of posing the photograph serves to highlight the importance of the events as something worth remembering.

Musello draws on considerations such as these to identify three sub-genres in home mode photography.[53] In 'idealisation', there is formal posing in imitation of professional photography, a sub-genre often employed at family gatherings such as weddings. In 'natural portrayal', the intent is to record events 'as they actually happened', though the photographs may involve both candid and posed events; the 'reality' is frequently reconstructed for the camera after the event. In the 'demystification' sub-genre, the photographer aims to create an alternative image of a person, often through candid photography in situations which do not figure in the other two sub-genres – while sleeping, partially dressed, or in other 'embarrassing' situations. This form of photography is oriented by a recognition of the artificiality of much home mode photography, and is used as a minor countervailing theme to the other sub-genres.

Though artificial – as indeed all human products are – home mode photographs can tell the researcher a great deal about a family, so long as he or she is attuned to the conventions and sub-genres employed. Such an awareness enables the researcher to read beyond the surface appearance of the photograph to its deeper significance. There is a great deal that photographs do not tell us about their world. Hirsch argues, for example, that 'The prim poses and solemn faces which we associate with Victorian photography conceal the reality of child labour, women factory workers, whose long hours often brought about the neglect of their infants, nannies sedating their charges with rum, and mistresses diverting middle class fathers.'[54]

Of particular importance in interpretation is a knowledge of the representativeness of the photographs, which rests, in turn, on an understanding of why they were taken and why they were kept. Professional photographs have sometimes found their way into public or private archives, though this is far more common for photo-journalism and similar photographs, such as townscape and landscape photographs produced for postcard production. This is extremely unusual, on the other hand, for those produced within home mode photography.[55]

It is dangerous to assume that photographs which survive in archives and in private hands are representative of those that once existed. There will always be some degree of filtering on technical grounds, families retaining only the 'best' and discarding those which 'didn't come out'. Nevertheless, it is remarkable how often technically poor photographs are retained within a family collection, and King shows how the technical standards of most home mode photographers are extremely tolerant of such things as blurring, double exposure, poor lighting, tilted framing, and so on. King indeed goes so far as to suggest that such technical inadequacies are one of the main defining criteria of the genre.[56]

A central feature of home mode photography is the accumulation of a personal collection of photographs, though rarely are these available to researchers. The collection will arise from diverse sources, including pictures taken by the family, those sent by other family members, and those taken by professionals. Such collections are generally in inadequately labelled albums, but sometimes in a box or an old suitcase. 'Such a collection ostensibly permits home moders to recall, reflect on, share and compare these subjects over time, and rests on the implicit assumption that documenting and recalling such things is of inherent importance.'[57] Since photographs are used to reconstruct the self-images of individuals and families, the collection itself will be shaped by this same intent. Photographs, however good in technical or aesthetic terms, may be rejected and discarded if they do not 'fit' the image – and as the image changes over time, so the family photograph collection may be weeded and re-shaped.

The shape of the collection also reflects the family life cycle. A nuclear family collection may begin with the husband and wife taking pictures of one another, and proceed to young children and their development. As the children get older, the camera may come out only for major events, with a smaller number of pictures being taken. The family collection, therefore, will be patchy and fragmented, giving greater attention to some stages in the life cycle than others. Many such collections will also include a number of fragmentary photographs inherited from relatives, and so the family collection becomes a sedimented accumulation of fragmentary records structured around the life cycle typical of the family.

But family collections may become dispersed over the years with many items being permanently lost. An archaeological 'dig' into a family photograph album or box of snapshots may not be a dig through a representative selection of the photos taken or acquired by the family. Indeed, it may be extremely difficult for researchers to gain access to family collections. Photographs are generally subject to restricted access, unless they become available in flea markets and junk shops after house clearances. In the latter circumstances, their whole significance is changed, as the researcher does not know whether they have been weeded or if the seller has added photographs from other sources.

Family photographs, I have argued, are personal documents in exactly the same sense as, say, letters or a diary. Despite the fact that they are pictorial rather than alphanumeric, they are 'texts' which can be interpreted and assessed like any other text. Equally, like other personal documents, they may enter the public sphere through publication or exhibition; and the products of professional studio photography are, in any case, commercial documents produced within the private sphere of business. The categories introduced in figure 1.2 must be regarded as provisional guides to analysis and not as fixed and immutable categories.

In this book I have tried to illustrate the techniques of documentary analysis using a range of different sources. I have not presented detailed accounts of the techniques of content analysis, semiotic interpretation, chemical dating, sampling, and so on. All of these techniques are adequately covered in specialist sources. My aim has been to highlight the common threads that run through the various uses to which documents can be put in social research. To this end, I have introduced the four quality-appraisal criteria of authenticity, credibility, representativeness and meaning, approaching them in a systematic way but varying the order of presentation slightly from one case to another. An understanding of the issues discussed is essential if a researcher is to make sensible use of documents, though experienced researchers do not, of course, typically proceed in the formal and systematic way I have outlined. The use of documents over a period of time ensures – or should ensure – that appreciation of these issues becomes second nature. Researchers raise only those of them that are relevant to the particular source they are handling. Even this they will do in an almost instinctive way, without consciously thinking through the headings I have introduced. However, a researcher coming to documentary research for the first time or faced with a need to assess another's use of documents in an unfamiliar area will, I hope, find the systematic approach outlined here useful. The book will also have served its purpose if its readers are later able to dispense with it and operate in a more flexible though informed way.

Notes

Chapter 1   Social Research and Documentary Sources

1 This is the argument of Jennifer Platt in 'Evidence and proof in documentary research', *Sociological Review*, 29/1 (1981), pp. 31–66. As will become apparent, I am greatly indebted to her path-breaking article.

2 Such conversation obviously involves the visual sense and perhaps tactile and olfactory senses as well. The point I am making is that the auditory sense is the primary channel in conversation.

3 P. Thompson, *The Voice of the Past* (Oxford University Press, 1978; 2nd edn 1988).

4 A computer dug up from the ground in a thousand years time could evidence many things about the culture that produced it, because it survives as a collection of pieces of metal, glass and so on. But such a computer would be extremely unlikely to convey any evidence of what information was contained in its memory before it was switched off.

5 See W. G. Hoskins, *The Making of the English Landscape* (Hodder & Stoughton, London, 1955); P. Coones and J. Patten, *The Penguin Guide to the Landscape of England and Wales* (Penguin, Harmondsworth, 1986); and for an interesting study using physical evidence to reconstruct pre-historic demography, J. D. Willigan and K. A. Lynch, *Sources and Methods of Historical Demography* (Academic Press, New York, 1982).

6 E. J. Webb, D. T. Campbell, R. D. Schwartz, and L. Sechrest, *Unobtrusive Measures* (Rand McNally, Chicago, 1966), pp. 40–1, 55.

7 Completed questionnaires and schedules may appear to qualify as documents, but the point must be emphasised that they are directly initiated by the observer in proximate access to the subjects of study. They may, however, become documents if they survive and are used by later researchers. For the purposes of this book they have not been considered as a separate class of document.

8 The discussion that follows draws heavily on the work of Platt, and of Langlois and Seignobos: see Platt, 'Evidence and proof', and C. V. Langlois

and C. Seignobos, *Introduction to the Study of History* (Duckworth, London, 1908).

9 R. Millar, *The Piltdown Men* (Gollancz, London, 1972).

10 See J. C. Mitchell, 'Case and situation analysis', *Sociological Review*, 31/2 (1983), pp. 187–211. Mitchell rightly rejects the search for typicality, but he is not arguing against the general question of the assessment of representativeness.

11 See the discussion of describing a rain dance in W. G. Runciman, *A Treatise on Social Theory* (Cambridge University Press, 1983), vol. I, pp. 60–3.

12 For a useful attempt at moving towards a theory of 'questionnairing' and interviewing, and a general discussion of coding, see N. Bateson, *Data Construction in Social Surveys* (Allen & Unwin, London, 1983). I draw heavily on the spirit of Bateson's argument in the following discussion.

13 A. L. Bowley and A. R. Burnett-Hurst, *Livelihood and Poverty* (Bell, London, 1915). Bowley first introduced the idea of sampling in his *An Elementary Manual of Statistics* (Macdonald & Evans, London, 1910); but see also the interesting account in Langlois and Seignobos, *Introduction to the Study of History*.

14 B. S. Rowntree, *Poverty: A Study of Town Life* (Macmillan, London, 1901); C. Booth, *Life and Labour of the People in London*, 17 vols. (Macmillan, London, 1902).

15 The degree of accuracy is, of course, unknown, but the probability that a sample will yield accurate results – termed the 'precision' – can be calculated for numerical data so long as certain conditions are met. This calculation of the 'standard error' assumes that variables are normally distributed, and various 'non-parametric' approaches have attempted to overcome this limitation.

16 C. Wright Mills, *The Sociological Imagination* (Oxford University Press, New York, 1959); and see T. Nichols, 'Social class: official, sociological and Marxist', in *Demystifying Social Statistics*, ed. J. Irvine, I. Miles and J. Evans (Pluto Press, London, 1979), pp. 152–71.

17 The major theories of meaning will be discussed in the next chapter.

18 Langlois and Seignobos, *Introduction to the Study of History*, p. 17.

19 Ibid.

20 Thompson, *Voice of the Past*, p. 46; see also J. Tosh, *The Pursuit of History* (Longman, Harlow, 1984).

21 But Thompson (in his *Voice of the Past*) and others have stressed the value of oral history for the recent past, and it is possible to learn a great deal about the past from observation of physical evidence such as buildings.

22 A. Marwick, *The Nature of History* (Macmillan, London, 1970), pp. 135–6.

23 Langlois and Seignobos, *Introduction to the Study of History*, p. 46. Here and throughout their book the authors assume the historian to be a man.

24 Ibid., p. 66.

25 S. and B. Webb, *Methods of Social Study* (1932); Cambridge University Press, 1975), p. 100.

26 Langlois and Seignobos, *Introduction to the Study of History*, p. 65, attempts

a rather unsatisfactory distinction between 'material documents' (monuments and fabricated articles) and 'psychological documents', but this cannot be sustained.

27 Tosh, *Pursuit of History*, p. 30, makes a similar distinction between authorship and publication.

28 M. Weber, *Economy and Society* (2 vols, 1920–1; Bedminster Press, New York, 1968).

29 The classification in figure 1.2 was evolved for modern documents, in capitalist industrial societies. It is, of course, far less relevant to societies such as the Soviet Union, where the State/private distinction is hardly recognised.

30 This is not to imply that all organisations or rooms labelled 'archive' operate in this way: some government archives, for example, are closed to outsiders. The term is used here simply to describe the particular form of openness that exists in most public archives, libraries, museum, and record offices.

31 In practice they are also accessible to the medical records staff and medical secretaries who maintain them, but this is no different from any other closed document, whether private or state, which has to be bureaucratically processed.

32 Reference books such as *Who's Who* and *Burke's Peerage* are slightly different in character from the directories produced by particular organisations and concerning their own members. Burke's publishing organisation, for example, does not stand in the same relation to peers and baronets as does the (British) Institute of Directors, responsible for the *Directory of Directors*, to individual company directors.

33 'Restricted' is often used in government circles as a secrecy grading for documents and means, in effect, 'closed'. This difference in the meaning of the term 'restricted' from its use in figure 1.2 should be borne in mind.

Chapter 2   Assessing Documentary Sources

1 This whole discussion draws heavily on the works of Platt and of Langlois and Seignobos, to which I am greatly indebted: see Platt, 'Evidence and proof' and Langlois and Seignobos, *Introduction to the Study of History*.

2 Langlois and Seignobos, *Introduction to the Study of History*, p. 73.

3 Ibid., p. 80.

4 The 'Donation of Constantine' is discussed in Tosh, *Pursuit of History*, p. 52; on the 'Hitler' diaries see R. Harris, *Selling Hitler* (Faber, London, 1986). The general problem is discussed in I. Haywood, *Faking It* (Harvester, Brighton, 1987).

5 Platt, 'Evidence and proof', p. 34.

6 Ibid., p. 32.

7 Langlois and Seignobos, *Introduction to the Study of History*, pp. 156–7. The authors discuss credibility under the headings of 'good faith' and accuracy.

8 Ibid., p. 162.

9 G. W. Alport, *The Use of Personal Documents in the Psychological Sciences* (Social Science Research Council, New York, 1947).

10 J. A. Banks, 'Sociological theories, methods, and recent techniques', *Sociological Review*, 27 3 (1979), pp. 561–78.

11 See the useful discussion in R. Naroll, *Data Quality Control* (Free Press, Glencoe, 1962). Shorthand and tape recording as aids to memory are discussed in G. Kitson Clark, *The Critical Historian* (Heinemann, London, 1967), pp. 85–90.

12 Webb *et al.*, *Unobtrusive Measures*, pp. 54 ff.

13 This is how Karl Marx described the fate of the manuscript of K. Marx and F. Engels, *The German Ideology* (1846; Lawrence & Wishart, London, 1965). See also Clark, *Critical Historian*, p. 73.

14 Clark, *Critical Historian*, p. 73.

15 For some documents this period is extended to 100 or even 150 years. On the general issues of access see Clark, *Critical Historian*, p. 75.

16 A catalogue is a particular kind of index, generally arranged by class of document or by author. A calendar contains a summary or abstract of the document as well as the bibliographical and indexing details generally contained in a catalogue.

17 Langlois and Seignobos, *Introduction to the Study of History*, p. 28.

18 The problem of reconstructing the logic of an archive has been brilliantly explored in U. Eco, *The Name of the Rose* (Pan, London, 1984).

19 S. and B. Webb, *English Local Government from the Revolution to the Municipal Corporations Act*, 9 vols (Longman, Green, London, 1907–29).

20 Platt, 'Evidence and proof', p. 35.

21 Langlois and Seignobos, *Introduction to the Study of History*, p. 48.

22 Ibid., pp. 146 ff. See also L. C. Hector, *The Handwriting of English Documents* (Edward Arnold, London, 1958); and H. E. P. Grieve, *Examples of English Handwriting* (Essex Records Office Publications no. 21, 1954).

23 On the changing meaning of words and on specialised meanings see Clark, *Critical Historian*, pp. 63–5.

24 The dating of documents is further complicated by the fact that the change in the calendar involved the 'loss' of eleven days from 3 September to 14 September as the Julian calendar reckoned centennial years as leap years and so had resulted in an eleven-day discrepancy between the tropical and calendar years. It is for this reason that the financial year, still reckoned on the old basis, does not begin on Lady Day but on 6 April – eleven days later. The Gregorian calendar was introduced in Scotland in 1660, before the Union of Parliaments, and this means that care must be taken in comparing what appear to be contemporary documents from England and Scotland.

25 The coronation date, in this case 12 May 1953, is invariably much later than the actual date of accession.

26 This is the date calculated from the presumed creation of the world in 4000 BC, and so 1986 is equivalent to 5986 Anno Lucius.

27 Langlois and Seingobos, *Introduction to the Study of History*, p. 153.

28 I am referring to Dilthey's later work. See the discussion in W. Outhwaite, *Understanding Social Life* (Allen & Unwin, London, 1975), ch. 3.

29 For discussions of varying genres see H. M. Collins, *Changing Order* (Sage, London, 1985) and F. Burton and P. Carlen, *Official Discourse* (Routledge and Kegan Paul, London, 1979).

30 See H. G. Gadamer, *Wahrheit und Methode* (Mohr, Tübingen, 1960). Giddens has discussed this as the 'double hermeneutic': see A. Giddens, *The New Rules of Sociological Method* (Hutchinson, London, 1976), pp. 142ff.

31 See the discussion in A. Giddens, *Central Problems in Social Theory* (Macmillan, London, 1979), pp. 14–15.

32 The surface meaning is termed its denotation and the underlying meaning is termed its connotation.

33 J. Derrida, *L'Écriture et la différence* (Editions du Seuil, Paris, 1967).

34 K. Mannheim, *Ideology and Utopia* (1929; Routledge & Kegan Paul, London, 1936), pp. 136ff.

35 Giddens, *Central Problems*, pp. 15–16.

36 See the position advanced in B. Hindness, 'Models and masks: empiricist conceptions of scientific knowledge', *Economy and Society*, 2/2 (1973), and P. Q. Hirst, 'Recent tendencies in sociological theory', *Economy and Society*, 1/2 (1972). These writers are criticised in J. Scott, 'Sociological theorising and the Althusserian ideal', *Sociological Analysis and Theory*, 4/2 (1974).

37 Giddens, *New Rules*, p. 27.

38 This suggests particular problems for those approaches to textual analysis which stress coherence as a criterion: any coherence disclosed by the analyst may be, to a greater or lesser extent, the product of the analyst's own reading of the text. See J. Larrain, *The Concept of Ideology* (Hutchinson, London, 1979), pp. 135ff, and C. Sumner, *Reading Ideologies* (Academic Press, London, 1979). Sumner unfortunately sets up many straw men and fails to illustrate clearly alternatives to the approaches he rejects.

Chapter 3   The Use of Documents in Social Research

1 L. Alcock, *Arthur's Britain: History and Archaeology, AD 367–634* (Penguin, Harmondsworth, 1973).

2 Geoffrey of Monmouth, *The History of the Kings of Britain* (c.1136; Penguin, Harmondsworth, 1966).

3 I disregard the rest of Geoffrey's *History* and look only at the chapters concerned with Arthur.

4 Problems of copying errors are discussed in Alcock, *Arthur's Britain*, pp. 3–4.

5 For a reconstruction of the genealogy of the surviving copies of the Chronicle see G. N. Garmonsway, 'Introduction' to *The Anglo-Saxon Chronicle*, tr. G. N. Garmonsway (Dent, London, 1953).

6 Alcock, *Arthur's Britain*, p. 68.

7 Ibid., pp. 67–71.

8 Ibid., pp. 20, 55, 111. The Preface to this, the Penguin edition of Alcock's book suggests a simpler explanation. Instead of assuming an error in conversion it is possible to hypothesise a simple confusion between successive Easter tables. As each table covers a period of 19 years the date of Badon can be revised to 499 AD. See ibid., p. xvii and L. Alcock, *By South Cadbury is that Camelot* (Thames and Hudson, London, 1972), appendix.

9 Alcock, *Arthur's Britain*, pp. 359–60.

10 The background to this case is drawn mainly from L. Chester, S. Fay and H. Young, *The Zinoviev Letter* (Heinemann, London, 1967). It is discussed as a case of historical dispute in C. L. Mowat, *Great Britain since 1914* (Sources of History, London, 1971), pp. 199ff.

11 Chester, *Zinoviev Letter*, pp. 40–1.

12 This view is supported in C. Andrew, *Secret Service* (Heinemann, London, 1985), p. 308.

13 Chester, *Zinoviev Letter*, p. 73.

14 Chester et al. claim that the friend was, in fact, the 'master spy', Sydney Reilly, who was working closely with the Poles. Some qualified support for this is given in Andrew, *Secret Service*.

15 Nigel West, *MI5: British Security Service Operations 1909–1945* (Triad/Granada, London, 1983). Interestingly in an area where authorship is in dispute, 'Nigel West' is the pseudonym for Conservative MP Rupert Allason.

16 Andrew also points out that Mme Bellegarde's statement that a single sheet of paper had been stolen for the letter is incompatible with the known length of the surviving copies. See Andrew, *Secret Service*, p. 309.

17 Ibid., p. 308.

18 E. Durkheim, *Suicide* (1897; Free Press, Glencoe, 1951).

19 It should perhaps be made clear here that I do not accept that sociology and history are to be distinguished by their 'generalising' and 'particularising' concerns.

20 E. Durkheim, *The Division of Labour in Society* (1893; Free Press, Glencoe, 1951) and *The Rules of the Sociological Method* (1895; Free Press, Glencoe, 1938).

21 I follow here the interpretation of Durkheim's argument given in W. Pope, *Durkheim's Suicide* (University of Chicago Press, 1976), part I.

22 Durkheim also explored variations in marital status as responsible for anomie among men. Marriage restrains men's passions, and so single men are less restrained and more prone to unfulfilment. Women were seen by Durkheim as more restrained in their wants by biology, and as a result marriage leads to excessive regulation for women. While married men show low rates of suicide, other things being equal, married women show high rates.

23 Durkheim, *Suicide*, p. 39. The tables produced by Mauss are table XXI on p. 178 and table XXII on p. 196 of the 1951 translation of his book.

24 Ibid., p. 47.

25 Ibid., pp. 52–3.

26 J. Douglas, *The Social Meanings of Suicide* (Princeton University Press, New Jersey, 1967), pp. 171–2. The title of this section of my chapter is taken from Douglas's influential book.

27 H. Morselli, *Suicide* (Appleton, New York, 1903; originally Milan, 1879).

28 Durkheim, *Suicide*, table XVII, p. 150.

29 Douglas, *Social Meanings of Suicide*, pp. 183 ff.

30 See the empirical studies in J. M. Atkinson, *Discovering Suicide* (Macmillan, London, 1978), chs 5, 6 and 7, and S. Taylor, *Durkheim and the Study of Suicide* (Macmillan, London, 1982), chs 4 and 5.

31 Douglas, *Social Meanings of Suicide*, p. 179.

32 Ibid., p. 180. Douglas goes even further and argues that there may be no consistency in the meaning given to the concept of 'death', of which 'suicide' is supposed to be a sub-type. This is, he claims, a particular problem if comparisons with non-Western societies are to be made.

33 Taylor, *Durkheim*, p. 45.

34 Atkinson, *Discovering Suicide*.

35 J. I. Kitsuse and A. V. Cicourel, 'A note on the uses of official statistics', *Social Problems*, 11 (1963), pp. 131–9.

36 The best-known formulation of this is to be found in K. R. Popper, *Objective Knowledge* (Clarendon Press, Oxford, 1972). See also the different views of M. Hesse, *The Structure of Scientific Inference* (Macmillan, London, 1974) and R. Harré, *The Principles of Scientific Thinking* (Macmillan, London, 1970).

37 Though it is recognised that the calendar year and the solar year move out of step with one another in such a way that an 'extra' day must be included in the calendar once in every four years.

38 L. Laing and J. Laing, *The Origins of Britain* (Routledge & Kegan Paul, London, 1980), pp. 247–8.

39 For a discussion of the problem of conceptualising who is to count as a woman see H. Garfinkel, *Studies in Ethnomethodology* (Prentice-Hall, New Jersey, 1967). For a more general view see A. Oakley, *Sex, Gender and Society* (Maurice Temple Smith, London, 1972). The distinction I am making between reporting and describing is closely related to that made in W. G. Runciman, *Treatise on Social Theory*.

40 M. Weber, '"Objectivity" in social science and social policy' (1904), in his *The Methodology of the Social Sciences* (Free Press, Glencoe, 1949).

41 See the related views in E. H. Carr, *What is History* (1961; Penguin, Harmondsworth, 1964), pp. 10 ff; and G. Kitson Clark, *The Critical Historian* (Heinemann, London, 1967), pp. 41–4.

42 H. H. Bruun, *Social Values and Politics in Max Weber's Methodology* (Munksgaard, Copenhagen, 1972); W. G. Runciman, *A Critique of Max Weber's Philosophy of Social Science* (Cambridge University Press, 1972). Weber uses the generic term 'value' perhaps with undue deference to the work of Rickert.

43 See A. W. Gouldner, 'Anti-Minotaur: the myth of a value-free socio-logy', *Social Problems*, 9 (1962), pp. 199–213; H. Becker, 'Whose side are we on?', *Social Problems*, 14 (1967), pp. 239–47; A. W. Gouldner, 'The sociologist as partisan', *American Sociologist*, 3 (1968), pp. 103–16.

44 See the whole-hearted embracing of this in R. Anderson, W. Sharrock and R. Watson, *The Sociology Game* (Longman, Harlow, 1985), ch. 3. My own discussion draws heavily on the important work of Runciman, *Treatise on Social Theory*, though I differ from him on certain crucial points and emphases. It should be recognised that all social and historical concepts are 'contestable' in the sense that Lukes adopts from Gallie. Contestability is not an attribute of particular concepts, such as 'power', but it is inherent in the very nature of social science concept formation: see S. Lukes, *Power: A Radical View* (Macmillan, London, 1974).

45 See the discussions in I. Lakatos and A. Musgrave (eds), *Criticism and the Growth of Knowledge* (Cambridge University Press, 1970).

Chapter 4   The Official Realm: Public and Private

1 M. Foucault, *Madness and Civilization* (1964; Tavistock, London, 1967), pp. 49–51; J. Douglas, *American Social Order* (Free Press, Glencoe, 1972), pp. 52 ff.

2 M. Weber, *The Protestant Ethic and the Spirit of Capitalism* (1904–5; Allen & Unwin, London, 1930); R. K. Merton, *Science, Technology and Society in Seventeenth-Century England* (1938; Harper & Row, New York, 1970); and J. Habermas, 'Technology and science as "Ideology"' (1968), in his *Towards a Rational Society* (Heinemann, London, 1971).

3 Douglas, *American Social Order*, p. 90.

4 H. S. Becker, *Outsiders* (Free Press, Glencoe, 1963), p. 9, emphasis removed.

5 Becker, *Outsiders*, ch. 8.

6 I. Taylor, P. Walton and J. Young, *The New Criminology* (Routledge & Kegan Paul, London, 1973), p. 168.

7 Taylor et al., *New Criminology*, pp. 170, 273. Compare the Miliband–Poulantzas debate, partly reprinted in J. Urry and J. Wakeford (eds), *Power in Britain* (Heinemann, London, 1973).

8 K. G. Robertson, *Public Secrets* (Macmillan, London, 1982), p. 3.

9 See H. Parris, *Constitutional Bureaucracy* (Allen & Unwin, London, 1969).

10 A spy fever whipped up in such scaremongering books as W. Le Queux, *Spies of the Kaiser* (Hurst and Blackett, London, 1909) and *Invasion 1910* (Eveleigh Nash, London, 1906).

11 Robertson, *Public Secrets*, p. 58.

12 Tosh, *Pursuit of History*, pp. 35, 41; see also the general review in M. T. Clanchy, *From Memory to Written Record, England 1066–1307* (Edward Arnold, London, 1979).

13 The first published version of Domesday Book was in 1783, and there is now a series of widely available county volumes published by Phillimore. See the important discussions in V. H. Galbraith, *Domesday Book* (Clarendon Press, Oxford, 1974) and H. C. Darby, *Domesday England* (Cambridge University Press, 1977).

14 R. A. Kent, *A History of British Empirical Sociology* (Gower, Farnborough, 1981), p. 30; P. Corrigan and D. Sayer, *The Great Arch* (Basil Blackwell, Oxford, 1985), pp. 125–6.

15 G. R. Elton, *The Tudor Revolution in Government* (Cambridge University Press, 1953).

16 Publication of 'Calendars', the official index and summary of the State Papers, began in 1802 and it was intended to cover all records from Henry VIII onwards. The State Papers from 1547 were themselves published by the PRO soon after its formation. See J. J. Bagley, *Historical Interpretation 2: Sources of English History, 1540 to the Present Day* (Penguin, Harmondsworth, 1971), pp. 68–71.

17 Only since 1878 has Hansard had its own reporters in the Gallery of the House. The verbatim transcripts have, in fact, been corrected and edited to omit repetitions and slips of the tongue. Hansard is not, therefore, a fully authentic record of the verbal exchanges.

18 After the Reformation, effectively from 1558, records of the Presbyterian Church of Scotland were completely separate from the Church of England. Scottish Church records are now stored in New Register House, Edinburgh.

19 The English Church inherited the English records of the Catholic Church, but the latter obviously maintained separate records after the formation of the established Anglican Church.

20 Poll books date from 1720 and lasted until 1870, when the secret ballot was introduced. Unlike the electoral register, which simply shows home, address, and qualification to vote, poll books also show for which candidate(s) each person voted.

21 Bagley, *Historical Interpretation 2*, p. 52.

22 See the discussion in S. and B. Webb, *English Local Government*.

23 Some large ecclesiastical parishes, especially in the north and west, were subdivided into two or more civil parishes, but in each case the focus was a church or its chapel of ease.

24 The main apprentice records, however, were maintained by the 'companies' and 'guilds' of the boroughs. Borough records themselves were similar to those of the parishes, though borough administration was separate from church organisation.

25 A Giddens, *A Contemporary Critique of Historical Materialism* (Macmillan, London, 1981), pp. 165, 169, 174.

26 The Catholic Church in Britain began its own system of registration in 1563.

27 The parish registers were used in this way only in the 1801 census, which is discussed in the following chapter. An important limitation on the registers is that from 1653 to 1660 the Bishop's transcripts, and in some cases the parish

registers themselves, were not maintained, as the abolition of the monarchy in this period had also involved the abolition of bishops and the disestablishment of the Church

28 A. M. Carr-Saunders, *World Population* (Clarendon Press, Oxford, 1936), ch. 1; M. W. Flinn, *The European Demographic System* (Harvester, Brighton, 1981), pp. 5–6.

29 Quoted in D. Lawton, 'Introduction', in *The Census and Social Structure*, ed. D. Lawton (Frank Cass, London, 1978), p. 12. The whole debate is discussed in D. V. Glass, *Numbering the People* (Saxon House, Farnborough, 1973).

30 M. Shaw and I. Miles, 'The roots of statistical knowledge', in *Demystifying Social Statistics*, eds J. Irvine, I. Miles and J. Evans (Pluto Press, London, 1979).

31 Scottish civil registration began in 1858 and Irish in 1864. A GRO for Scotland was formed as a separate body in 1861, under the authority of the Secretary of State for Scotland. This is currently administered through the Scottish Home and Health Department. A separate Irish GRO also existed and, following the partition of Ireland, the Northern Ireland Department of Finance took over responsibility for the census and civil registration in the North. Under the direct rule of the Westminster government the Secretary of State for Northern Ireland became the supervising minister.

32 From 1861 the Scottish census was separated from that for England and Wales, but it was run as a parallel operation.

33 S. J. Woolf, 'Towards the history of the origins of statistics', in J. C. Perrot and S. J. Woolf, *State and Statistics in France, 1789–1815* (Harwood Academic Publications, London, 1984).

34 This discussion draws on J. C. Perrot, 'The golden age of regional statistics', in Perrot and Woolf, *State and Statistics in France*.

35 The Swedish census included Finland until 1809. A census in Iceland began in 1703 but was intermittent.

36 The census of Ireland began in 1813.

37 A census of French Canada had been undertaken about every five years from 1665 to 1754, but a full Canadian census did not begin until 1871. The Japanese census was recast on modern lines in 1873.

38 Other countries adopting civil registration in the twentieth century include Norway (1906), Portugal (1910), and Denmark (1924). The United States had begun a partial system of death registration in 1901. Some general information relevant to these points can be found in N. Currer-Briggs, *Worldwide Family History* (Routledge & Kegan Paul, London, 1982).

39 V. A. Gattrell and T. B. Hadden, 'Criminal statistics and their interpretation', in *Nineteenth-Century Society*, ed. E. A. Wrigley (Cambridge University Press, 1972).

40 Table 1 in Gattrell and Hadden, 'Criminal statistics', lists the main series available in the nineteenth century.

41 Kent, *British Empirical Sociology*, pp. 13ff.

42 This gave only partial coverage of the country, being based on just 112

parishes and using no sampling methods or explicit criteria for selection. The Board of Agriculture pioneered government research in other areas through its series of county investigations of the state of agriculture.

43 K. Marx, *Capital*, vol. 1 (1867; Penguin, Harmondsworth, 1976).

44 Domesday Book, however, gives little detailed attention to geographical boundaries, concentrating on the manorial and economic boundaries of the major units of land ownership.

45 See W. G. Hoskins, *Fieldwork in Local History* (Faber, London, 1967), ch. 2.

46 J. B. Harley, *Maps for the Local Historian* (National Council for Social Service, London, 1972); J. West, *Town Records* (Phillimore, Chichester, 1983), ch. 6; A. G. Hodgkiss, *Discovering Antique Maps* (Shire Publications, Aylesbury, 1981); D. Smith, *Maps and Plans* (Batsford, London, 1988); P. Hindle, *Maps for Local History* (Batsford, London, 1988).

47 W. Camden, *Britannia* (1607), W. Bowyer, London, 1772, which included maps by Saxton and Norden; J. Speed, *The Theatre of the Empire of Great Britain* (1611), 2 vols (Phoenix House, London, 1953).

48 A definitive listing is the *Catalogue of Printed Maps, Charts and Plans* (British Museum, London, 1967), 15 vols. A useful shorter gazeteer can be found in West, *Town Records*, ch. 6. See also J. Howgego, *Printed Maps of London circa 1553–1850* (Dawson, Folkestone, 1978).

49 The later series appeared in 1903, 1918, 1931, 1945 and 1952. The Fifth Series of 1931–9 covered only the south of England, as the Ordnance Survey was forced to concentrate on making 'war revisions' to the earlier series.

50 Sparsely populated mountain and moorland areas were mapped only at the six-inch scale, but many urban areas, including the whole of London, were mapped at five feet to the mile (1:1,056).

51 In the current (1986) series, a 1:2,500 map covers an area of 2 km by 1 km, and a 1:250 urban map covers an area of 500 m by 500 m.

52 Computerisation and digital mapping began in the 1960s, and large-scale maps became available on tape and microfilm. The Ordnance Survey subsequently introduced a facility for producing customised 'unpublished' maps. This parallels in an interesting way the progression in publication of census data which is discussed in the following chapter.

53 R. Tooley, *Maps and Mapmakers* (Batsford, London, 1949); A. R. Hinks, *Maps and Surveys* (Cambridge University Press, 1913); L. Bagrow, *History of Cartography* (Watts, 1964).

54 The land tax began in 1692 but was not a permanent tax at that time.

55 These personal documents are discussed in ch. 8.

56 As already noted, the Church of England has an ambiguous position between the State and the private sphere. Most other churches are assimilable to private bodies.

57 Prior to the 1844 Act, company formation required a Royal Charter or an Act of Parliament. See J. Scott, *Capitalist Property and Financial Power* (Wheatsheaf, Brighton, 1986), ch. 2.

58 The range of British company records is surveyed in J. Armstrong and S.

Jones, *Business Documents* (Mansell, London, 1987). The archival records of early companies are comprehensively covered in L. Richmond and B. Stockford, *Company Archives* (Gower, Farnborough, 1985).

59 See J. Scott, *Capitalist Porperty*, pp. 132–4, which draws on L. Loss, *Securities Regulation* (Little, Brown, New York, 1961).

60 M. Weber, *Economy and Society*. See also S. Pollard, *The Genesis of Modern Management* (1965; Penguin, Harmondsworth, 1968) and Giddens, *Contemporary Critique*, p. 176.

61 For discussions of various classes of business records, see J. Rule, D. Caplovitz, and P. Barker, 'The dossier in consumer credit', I. Berg and J. Salvate, 'Record keeping and corporate employees', H. L. Ross, 'Personal information in insurance files', all in *On Record*, ed. S. Wheeler (Russell Sage Foundation, New York, 1969).

62 D. A. Goslin and N. Bordier, 'Record keeping in elementary and secondary schools', in *On Record*, ed. Wheeler.

63 B. R. Clark, 'The dossier in colleges and universities', in *On Record*, ed. Wheeler.

64 R. Alvarez and W. E. Moore, 'Information flow within the professions: some selective comparisons of law, medicine and nursing', in *On Record*, ed. Wheeler.

65 Promissory notes and bills of exchange, from which paper currency and cheques evolved, are similar in nature to these certified copies, though they may not always be 'personalised' or registered in the names of particular individuals: a bank note, for example, is freely transferable without the need to register its current ownership.

Chapter 5   Administrative Routines and Situated Decisions

1 C. Hakim, 'Research based on administrative records', *Sociological Review*, 31/3 (1983), pp. 489–519. I use the term 'recurrent' in place of Hakim's term 'routine' in order to avoid confusion with my own notion of administrative routines.

2 Ibid., p. 492.

3 P. M. Blau, *The Dynamics of Bureaucracy* (University of Chicago Press, 1955).

4 Kitsuse and Cicourel, 'Note on the uses of official statistics'.

5 B. Hindess, *The Use of Official Statistics in Sociology* (Macmillan, London, 1973).

6 See W. A. Armstrong, 'The use of information about occupation', in *Nineteenth Century Society*, ed. E. A. Wrigley (Cambridge University Press, 1972), pp. 192–3.

7 C. Davies, 'Making sense of the census in Britain and the USA', *Sociological Review*, 28/3 (1980), p. 585.

8 J. A. Banks, 'The social structure of nineteenth century England as seen

through the census', in *The Census and Social Structure*, ed. D. Lawton (Frank Cass, London, 1978), pp. 190–1. See also J. M. Bellamy, 'Occupational statistics in the nineteenth century censuses', in the same source.

9 The SIC was first used in the census report for 1951, and was revised in 1958, 1968 and 1980. The latest revision was partly concerned with comparability with the NACE (Nomenclature générale des activités economiques dans les Communautés Européennes) classification of the European Community: see *Statistical News*, 47 (November 1979). The current classification has 27 'orders' subdivided into 'minimum list headings'.

10 S. R. Szreter, 'The genesis of the Registrar-General's social classification of occupations', *British Journal of Sociology*, 25/4 (1984), p. 525. This section of my book draws heavily on Szreter's important paper.

11 Ibid.

12 The definitive edition is C. Booth, *Life and Labour of the People in London*, 17 vols (Macmillan, London, 1902).

13 Szreter, 'The genesis . . .', p. 526; D. Mackenzie, 'Eugenics and the rise of mathematical statistics in Britain', in *Demystifying Social Statistics*, eds J. Irvine, I. Miles and J. Evans (Pluto Press, London, 1979). Galton's most important works in this area are *Hereditary Genius* (Macmillan, London, 1869) and *Natural Inheritance* (Macmillan, London, 1889).

14 For purposes of the civil registration of births this was normally, and remains, the father's occupation. The social class of those entering a marriage contract is similarly classified by paternal occupation.

15 It is important to recognise that he regarded occupation as an indicator of class and not a determinant of it.

16 The Registrar-General's Classification is published in a new edition approximately every ten years. The number of OPCS 'occupational unit groups' in 1971 was 223 and in 1981 it was 549. These are derived from occupational groups which can also be converted into the 404 groups derived from CODOT. Thus, a single code book enables an individual's occupation to be classified in such a way that the result can be related to the 1981 census and to Department of Employment statistics. Official publications now frequently translate from one format to the other.

17 *Classification of Occupations, 1970* (HMSO, London, 1970), p. x.

18 E.g. see W. A. Armstrong's important 'The use of information . . .'.

19 Szreter, 'The genesis . . .', pp. 530, 533; F. Bechhofer, 'Occupations', in *Comparability in Social Research*, ed. M. Stacey (Heinemann, London, with the British Sociological Association and the SSRC, 1969); C. Marsh, 'Social class and occupation', in *Key Variables in Social Investigation*, ed. R. Burgess (Routledge & Kegan Paul, London, 1986), p. 133.

20 The Classification also uses the variable economically active/inactive.

21 The number of SEGs was thirteen in 1951 and sixteen from 1961. With an additional category for 'inadequately described occupations' there are currently seventeen SEGs in all.

22 Bechhofer, 'Occupations', p. 113.

23 Kitsuse and Cicourel, 'Note on the uses of official statistics', p. 138. See also A. V. Cicourel, *The Social Organisation of Juvenile Justice* (Wiley, New York, 1968); E. Bittner, 'The police on Skid Row', *American Sociological Review*, 32 (1967), pp. 699–715.

24 S. Box, *Deviance, Reality and Society* (Holt, Rinehart & Winston, London, 1971), p. 69.

25 N. Walker, *Crimes, Courts, and Figures* (Penguin, Harmondsworth, 1971).

26 Some published statistics, of course, derive from court and prison records, but these also depend, ultimately, on the crime having been brought to the attention of the police.

27 J. Hanmer and S. Saunders, *Well-Founded Fear* (Hutchinson, London, 1984); M. Hepworth, *Blackmail* (Routledge & Kegan Paul, London, 1975).

28 Strictly speaking, of course, a court will decide only that guilt has not been proven.

29 B. Hindess, *Use of Official Statistics*. This is Hindess's summary of the ethnomethodologists' position rather than an argument with which he agrees.

30 Becker, *Outsiders*.

31 V. A. C. Gatrell, 'The decline of theft and violence in Victorian and Edwardian England', in *Crime and the Law*, eds V. A. C. Gatrell, B. Lenman and G. Parker (Europa, London, 1980).

32 P. Wiles, 'Criminal statistics and sociological explanations of crime', in *Crime and Delinquency in Britain*, eds W. G. Carson and P. Wiles (Martin Robertson, Oxford, 1971), p. 186.

33 M. Bulmer, 'Why don't sociologists make more use of official statistics?', *Sociology*, 14/4 (1980), pp. 511–13. See also Hindess. *Use of Official Statistics*, p. 40.

Chapter 6   Explorations in Official Documents

1 On the history of parish registration see W. E. Tate, *The Parish Chest* (Cambridge University Press, 1969), ch. 1. Catholic registration began in 1563 as a completely separate system. The background to registration is discussed more fully in ch. 4 above.

2 Ministers were empowered to act as registrars for marriages at which they officiated and sent a quarterly transcript to the local registrar, who forwarded it to the GRO. After 1837, therefore, birth and death registration was a purely civil matter, while marriage registration could be either parochial or civil.

3 Protestant civil registration in Ireland began in 1845.

4 In the early years some parish registers recorded all three events, chronologically, in a single register.

5 This system was adopted for marriages in 1754 and for baptisms and burials in 1837.

6 Actually three separate indexes. There are also separate registers and

indexes for military families and for births at sea, in the air and overseas.

7 In Scotland the copy registers are on open access.

8 The father is not always named if the child is illegitimate, and the mother is given under her own surname.

9 Some 'short' certificates are issued, on request, containing an abbreviated form of entry.

10 D. C. Jones, *Social Surveys* (Hutchinson, London, no date), pp. 25–8.

11 The registration districts were the Poor Law union districts, divided into smaller 'enumeration districts'.

12 See D. M. Thompson, 'The religious census of 1851' and M. Goldstrom, 'Education in England and Wales', both in *The Census and Social Structure*, ed. D. Lawton (Frank Cass, London, 1978).

13 All small area statistics are available in computer form at the Economic and Social Research Council Data Archive. See C. Hakim, *Secondary Analysis* (Allen & Unwin, London, 1982), ch. 3.

14 J. Steinberg, 'Government records: the census bureau and the social security administration', in *On Record*, ed. S. Wheeler (Russell Sage Foundation, New York, 1969).

15 The Bureau of the Census is now located in the Department of Commerce.

16 Fire has ravaged the French civil records of vital events. During the Commune in Paris in 1871 all pre-1859 Parisian records were destroyed. There has been some attempt to reconstruct these lost records from other sources.

17 In the case of church and chapel weddings, the local registrar works from a copy register.

18 See the discussions of these in numerous family history guides, especially D. J. Steel, *Discovering Your Family History* (BBC, London, 1980); D. Iredale, *Discovering Your Family Tree* (Shire Publications, Aylesbury, 1970), ch. 4; and G. Hamilton-Edwards, *In Search of Ancestry* (Phillimore, Chichester, 1974), chs 3 and 5. The largest collection of private and commercial parish register copies in Britain is to be found at the Society of Genealogists: see *Parish Register Copies*, pts I and II (Society of Genealogists, London, 1985 and 1974). For a discussion of printed copies and the bishops' transcripts see D. J. Steel, *National Index of Parish Registers*, vol. I: Sources of Births, Marriages, and Deaths before 1837 (Society of Genealogists, London, 1968), chs 5 and 6.

19 Tillott has suggested that such errors are slight. See P. M. Tillott, 'Sources of inaccuracy in the 1851 and 1861 censuses', in *Nineteenth Century Society*, ed. E. A. Wrigley (Cambridge University Press, 1972), p. 83. See also W. A. Armstrong, 'The census enumerator's books: a commentary', in *The Census and Social Structure*, ed. D. Lawton (Frank Cass, London, 1978), pp. 30–2.

20 On the editing of twentieth-century returns see B. Benjamin, *The Population Census* (Heinemann, London, 1970), pp. 143–9.

21 M. Drake, 'The census 1801–1901', in *Nineteenth Century Society*, ed. E. A. Wrigley (Cambridge University Press, 1972), pp. 25–6.

22 Ibid., p. 29.

23 In the early censuses ages were officially rounded down to the nearest five years, causing great difficulty in the interpretation of such data. In a general survey of the problem of accuracy, Tillott, 'Sources of inaccuracy', p. 85, claims that there were, however, few discrepancies between the ages recorded in the census and those which can be calculated from parish registers.

24 Drake, 'The census 1801–1901', p. 29.

25 For general discussions of the form and content of the parish registers see Steel, *National Index*, vol. 1, ch. 2.

26 See Bellamy, 'Occupational statistics'.

27 D. V. Glass, 'A note on the under-recording of births in Britain in the nineteenth century', *Population Studies*, 5 (1951–2), pp. 70–88.

28 C. D. Rogers, *The Family Tree Detective*, 2nd edn (Manchester University Press, 1985).

29 Drake, 'The census 1801–1901', pp. 21–2.

30 On the problem of drawing samples from the census see W. A. Armstrong, 'Social structure from the early census returns', in *An Introduction to English Historical Demography*, ed. E. A. Wrigley (Weidenfeld & Nicolson, London, 1966).

31 Some small chapels celebrating few marriages may still be using their original register, which will not, therefore, be available in the local registration offices. On the gaps in registers see D. E. C. Eversley, 'Exploitation of Anglican parish registers by aggregative analysis', in Wrigley (ed.), *English Historical Demography*, pp. 45 ff.

32 See Parochial Registers and Records Measure (No. 2), 1978.

33 This is true also of the extremely useful International Genealogical Index, which is far from complete but is believed to be generally reliable. See J. Gibson and M. Walcot, *Where to Find the International Genealogical Index* (Federation of Family History Societies, Plymouth, 1985).

34 Some surname indexes and census transcripts do include an occupation index, but this is not usual.

35 Bechhofer, 'Occupations', p. 104.

36 Ibid., pp. 108–9

37 C. Hakim, 'Census reports as documentary evidence', *Sociological Review*, 28/3 (1980), p. 566. This is reflected in the Registrar-General's Classification, where clerks were allocated to Class I in 1911, Class II in 1921, and Class III in 1931 and after. In the nineteenth century, 'clerk' often meant 'clerk in holy orders', i.e. a clergyman or cleric.

38 Davies, 'Making sense of the census', pp. 595–9. See also Banks, 'The social structure', pp. 190–1.

39 C. Marsh, *The Survey Method* (Allen & Unwin, London, 1982), p. 144.

40 See A. Oakley and R. Oakley, 'Sexism in official statistics', in *Demystifying Social Statistics*, eds J. Irvine, I. Miles and J. Evans (Pluto, London, 1979).

41 Family reconstitution is discussed in E. A. Wrigley and R. S. Schofield,

'Nominal record linkage by computer and the logic of family reconstitution', in *Identifying People in the Past*, ed. E. A. Wrigley (Edward Arnold, London, 1973); and E. A. Wrigley, 'Family reconstitution', in *An Introduction to English Historical Demography*, ed. E. A. Wrigley (Weidenfeld & Nicolson, London, 1966). Community reconstitution is discussed in A. Macfarlane, S. Harrison and C. Jardine, *Reconstructing Historical Communities* (Cambridge University Press, 1977).

42 For a genealogist's discussion of this see Steel, *National Index*, vol. I, ch. 2, app. iii and iv.

43 I. Winchester, 'On referring to ordinary historical persons', in E. A. Wrigley (ed.), *Identifying People in the Past*.

44 See Wrigley and Schofield, 'Nominal record linkage'. A related discussion can be found in P. Laslett, 'Introduction: the history of the family', in *Household and Family in Past Times*, ed. P. Laslett with R. Wall (Cambridge University Press, 1972), pp. 86–9. Any errors made in the mechanistic application of rules can be assumed to be minimal when the rules are well founded and the number of cases is large. Where the researcher is dealing with one or a small number of cases, errors of identification can be much more damaging.

45 Winchester, 'On referring . . .'. Winchester makes the stronger point that we may legitimately question the very idea of a 'real' identity, as all identities are socially constructed in specific situations.

46 Eversley, 'Exploitation of Anglican parish registers'. The work of Wrigley and Schofield, which began as a relational study of family reconstitution, produced a massive volume of aggregate material from English parish registers. See E. A. Wrigley and R. Schofield, *The Population History of England* (Edward Arnold, London, 1981).

47 Hakim, 'Census reports as documentary evidence', p. 553.

48 The classification is described in J. R. Hall and D. Caradog Jones, 'The social grading of occupations', *British Journal of Sociology*, 1/1 (1950), pp. 31–55, and in C. Moser and J. R. Hall, 'The social grading of occupations', in *Social Mobility in Britain*, ed. D. V. Glass (Routledge & Kegan Paul, London, 1954).

49 See the list printed in A. N. Oppenheim, *Questionnaire Design and Attitude Measurement* (Heinemann, London, 1966), pp. 276–84.

50 Hall and Jones say that they re-classified only the farmer in 'The social grading', p. 41. Moser and Hall in 'The social grading', p. 35, say that they re-classified farmer, coal hewer, and railway porter.

51 J. Goldthorpe, D. Lockwood, F. Bechhofer and J. Platt, *The Affluent Worker in The Class Structure* (Cambridge University Press, 1969). See also Bechhofer, 'Occupations', pp. 115–17.

52 J. H. Goldthorpe and K. Hope, *The Social Grading of Occupations* (Oxford University Press, 1974), p. 24.

53 They actually generated 125 categories, but deleted one which they regarded as being specific to female employment. The implications of this are discussed later in this chapter.

54 J. Goldthorpe, 'Social mobility and class formation', CASMIN Paper no. 1 (Institut für Sozialwissenschaft, Mannheim, 1985), and personal communication.

55 For a use of the schema in a cross-national analysis see R. Erikson, J. Goldthorpe and L. Portocarero, 'Intragenerational class mobility in three Western European societies', *British Journal of Sociology*, 30/4 (1979), pp. 415–41.

56 R. Penn, 'The Nuffield class categorisation', *Sociology*, 15/2 (1981), pp. 265–71; J. Goldthorpe, 'The class schema of "social mobility and class structure in modern Britain": a reply to Penn', *Sociology*, 15/2 (1981), pp. 272–80. An approach to theorising the separation of an upper class from a middle class is set out in J. Scott, *Corporations, Classes, and Capitalism*, 2nd edn (Hutchinson, London, 1985), ch. 8. See also J. Scott, *The Upper Classes* (Macmillan, London, 1982).

57 Armstrong, 'The use of information . . .'.

58 J. Goldthorpe, 'Women and class analysis: in defence of the conventional view', *Sociology*, 17/4 (1983), pp. 465–88.

59 Ibid., p. 468.

60 See the congruent, though differently constructed position in R. E. Pahl, *Divisions of Labour* (Basil Blackwell, Oxford, 1984).

61 Goldthorpe, 'Women and class analysis', p. 469.

62 Hakin has claimed that the Registrar-General's Classification is, for this reason, preferable, as one quarter of the OPCS occupational units are geared to female occupations.

63 In his original paper Goldthorpe unsatisfactorily resolves this problem by claiming that the fact that women's employment tends to be intermittent, limited, and inferior in conditions to that of men means that it is misleading to regard apparently similar occupations held by men and women as being truly equivalent. The argument discussed in this paragraph is contained in J. Goldthorpe, 'Women and class analysis: a reply to the replies', *Sociology*, 18/4 (1984), pp. 491–9, and especially in J. Goldthorpe and C. Payne, 'On the class mobility of women', unpublished paper (Nuffield College, Oxford, 1985). The argument is elaborated in R. Erikson, 'Social class of men, women, and families', *Sociology*, 18/4 (1984), pp. 500–14.

64 See, in particular, M. Stanworth, 'Women and class analysis: a reply to Goldthorpe', *Sociology*, 18/2 (1984), pp. 159–70; E. Garnsey, 'Women's work and theories of class stratification', *Sociology*, 12/2 (1978), pp. 223–43; L. Murgatroyd, 'Women, men, and the social grading of occupations', *British Journal of Sociology*, 25/4 (1984), pp. 46–60. Related positions can be found in N. Britten and A. Heath, 'Women, men and social class', in E. Gamarnikow, D. Morgan, J. Purvis and D. Taylorson, *Gender, Class and Work* (Heinemann, London, 1983); A. Heath and N. Britten, 'Women's jobs do make a difference', *Sociology*, 18/4 (1984), pp. 475–90; A. Dale, G. N. Gilbert and S. Arber, 'Integrating women into class theory', *Sociology*, 19/3 (1985), pp. 384–409.

65 Britten and Heath's 'joint classification' moves in this direction, though

Goldthorpe shows a number of problems with it. See Goldthorpe, 'Women and class analysis'. It is worth pointing out here that the census authorities recognised an ambiguity over the concepts of 'family' and 'household' as early as 1851. It was seen that 'family' was used by people to refer to a co-residing group which included both servants and lodgers. Later censuses, therefore, employed the term 'household'.

66 A. M. Carr-Saunders and D. Caradog Jones, *A Survey of the Social Structure of England and Wales* (Oxford University Press, 1927); *idem.*, the same title (Oxford University Press, 1937); A. M. Carr-Saunders, D. Caradog Jones and C. A. Moser, *A Survey of Social Conditions in England and Wales* (Oxford University Press, 1958).

67 D. V. Glass, *Social Mobility in Britain*.

68 In addition to the sources referred to in note 66 above, I shall discuss D. C. Marsh, *The Changing Social Structure of England and Wales* (Routledge & Kegan Paul, London, 1958; rev. edn 1965). Similar approaches can be found in A. H. Halsey, *Trends in British Society* (Macmillan, London, 1972), and in such official sources as *Facts in Focus* (1974–8), *Social Trends* (from 1970), and *Key Data* (from 1979).

69 It is referred to by the original title on p. xvi of the 1927 edition.

70 The books draw on Inland Revenue and similar statistics to depict the distribution of income and wealth and the extent of poverty. I am concerned here only with their use of census and registration data.

71 Carr-Saunders and Jones, *Survey*, 1927 edn, p. 8.

72 Intercensal estimates from civil registration allow them to bring some series forward to 1955.

73 Carr-Saunders and Jones, *Survey*, 1927 edn, p. 11.

74 Ibid., p. 17.

75 Ibid., p. 27.

76 Ibid., pp. 50–1.

77 Ibid., pp. 69, 71.

78 Ibid., p. 71.

79 Ibid., p. 72.

80 Ibid. (with Moser), 1958 edn, p. 115.

81 Ibid., p. 117.

82 Marsh, *Changing Social Structure*, p. 198.

83 C. A. Moser and W. Scott, *British Towns* (Oliver & Boyd, Edinburgh, 1961).

84 Scottish towns were excluded because of different recording practices followed by the GRO in Scotland. Moser and Scott, *British Towns*, app. C.

85 Moser and Scott initially say that they analysed 60 variables, but their printed table includes only 57. Three variables seem to have been added after the initial analysis but were used in later interpretation of the results. They refer to 1,653 correlations, which would suggest 58 variables.

86 See K. Hope, *Methods of Multivariate Analysis* (University of London Press, 1968).

87 On Conservative voting see the analogous study of H. Pelling, *The Social Geography of British Elections* (London, Macmillan, 1967).

88 These four components accounted for 60 per cent of the variance, the first component alone accounting for 30 per cent. Two further components were identified but could be given no interpretation.

89 The only other town which could not be classified was Huyton near Liverpool. This town had experienced a massive tenfold population increase between 1931 and 1951.

90 H. J. Dyos, *Victorian Suburb* (Leicester University Press, 1961). See also Lawton's study of Liverpool, 'Census data for urban areas', in Lawton, *Census and Social Structures*, pp. 82–141.

91 M. Anderson, *Family Structure in Nineteenth-Century Lancashire* (Cambridge University Press, 1971). Note that Anderson (p. 200, n. 3) uses SEGs to reject Armstrong's claims for the Registrar-General's schema.

92 J. Foster, *Class Struggle in the Industrial Revolution* (Methuen, London, 1974).

93 See the general reviews in D. Gittins, *Fair Sex* (Hutchinson, London, 1982), and J. Lewis, *Women in England* (Wheatsheaf, Brighton, 1984). General reviews of the need to incorporate this dimension are D. H. J. Morgan, 'Gender', in *Key Variables in Social Research*, ed. R. G. Burgess (Routledge & Kegan Paul, London, 1986), and Oakley and Oakley, 'Sexism in official statistics'.

94 For a discussion of some of the problems in this area see the papers in *Archives and the Historian*, ed. D. Reeder (Centre for Urban History, University of Leicester, 1989).

95 Garfinkel, *Studies in Ethnomethodology*, pp. 191–2.

96 Ibid., p. 194.

97 Ibid., p. 199.

98 Ibid., p. 200.

99 Ibid.

100 For a particularly strident view of this use of medical records see S. Raffel, *Matters of Fact* (Routledge & Kegan Paul, London, 1979).

101 A. V. Cicourel and J. I. Kitsuse, *The Educational Decision-Makers* (Bobbs-Merrill, New York, 1968).

102 Ibid., p. 53.

103 Ibid., pp. 71–2

104 Ibid., pp. 82–3. Here and elsewhere I have Anglicised the spelling of 'counsellor'.

105 Ibid., p. 129. The nature of the files is discussed on pp. 123ff.

106 S. Macintyre, 'Some notes on record taking and making in an antenatal clinic', *Sociological Review*, 26/3 (1978), pp. 595–611.

107 Ibid., p. 598.

108 Ibid., p. 600.

109 Ibid., p. 603.

110 Ibid., p. 607.

111 See the classic statement of O. R. Holsti, *Content Analysis for the Social Sciences and Humanities* (Addison-Wesley, Reading, Mass., 1969).

112 Ibid., pp. 116–19.

113 It is also, of course, necessary to draw on external evidence such as whether the patient actually was in a Swiss hospital at the time.

114 On content analysis see also J. Curran, *Messages and Meanings*, Unit 6 for Open University Course 'Mass Communications and Society', (Open University Press, Milton Keynes, 1977).

115 D. Strinati, *Capitalism, the State, and Industrial Relations* (Croom Helm, London, 1985).

116 C. M. Vogler, *The Nation-State: The Neglected Dimension of Class* (Gower, Farnborough, 1985).

117 The Donovan Report was published as *Royal Commission on Trades Unions and Employers' Associations, 1965–68: Report* (Cmnd. 3623, HMSO, London).

118 See especially Strinati, *Capitalism*, ch. 5. *Petit-bourgeois* capital was claimed to be 'paternalist', as was money capital, and foreign capital to be 'liberal'.

119 Vogler, *The Nation-State*, p. 89. Her allocation rules for inferring the meaning of 'we' from its context are set out in table 3.2 and exemplified through examples in an appendix to her book.

120 Ibid., p. 96.

121 The logic of her conclusion should be to re-examine all the 'practical' documents, not simply those which do not 'fit'.

Chapter 7   The Public Sphere and Mass Communication

1 The discussion here and elsewhere draws heavily on R. Williams, *The Long Revolution* (1961; Penguin, Harmondsworth, 1965).

2 C. Campbell, *The Romantic Ethic and the Spirit of Modern Consumerism* (Basil Blackwell, Oxford, 1987), and M. Ossowska, *Bourgeois Morality* (Routledge, London, 1986).

3 B. Rosenberg and D. M. White (eds), *Mass Culture* (Free Press, New York, 1957).

4 S. Koss, *The Rise and Fall of the Political Press in Britain*, two vols (Hamish Hamilton, London, 1981 and 1984); Williams, *Long Revolution*, pt. II, ch. 3; G. Murdock and P. Golding, 'The structure, ownership and control of the Press, 1914–76', in G. Boyce et al., *Newspaper History* (Constable, London, 1979).

5 West, *Town Records*, p. 225.

6 Williams, *Long Revolution*, p. 213.

7 W. P. Davison, J. Boglin and F. T. C. Yu, *Mass Media* (Praeger, New York, 1976); and E. Emey, *The Press and America* (Prentice-Hall, Englewood Cliffs, New Jersey, 1972).

8 A. Smith, *The Newspaper: An International History* (Thames & Hudson, London, 1979), p. 165.

9 Williams, *Long Revolution*.

10 R. Williams, *Communications* (Penguin, Harmondsworth, 1966), p. 25.

11 L. Jacobs, *The Rise of the American Film* (1931; Teachers' College Press, New York, 1968); M. Huettig, *Economic Control of the Motion Picture Industry* (University of Pennsylvania Press, Philadelphia, 1944); J. Wasko, 'D. W. Griffith and the banks: a case study in film-financing', in *The Holywood Film Industry*, ed. P. Kerr (Routledge & Kegan Paul, London, 1986).

12 B. Paulu, *Radio and TV Broadcasting on the European Continent* (University of Minnesota Press, Minneapolis, 1967).

13 G. Murdock and P. Golding, 'Mass communication and class relations', in J. Curran et al., *Mass Communications and Society* (Edward Arnold, London, 1977); and *idem.*, 'For a political economy of mass communications', *Socialist Register, 1973* (Merlin Press, London, 1974).

14 EMI is now (1989) a part of the Thorn group which is, however, selling off such areas as cinema and television production.

15 Koss, *Rise and Fall*, vol. 2.

16 For general evidence on this see J. Scott, *Corporations* (Hutchinson, London, 1985) and *Capitalist Property* (Harvester, Brighton, 1986).

17 J. Scott and C. Griff, *Directors of Industry* (Polity Press, Cambridge, 1984), p. 82.

18 A. Mattelart, *Multinational Corporations and the Control of Culture* (1976; Harvester, Brighton, 1979).

19 J. Aldridge and J. Tregorran (pseuds.), *Ambridge: An English Village Through the Ages* (Eyre Methuen, London, 1981).

20 P. Knightley, *The First Casualty* (Deutsch, London, 1975); Glasgow Media Group, *War and Peace News* (Open University Press, Milton Keynes, 1985); D. E. Morrison, *Journalists at War* (Sage, London, 1988); V. Adams, *The Media and the Falklands Campaign* (Macmillan, London, 1986).

21 D. MacShane, *Using the Media* (Pluto, London, 1979).

22 See M. Harrison, *TV News: Whose Bias?* (Policy Journals, Hermitage, Berks., 1985), a study of television news which relies heavily on written scripts and transcripts of the non-surviving broadcasts.

23 See the useful overview of studies in D. McQuail, *Mass Communications Theory*, 2nd edn (Sage, London, 1987), pp. 218–22.

24 D. Morley, *Family Television* (Comedia Publishing, London, 1986), p. 43.

25 *Report on the British Press* (PEP, London, 1938); *Royal Commission on the Press*, Cmd. 7700 (1949).

26 I am of course involved in an attempt to interpret the internal meaning of the PEP text. There is no escape from the hermeneutic circle.

27 The data are contained in the PEP *Report*, pp. 126–9.

28 Research by R. Silverman, a researcher appointed by the Commission, is contained in appendix vii, pp. 238–359, of its Report.

29 Silverman, p. 238.

30 My discussion concentrates on the inter-war years. Data for 1947 were slightly problematic because of the persistence of wartime restrictions on the availability of newsprint. All papers declined in size between 1937 and 1947.

31 See, for example, Glasgow Media Group, *Bad News* (Routledge & Kegan Paul, London, 1976).

32 Silverman, p. 359.

33 Cmd. 7700, p. 176.

34 Williams, *Communications*, ch. 3.

35 See R. K. Merton, 'Studies in radio and film propaganda', in his *Social Theory and Social Structure*, revised edition (Free Press, Glencoe, 1957), pp. 509–28; B. Berelson, *Content Analysis in Communications Research* (Free Press, Glencoe, 1951).

36 M. Ferguson, 'Imagery and ideology: the cover photographs of traditional women's magazines', in *Hearth and Home: Images of Women in the Mass Media*, ed. G. Tuchman, A. K. Daniels and J. Benet (Oxford University Press, New York, 1978). See also M. Ferguson, *Forever Feminine* (Heinemann, London, 1982).

37 Ferguson, *Imagery and Ideology*, p. 107.

38 G. Tuchman, 'The symbolic annihilation of women in the media', in *Hearth and Home*, ed. Tuchman et al.

39 Ibid., p. 13. See also M. Cantor, 'Where are the women in public broadcasting?', in *Hearth and Home*, ed. Tuchman et al.

40 J. Lemon, 'Dominant or dominated? Women on prime time television', in *Hearth and Home*, ed. Tuchman et al.

41 Ibid., pp. 54–9.

42 Glasgow Media Group, *Bad News*.

43 See, for example, T. A. van Dijk, ed., *Discourse and Communication* (de Gruyter, Berlin, 1985); J. Williamson, *Decoding Advertisements* (Marion Boyars, London, 1978).

44 The word 'directory' has also been used to mean a book of rules of conduct, especially a religious codification, which 'directs' our behaviour. This usage is now archaic.

45 It is important to add the qualification that many people are 'ex-directory', i.e. they choose not to be listed.

46 Specialist directories include the *Directory of Directors, Kelly's Manufacturers and Merchants Directory*, the *Million Dollar Directory*, and *Crockford's Clerical Directory*. The list is diverse and almost endless.

47 Many directories which include a brief almanac section go under the name of 'Diary' when they also include space for keeping a personal diary of appointments, etc. See, for example, *The Solicitors' Diary*.

48 In addition to this 'Complete Edition' a 'Short Edition' is published.

49 Specialist yearbooks include *Dod's Parliamentary Companion*, the *Stock Exchange Official Year Book, Wisden Cricketers' Almanack*; there are numerous others.

50 The *Stock Exchange Official Year Book* is a similar source covering all quoted companies, though it began as the official record of the stock

exchange and is still regarded as a publication of record for stockbrokers rather than a manual for investors. The rise of corporate and institutional investors has, of course, blurred this distinction.

51 Other examples in Britain are the AA and RAC membership manuals, the *Good Food Guide*, and the 'spotter' books of Ian Allan, specialist manuals for those interested in the day-to-day business operations of the transport industry.

52 Fairly comprehensive lists of books currently published can be found in *Willing's Press Guide* and the *Directory of Directories*, though many ephemeral items escape such compilations. In this chapter I will sometimes make reference to government publications which are similar in origin and form to privately generated reference books: examples are the *Army List* and the *Civil Service Yearbook*.

53 See J. Norton, *Guide to the National and Provincial Directories of England and Wales* (Royal Historical Society, London, 1950); C. W. F. Goss, *The London Directories* (Denis Archer, London, 1932); G. Shaw, *British Directories as Sources in Historical Geography* (Geo Abstracts, Norwich, 1982).

54 The first modern directory appeared in 1677, though a very early example is known from 1538.

55 See M. Daunton, *Royal Mail* (Athlone Press, London, 1985).

56 Edinburgh in the late eighteenth century was the first city to have a strong Post Office link to its directory. On the general process see Shaw, *British Directories*, pp. 10–12.

57 Mid- and North Wales were not covered; and Scotland, except Edinburgh, was virtually untouched.

58 J. Vaughan, *The English Guide Book, 1780–1870* (David & Charles, Newton Abbot, 1974); Bagley, *Historical Interpretation 2*, pp. 191–200. Such guides mushroomed in the twentieth century with the spread of car ownership and the rise of mass travel. The older volumes were joined by Methuen's 'Little Guides', Arthur Mee's 'King's England', and numerous other publications, including '*Contour' Road Book* and the road books produced by 'Autocar', Dunlop, and the AA.

59 While the volume of mail carried today is, of course, greater than that carried in the nineteenth century, usage of the postal system has not grown in proportion with the scale of business.

60 Only Hull remains outside the national system with a network of its own.

61 See the reprints in *Three Victorian Telephone Directories* (David & Charles, Newton Abbot, 1970).

62 British Telecom was split from the Post Office in 1981 and was subsequently privatised, though retaining its monopoly. For commercial users the new Mercury system, operated by Cable & Wireless, offers alternative channels of international communication and it is spreading within Britain. It remains to be seen whether this will mean the end of the comprehensive telephone directory.

63 For general sources on the telephone see the papers in I. de Sola Pool (ed.),

The Social Impact of the Telephone (MIT Press, Cambridge, Mass., 1971), especially S. H. Aronson, 'Bell's electrical toy', C. R. Perry, 'The British experience 1876–1912', and J. Attali and Y. Stourdze, 'The birth of the telephone and economic crisis'.

64 See the history and bibliography by R. Pinches in *Burke's Family Index*, comp. Montgomery-Massingberd (Burke's Peerage, London, 1976).

65 Debrett published, for a short period, *Titled Men* as a biographical 'pocket companion' to its main volume.

66 The earliest volumes were published as *The Upper 10,000*. The book ceased publication in 1977 and was re-launched in 1982 as *Debrett's Handbook: Distinguished People in British Life*, the Debrett organisation having been acquired by Kelly's (itself part of a large conglomerate).

67 *Who Was Who* does not cover deaths prior to 1897, and so it is not a comprehensive listing.

68 Periodic supplements to *Burke's Landed Gentry* covering Irish and American families were published.

69 This originated in France as *Annuaire de la Noblesse en France*.

70 E. D. Baltzell, *Philadelphia Gentlemen* (Free Press, New York, 1958), pp. 18–20; C. Wright Mills, *The Power Elite* (Oxford University Press, New York, 1956), pp. 55–7; D. Wecter, *The Saga of American Society* (Scribner's, New York, 1932).

71 Volumes for other areas have been published, but they were discontinued in the 1920s.

72 Members of the political and administrative leadership are included automatically, without application, subscription or references.

73 *Sunday Times*, 6 July 1980.

74 J. B. Morton's 'Beachcomber' column in the *Daily Express* included parodies on the lists of Huntingdonshire cabmen.

75 The *Guardian*, 7 April 1987.

76 Shaw, *British Directories*, p. 31.

77 M. Morgan, *Historical Sources in Geography* (Butterworth, London, 1979). The coverage of directories was thus similar to the nineteenth-century electoral and rating registers.

78 Norton, *Guide*; Goss, op. cit.

79 Norton, *Guide*, pp. 20–2.

80 Moreover, as previously noted, some subscribers may be ex-directory.

81 Typical examples of such research include G. W. Domhoff, *Who Rules America?* (Prentice-Hall, Englewood Cliffs, New Jersey, 1967), *The Higher Circles* (Harper & Row, New York, 1970) and *The Bohemian Grove and Other Retreats* (*idem.*, 1974).

82 Baltzell, *Philadelphia Gentlemen*, p. v.

83 D. Boyd, *Elites and their Education* (National Foundation for Educational Research, London (1973).

84 C. Bell, 'Some comments on the use of directories in research on elites, with particular reference to the twentieth-century supplements of the *DNB*, in *British Political Sociology Yearbook*, vol. I, ed. I. Crewe (Croom Helm, London, 1974).

85 M. Useem, *The Inner Circle* (Oxford University Press, New York, 1984).
86 This typology is modified from Bell, 'Some comments . . .', p. 170.
87 C. Miller, *Who's Really Who* (Blond & Briggs, London, 1983; rev. edn Sphere, London, 1984).

Chapter 8   Personal Documents

1 See the account of an archaeological dig through a household's accumulated documents in M. Reeves, *Sheep Bell and Ploughshare* (Moonraker Press, Bradford on Avon, 1978). See also R. Parker, *Cottage on the Green* (Research Publishing, Cambridge, 1973).
2 See the discussion of this in K. Plummer, *Documents of Life* (Allen & Unwin, London, 1983).
3 See J. Warrington (ed.), *The Paston Letters* (Dent, London, 1924).
4 Bagley, *Historical Interpretation 2*, p. 87.
5 J. Evelyn, *The Diary of John Evelyn* (c.1636–1706), 6 volumes (Clarendon Press, Oxford, 1955); S. Pepys, *The Diary of Samuel Pepys* (1660–1669), 11 volumes (G. Bell & Sons, London, 1970–83).
6 Ralph Josselin will be discussed more fully below. See A. Macfarlane (ed.), *The Diary of Ralph Josselin, 1611–1683* (British Academy Records of Economic and Social History, London, new series III, 1976); J. Woodforde, *The Diary of a Country Parson* (1758–1802), 5 volumes (Oxford University Press, 1924–31); G. Fox, *Journal of George Fox* (1690) (Cash, London, 1852); J. Wesley, *The Journal of the Rev. John Wesley*, 8 volumes (Robert Culley, London, 1909–16).
7 See Namier's discussion of the Duke of Newcastle's documents in L. Namier, *The Structure of Politics at the Accession of George III* (1929; 2nd edn, Macmillan, London, 1957).
8 Harris, *Selling Hitler*.
9 Namier, *Structure of Politics*.
10 W. Plomer, Introduction to *Kilvert's Diary, 1870–1879* (Penguin, Harmondsworth, 1977), p. 6. The full version of the surviving diary was published between 1938 and 1940.
11 J. Burnett, *Destiny Obscure* (Allen Lane, London, 1982), p. 11. See also D. Vincent, *Bread, Knowledge and Freedom* (Europe, London, 1981), p. 6.
12 A. Macfarlane, *The Family Life of Ralph Josselin* (Cambridge University Press, London, 1970), pp. 5–6.
13 Bagley, *Historical Interpretation 2*, p. 87.
14 Plummer, *Documents of Life*, p. 18.
15 A. Ponsonby, *English Diaries* (1923) and *More English Diaries* (1927); W. Matthews, *British Diaries* (1950) and *British Autobiographies* (University of California Press, 1955); R. A. Fothergill, *Private Chronicles* (Oxford University Press, London, 1974).
16 T. Ashworth, *Trench Warfare, 1914–18* (Macmillan, London, 1980).
17 J. Burnett (ed.), *Annals of Labour* (Indiana University Press,

Bloomington, 1974); J. Burnett, D. Vincent and D. Mayall (eds), *The Autobiography of the Working Class* (Harvester Press, Brighton, 1984).

18 Vincent, *Bread, Knowledge and Freedom*, p. 8; Burnett, *Destiny Obscure* and *Useful Toil* (1974); Penguin, Harmondsworth, 1977).

19 *Bread, Knowledge and Freedom*, pp. 8–9.

20 W. I. Thomas and F. Znaniecki, *The Polish Peasant in Europe and America* (1918–20); Dover Publications, New York, 1958).

21 W. I. Thomas, 'Comments on Blumer's analysis', in *Critiques of Research in the Social Sciences, No. 1: An Appraisal of Thomas and Znaniecki's The Polish Peasant in Europe and America*, ed. H. Blumer (Transaction, New Jersey, 1979), p. 104.

22 Ibid., p. 105.

23 R. Towler, *The Need For Certainty* (Routledge & Kegan Paul, London, 1984); J. Robinson (Bishop of Woolwich), *Honest to God* (SCM Press, London, 1963).

24 Macfarlane (ed.), *Diary of Ralph Josselin*.

25 Thomas and Znaniecki, *Polish Peasant*.

26 Vincent, *Bread, Knowledge and Freedom*, p. 11.

27 Burnett, *Destiny Obscure*.

28 See A. Macfarlane, *The Origins of English Individualism* (Basil Blackwell, Oxford, 1978), and his reply to his critics in 'Individualism reconsidered, or the craft of the historian', in his *The Culture of Capitalism* (Basil Blackwell, Oxford, 1987), pp. 191–222.

29 Macfarlane et al., *Reconstructing Historical Communities*; Macfarlane (ed.), *Diary of Ralph Josselin*; Macfarlane, *Family Life of Ralph Josselin*.

30 Macfarlane (ed.), *Diary of Ralph Josselin*, pp. 17–18.

31 Ibid., p. xxi.

32 Macfarlane, *Origins of English Individualism*, pp. 64–6.

33 Macfarlane's own text involves a discrepancy in the age of Josselin between pages 81 and 106; internal evidence suggests that the age on the latter page is the correct one.

34 Macfarlane (ed.), *Diary of Ralph Josselin*, p. xxii.

35 Relevant sources on the history of art include R. J. Gettens and G. L. Stout, *Painting Materials* (1942; Dover Press, New York, 1955); W. G. Constable, *The Painter's Workshop* (Oxford University Press, London, 1954); Mrs Merrifield, *The Art of Fresco Painting* (1841: Alec Tiranti, London, 1966).

36 J. Berger, *Ways of Seeing* (Penguin, Harmondsworth, 1972), pp. 84–7.

37 C. B. Macpherson, *The Political Theory of Possessive Individualism* (Oxford University Press, London, 1962).

38 Only in the seventeenth century did the pure landscape painting emerge as a genre distinct from the portrait with background.

39 On the development of photography see B. Coe, *The Birth of Photography* (Ash & Grant, London, 1976); J. Hannavy, *The Victorian Professional Photographer* (Shire Publications, Aylesbury, 1980); *idem*, Masters of Victorian Photography (David & Charles, Newton Abbott, 1976). See also West, *Town Records*, ch. 12.

40 B. Coe, *George Eastman and the Early Photographers* (Priory Press, London, 1973); C. Ackerman, *George Eastman* (1930); B. Coe and P. Gates, *The Snapshot Photograph: The Rise of Popular Photography, 1888–1939* (Ash & Grant, London, 1977).

41 G. King, *Say 'Cheese'* (Collins, Glasgow, 1986), p. 16.

42 I. Haywood, *Faking It* (Harvester, Brighton, 1987).

43 Berger, *Ways of Seeing*, pp. 20–3.

44 Ibid., pp. 19–20.

45 N. Barley, *The Innocent Anthropologist* (1983; Penguin, Harmondsworth, 1986), pp. 96–7.

46 For information relevant to dating photographs in this way see W. Welling, *Collectors' Guide to Nineteenth-Century Photographs* (Macmillan, New York, 1976), which contains lists of British and American photographers of the 1840s and 1850s; *A Directory of London Photographers, 1841–1908* (ALLM Press, Bushey, 1986); and D. Cory, 'The carte de visite', in D. Joice, *Bygones 5* (Boydell Press, Woodbridge, 1980), which contains a list of Norwich photographers.

47 C. Musello, 'Family photographs', in *Images of Information*, ed. J. Wagner (Sage, Beverley Hills, 1979), p. 101.

48 R. E. Pahl, *Divisions of Labour*, pp. 73–85.

49 King, *Say 'Cheese'*, p. 38.

50 D. Steel, 'Identification and dating: a survey', in D. Steel and L. Taylor, *Family History in Focus* (Lutterworth Press, Guildford, 1984), p. 44.

51 J. Hirsch, *Family Photographs* (Oxford University Press, New York, 1981, pp. 12–13.

52 Musello, 'Family photographs', p. 106.

53 Ibid., pp. 110–12.

54 Hirsch, *Family Photographs*, p. 42.

55 Private archives of professional photographers include the Francis Frith Collection, the Hulton Picture Library, the Mansell Collection, and the Mary Evans Picture Library. County record offices, libraries and museums occasionally have collections. Sources are listed in H. and M. Evans and A. Nelkin, *Picture Researchers' Handbook* (David & Charles, Newton Abbott, 1975), R. Eakins, *Picture Sources, UK* (Macdonald, London, 1985) and J. Wall, *Directory of British Photographic Collections* (Heinemann, London, 1977). Published collections include G. Winter (ed.), *Past Positive* (Chatto & Windus, London, 1971; published as *idem*, *A Cockney Camera*, Penguin, Harmondsworth, 1975 and *idem*, *A Country Camera*, (David & Charles, Newton Abbott, 1971); D. Souhami, *A Woman's Place* (Penguin, Harmondsworth, 1986); J. Thompson, *Street Life in London* (1877–8; E.P. Publishing, Wakefield, 1973); T. Annan, *Photos of Old Closes and Streets of Glasgow* (1877?; Constable, London, 1977).

56 King, *Say 'Cheese'*, ch. 3.

57 Musello, 'Family photographs', p. 112. See also the discussion of the role of photo collections in families in R. Firth, *Families and Their Relatives* (Routledge & Kegan Paul, London, 1970).

Index

Only substantive references in footnotes have been indexed, purely bibliographical references have been ignored. References to British source material are subsumed in the general headings, but those for other countries have been indexed separately.

access, and classification of documents 14–15, and representativeness 26, 106; *see also* archives
accuracy 23–4; *see also* credibility
Acts of Parliament 11, 17, 27, 29
administrative routines 52, 83ff., 90, 124, 125, 127, 146
age in official documents 104–5, 108, 213n.
Alcock, Lesley 38ff., 54
Aldridge, Jennifer (pseud.) 144
almanacs 156ff.
Althusser, Louis 32, 33
Anderson, Michael 122
Andrew, Christopher 47
archaeological sources and methods 4–5, 55; *see also* physical evidence
Archers, The 144–5
archives 14, 17, 25, 27, 63, 65, 78, 106–7, 167, 178, 195–6, 200n.; *see also* access
Armstrong, W. 115
Arthurian legend 38ff., 54
Ashworth, Tony 178
audience and interpretation of meaning 33ff., 133, 148–9; *see also* content

Australia, vital registration 72
Austria, suicide statistics 50, vital registration 72
authenticity, definition of 6, 7, assessment of 19ff., in Durkheim's work 50, of census and vital registration data 102–3, of diaries 175–6, 182–3, in directories and yearbooks 163–4, in newspapers 143–5, in photographs 188–91; *see also* Zinoviev letter
author of text, and intended meaning 13, 33–4; *see also* authorship, audience, content
authorship, and classification of documents 14, and authenticity 20–2, of British Historical Miscellany 40, in newspapers and books 144–5, 163–4

Badon, battle of Mount 40–1, 54, 203n.
Bagley, John J. 177
Baltzell, E. Digby 169
baptism, and birth records 68, 211n., contents of registers 98, 211n.; *see also* vital registration

Barley, Nigel 190
Barthes, Roland 31–2
Becker, Howard 61, 94
Bede 40
Belgium, mapping 75, suicide statistics 50, vital registration 72
Bell, Colin 170
Berger, John 188
Beveridge, William 111
bias 9, 12, 28, 91, 148, 151, 155; *see also* credibility, sincerity, values in social science
biographical reference books: *see* directories
bishop's transcripts 69, 97, 206n.; *see also* vital registration
Blau, Peter 83
Booth, Charles 9, 87, 122
Bowley, Sir Arthur L. 8–9
Box, Stephen 91
Boyd, Stephen 91
Boyd, David 169–70
British Museum 40
bureaucracy 14, 69, 78, 80–1; *see also* administrative routines, surveillance
burial and death records 68, 211n., contents of registers 99; *see also* vital registration
Burnett, John 176, 178, 181
business documents 16, 26, 60, 78, 132–5

cabinet papers 24
Camden, William 75
Camlann, battle of 40, 42
Canada, vital registration in 73, census 207n.
Carr–Saunders, Alexander 111, 118–20
Catholic Church, vital registration in England 206n.
censorship 146
census of population 17, 28, 71, 99–101, origins of census 60, 70, and occupational classification 86,

statistics 100, enumerators' books 99–101, 103ff., authenticity 102–3, credibility 103–5, representativeness 105–7, meaning 107–11
certificates 82, 98; *see also* personal documents
Chester, Louis 44–7
Church of England 14, 66, records of 66, 78; *see also* parish records
Cicourel, Aaron 125–7
cinema 137, 141
civil society 69
class consciousness 132–5
Cobbett, William 65, 139
coding, and administrative categories 9–10
companies and company records: *see* business documents
conceptual and technical instruments 84–5, 90, 95, 109
content analysis 32, 130ff., 147ff.
content, intended, internal and received 34, 130, 133, 148, 155; *see also* audience, author, content analysis
copies and copying: *see* soundness
county records 69–70
County Records Offices 27, 65
credentialism and education records 81
credibility, definition of 6, 7, assessment of 22ff., in Durkheim's work 51–2, of census and vital registration data 103–5, of directories and yearbooks 164–6, of newspapers and television 145–6, of photographs 188–91
criminal records and statistics 36, 67, 73, 91–5, representativeness of 91–4
Culloden, battle of and development of mapping 75

data construction 8ff., 28, 54
dating, systems of 29–30, 41–2, 54–5

Davies, Celia 86, 108
Defoe, Daniel 21, 139
Denmark, census 72, vital registration 207n.
Department of Health and Social Security 123
Derrida, Jacques 32
destruction of documents 8, 25
deviance 60
diaries 11, 15, 174ff., and autobiographies 175, 180–1, and presentation of self 177, authenticity of 175–6, 182–3, credibility of 176–7, 184–5, representativeness of 178–9, meaning of 179ff.
Dilthey, Wilhelm 11
Dionysiac system 41, 54; *see also* dating
directories 16, 36, 37, 156, 157f, 200n., 220n., Post Office directories 158–9, 166, authenticity of 175–6, credibility of 164–6, representativeness of 166–8, meaning of 168–9
documents, definition of 5, 10ff., classification of 13–17, as resource and topic 36–7, 38, 94, 129, 156
Domesday Book 64
Douglas, Jack 53
Drake, Michael 104
Durkheim, Emile 1, study of suicide 48ff., 54, 91
Dyos, H. James 122

Easter tables 40; *see also* dating systems
Eden, Sir Frederick 74
education records 70, 79, 81, 125–7
electoral records 67, 206n.
electronic documents 12; *see also* survival
Emerson, Peter 187
Engels, Friedrich 25, and authorship of Marx's works 37

environmentalist views and class 86–8, 119
ephemera 13, 25, 173
ethnomethodology and official statistics 94–5
eugenics: *see* hereditarian views

family reconstitution 109, 183
Farr, William 86
Federal Trade Commission 80
feminism 58, 116–17, 135
Ferguson, Marjorie 153–4
film as a document 147, origins of 188; *see also* cinema
Foreign Office 44ff.
forgery 21, 44ff., 102, 188; *see also* Hitler diaries
Foster, John 122
Foucault, Michel 32
France, census 72, 101, surveys and statistics 64, 71–2, government finance 63, maps 75, suicide statistics 50, 51, telephone system 161, vital registration 69, 72, 101, 212n.
Frith, Francis 186

Galton, Sir Francis 87
Garfinkel, Harold 123–5
Gatrell, V. A. C. 94
gender and census data 108, 123
gender stereotyping 148, 154–5
General Register Office 17, 71, 85ff., 106
Geoffrey of Monmouth 38ff.
Germany, early surveys, 64, peerage directories 162, suicide statistics 50, vital registration 72
Giddens, Anthony 33
Gildas 40–2
Glasgow Media Group 155
Glass, David 113, 118, 120
Goldthorpe, John 113ff.
Gregorian calendar, introduction of 29

Hakim, Catherine 83, 111
Hall–Jones classification 111–12, 118
handwriting, reading of 28, 107
Hansard 17, 65, 206n.
head of household in census 88,
    108–9, 115–17, 216n.
hereditarian views and class 86–8
hermeneutic interpretation 31ff., 54;
    see also meaning
Hindess, Barry 84
Hirsch, Julia 195
historical method, and documentary
    sources 10–11, 38, 66
Hitler diaries 21, 175–6
Holsti, Ole 130–1
Hope, Keith 113
Hope–Goldthorpe scale 113

Iceland, census 207n.
indexes and catalogues of documents
    27, 107, 167, 178, 201n., 206n.
industrial and employment
    classifications 86; *see also* Standard
    Industrial Classification
International Genealogical Index
    (Mormon archive) 102–3, 106,
    213n.
interpretation 30ff., 147, of suicide
    52–3; *see also* meaning
interviews 6–7, 10
Ireland, census 207n., vital
    registration 72, 207n., 211n.
Italy, census 72, suicide statistics 50,
    vital registration 69, 72

Jaffé, Edgar 56
Japan, census in 72, 207n.
joint stock company legislation 79–80;
    see also business records
Jones, D. Caradog 118–20, 122
Josselin, Ralph, diary of 175, 179,
    181–5

King, Graham 192, 195
Kitsuse, John 125–7

labelling theory 61–2, 94
landownership 64, 66, documents of
    landed families 15–16, 78, enclosure
    and tithe documents 67, 77–8,
    estate maps 75, land tax 77, 208n.
landscape and human action 5, 6
Langlois, Charles 10–11, 20, 22, 28
Lemon, Judith 155
letters and correspondence 11, 15, 79,
    174ff., classification of 180,
    representativeness of 178–9; *see
    also* Zinoviev letter
liberalism 58
Library of Congress 17
loss of documents 26, 147; *see also*
    representativeness

Macfarlane, Alan 181ff.
Macintyre, Sally 127–9
magazines 152–4
Malthus, Thomas 70
Mannheim, Karl 33, 35
manorial records 66
maps 13, 75–7; *see also* Ordnance
    Survey
marriage records 68, 104, 211n.,
    contents of registers 98–9; *see also*
    vital registration
Marsh, David 121
Marx, Karl 1, 25, 135, authorship of
    works 37, Marxism 58, 118, 120
mass communications 130, 137ff.; *see
    also* cinema, newspapers, television
Mattelart, André 143
Matthews, W. 178
Mauss, Marcel 49
meaning, definition of 6, 8,
    measurement of 9–10, assessment
    of 28–35, 54, in Durkheim's work
    52–3, in census and vital
    registration data 107–11, in
    directories and yearbooks 168–9, of
    photographs 191ff.; *see also*
    interpretation
measurement 8ff.
mediate access by observer 4ff.

medical records 16, 61, 79, 123–5, 127–9, medical categories 61, 91 medical statisticians 87; *see also* suicide
M.I.5 (British security agency) 46
microfilm records 20, 100, 101, 103, 143–4
Mills, C. Wright 9
misprints and technical errors 20, 103, 143–4, 189
moral accounting 60
Mormon Church: *see* International Genealogical Index
Morselli, Henri 51
Moser, Claus 120ff.
Musello, C. 194

Namier, Sir Lewis 176
National Registration (1939) 71
Nennius 40–1
Netherlands, vital registration in 69, 72
New Zealand, vital registration in 72
newspapers 15, 16, 23, 43ff., 136, 147, 156, development of 137–40, ownership and control 139–40, 142–3, content analysis of 149–53, authenticity in 143–5, credibility of 145–6
nominal record linkage 109–10
Norway, census 72, vital registration 207n.
novels 34

observation: *see* mediate access, proximate access
occupational titles and classification 28, 85ff., 96ff., 105, 107–9, 111ff., 127–8, 168; *see also* Registrar General's Classification, social class
Office of Population, Censuses and Surveys 85, 96; *see also* General Register Office
official documents 59ff., 78–9, definition of 14, and sincerity 22,

weeding and destruction of 25, 46, 63, 101
Official Secrets Act 17, 62–3, thirty year rule 26
official statistics 61, 71ff., of crime 61, of suicide 49ff.
Old Style and New Style dates 29, 107, 201n.; *see also* dating systems
oral history 4, 174
Ordnance Survey 75–6

paintings 13, 185, 190; *see also* photographs
paper, deterioration of 25
paperback books 138
parish documents 67ff., 97; *see also* vital registration
Parliamentary papers: *see* Acts of Parliament, Hansard
participant observation 3–4, 7, 8
peerage and court directories 159–60, 161–2, 163ff.
Pepys, Samuel 175, 179
personal documents 173ff., definition of 14, 15, 173, and sincerity 23, destruction of 25, 176
photographs 13, origins of 186–8, snapshot photography 187–8, 192, 193ff., studio photography 192–3, and construction of reality 189–90, authenticity and credibility of 188–91, representativeness of 195–6, meaning of 191ff.
physical evidence 5, 7, 8; *see also* archaeological sources and evidence
police 73, records of 16, 67, and official statistics 91ff.
political arithmetic 70
Ponsonby, Arthur 178
poor law administration 60, 68, 73–4, 98, 99
population: *see* census of population, vital registration
Portugal, census 72, vital registration 207n.

poverty 61, 73; *see also* poor law administration
primary and secondary sources 23–4
private documents 14, 16; *see also* official documents
propaganda 22, 130
provenance 21, 40, 45; *see also* authorship
proximate access by observer 2–4, 5–6
Public Record Office 17, 27, 45, 46, 63, 65, 101
public sphere and reading public 136–7, 137ff.; *see also* audience

quality criteria: *see* authenticity, credibility, representativeness, meaning
quarter sessions 67
questionnaires 4, 7, 198n.

radio 137, 140, 141–2
radio carbon dating 55
Ranke, Leopold von 10
reactive and non-reactive research 3–4
Registrar General's Classification of occupations 85ff., 111ff., 119, 120–1, 128, 210n.
regnal years 29, 201n.
representativeness, definition of 6, 7–8, assessment of 24–8, in Durkheim's work 50–1, of census and vital registration data 105–7, in commercial publications 146–7, in directories and yearbooks 166–8, 170–2, of industrial documents 133–4, of personal documents 173, of photographs 195–6
Rowntree, B. Seebohm 9
Royal Commissions 17, 64, 74–5, 85, 132, 150

sampling 7–8, 8–9, 27
satire 21
Saussure, Ferdinand de 31, 33
scientific method: *see* social research
Scotland, Statistical Accounts 74,

census of population 207n., dating of documents 201n., military repression and mapping 76, vital registration 69, 72, 98, 106, 206n., 207n.
Scott, William 121–2
script: *see* writing
Secret Intelligence Service 45, 46
Securities and Exchange Commission 80
Seignobos, Charles 10–11, 20, 22, 28
semiotic analysis 31–2, 148
share registers 16, 80
shorthand 24, 179–80
Silverman, R. 150–1
sincerity 22–3, 165–6; *see also* credibility
Sinclair, John 74
situated decisions 52, 90ff.
social class 85ff., 111ff., measurement of 117ff., continuous versus discontinuous views 88, 113; *see also* occupational titles
social research, characteristics of 1–2, 33, 56ff.
Society of Genealogists 106
Sombart, Werner 56
soundness 19–20, and directories 164, and registration data 102–3
Soviet Union, and Zinoviev letter 43ff., 54
Spain, census 72, vital registration 69, 72
Speed, John 75
Speenhamland system 73–4
spelling and grammar mistakes 20, in registration data 97, 102–3
Standard Industrial Classification 86, 90, 210n.
State 60ff., 78–9, expansion of state activities 10, 59, 60, 63ff., and official documents 11–12; *see also* administrative routines
State papers 64–5, 67, 206n.
statistical data: *see* official statistics
Steel, Don 193

Stevenson, T. 88, 114, 115
storage of documents: *see* archives
Strinati, Dominic 132–5
stylisation 34
suicide, studies of 48ff., 54, 56
surveillance 60ff., 69, 75, 82, 160; *see also* State, official documents
survival 25–26, 106, and electronic media 167–8, 198n.; *see also* representativeness
Sweden, census 72, 207n., vital registration 72
Switzerland, vital registration 69, 72

taxation records 16, 17, 67, 85; *see also* landownership
Taylor, Ian 61
telephone and telephone directories 156, 160–1, 168, 174, 221n.; *see also* directories
television 137, 141ff., credibility of 145–6
text as a feature of a document 5
theatre 140–1
Thomas, William I 179, 180
Towler, Robert 179
trades unions 79, 132–5
Tregorran, John (pseud.) 144
Tuchman, Gaye 154

unemployment 84, 85, 107
United States, census in 72, 101, cinema 141, company legislation and records 80, dirctories and social registers 162–3, 169, education records 81, 125–6, mapping 77, newspapers 140, Polish migrants 179, suicide statistics 50, 51, telephone system 160–1, television 141–2, vital registration 73, 207n.
Useem, Michael 170

validity of interpretation 32–3, 131–2, 133, 134–5
values in social science 1–2, 57–8, 135
Vincent, David 178, 180–1
vital registration 60, 69, 70–1, 97–9, authenticity 102–3, credibility 103–5, representativeness 105–7, meaning 107–11; *see also* census of population
Vogler, Carolyn 132–5

Walton, Paul 61
Waterloo, battle of and dating 54–5, 56
Webb, Beatrice and Sidney, on documents and contemporary literature 11–12, and sampling 27
Webb, Eugene 5
Weber, Max 1, 135, and bureaucracy 14, and protestant ethic 60, and social science method 56–8
West, Nigel (pseud. of Rupert Allason) 47
Williams, Raymond 152–3
Winchester, Ian 109
women, absence in studies of class and class consciousness 123, 135, autobiographies of 178, concept of 56, employment of 105, 108–9, and social class 115–17, 127–8, 215n., in the mass media 150, 152–5
writing as a characteristic of documents 5, 12

yearbooks 157ff.
Young, Jock 61

Zinoviev letter 43ff., 54
Znaniecki, Florian 179, 180

Printed in the United States
140368LV00001B/17/A

9 780745 600703